# THE LAST CEMETERY IN BERLIN

## A Post-Holocaust Love Story
## In the Ruins of the Berlin Wall

### By

### Tania Wisbar and John Mahoney

Sept 8, 2008

To Fadra —
It took a while to
get this to you —
sorry about that but
hope you like this novel —
Best
Tania Wisbar

ISBN: 1-4033-9632-9 (e-book)
ISBN: 1-4033-9633-7 (Paperback)
ISBN: 0-7596-2917-X (Dustjacket)

Library of Congress Control Number: 2002095978

This book is printed on acid free paper.


Printed in the United States of America
Bloomington, IN


Cover photo of Weissensee Cemetery
By Theresa Hansen


A VRI Book

1stBooks – rev. 01/29/03

*The Last Cemetery in Berlin*

is dedicated to

Eva Kroy Wisbar, Maria B. Hansen, and Annenie Kaufmann

# FOREWORD

Much of this novel is based on actual events. The nations and agencies in the story are real but the characters are compilations of the many people met as we pursued our family's property claim in what had been the German Democratic Republic – East Germany – prior to the collapse of the Berlin Wall. Any similarity between the people in the novel and actual people is however purely coincidental.

This fascinating journey started with the United States Foreign Claims Commission. It took us along a path of history and of people that created the environment and the context for this work, a fictional account of what might have been, could have happened, and quite possibly did, at least in some world.

While this work is fictional, The Jewish Cemetery in Weissensee, Berlin, does exist and was essentially abandoned from the early 1940s until after German reunification in the 1990s. We trust that no one or no group will take offense that it is used as a major theme of this novel. It is our hope that all readers will understand that our intention is to honor Weissensee Cemetery's past and its future.

The shoe factory and its personnel are entirely fictional. On our visits to shoe factories we were treated with utmost courtesy. We learned from the many people who were willing to talk to us to respect the great challenges they faced in the first years of the reunified Germany. We continue to believe that in too many instances the people of the former East Germany were treated with undue harshness. We remember them and we wish them the very best.

We extend our gratitude to many people for help of many kinds, some of whom are: Leorah Krojanker of Jerusalem, who is the most joyous of our many discoveries; Norbert and Stephanie Dall, Dall & Associates, who were there with us; Michael Raboin, formerly of the United States Foreign Claims Commission; Jason Pohland, Standard Films, Berlin, another relative previously unknown; Dr. Heike Shroll, *Landesarchiv*, Berlin; Prof. Dr. Detlef Garz, Johann Gutenberg University of Mainz; Raymond Hansen, writer and friend; Erik Hansen, writer and proofreader, Caryl Albert, friend and listener, all of Los Angeles; in their own special ways, Ekkehard and Elisabeth Faude, Libelle Verlag, Switzerland; and always to our sister, Maria B. Hansen, who took the journey with us.

# PROLOGUE

## IMPERIAL BEACH, CALIFORNIA
## AUGUST 2002

Floodwaters swirl down the medieval cobblestone streets of Fehleen, the tiny shoe factory town in the former East Germany.

The shoe factory, arrogantly large when it was built in 1885, is being rapidly, ignobly diminished by the confluence of two swollen rivers, each converging from one side on the ancient, multi-storied brick building.

Eyeless windows, broken out or boarded up with haphazard materials create a large mask observing the frantic and useless rescue efforts that are taking place. The building withstood two wars, five different forms of government – only a few democratic, - strikes, boycotts and deaths, natural and unnatural, of its owners. Among them my wife's family.

But the shoe factory building in Germany will not survive this day's disaster by water, a disaster I am watching on television in our small beach house 6,000 miles away in San Diego County.

Carried along by the fast-moving rivers are literally the flotsam and jetsam of the small city's life – a café awning, a partially submerged car, house gates, road signs with warning lights still blinking as they bob up and down with the surge. It is a virtual water parade of ordinary items freed from their predictable places of ordinary rest that carom downstream toward the legendary if now derelict shoe factory.

In its better life, during the years my wife's family owned the shoe factory and even during the Nazi and Communist eras, in fact any time before German reunification in 1990, work in the factory nourished whole families, generation after generation. The plant stood as the centerpiece of the work world in the small city. And had it not been for the Nazis and later the Communists we probably would never have met, Lily Weitrek and I. She would be the Princess in Prinzline shoes and I only a former

1

philosophy professor and now a small beach town newspaper publisher.

As we watch, the television camera focuses on the floodwaters seeking the lowest level of the factory. Water rushes down the basement steps. There is much yelling. The picture begins to rock as if the cameraman is trying to keep his balance in a small boat. That must be the case inasmuch as many official-sounding voices bark orders to the television crew to vacate the area.

The news coverage shifts to cover the flood danger to larger and more important cities – Prague in the Czech Republic, Budapest in Hungary.

Others may weep for these cities; Lily will weep as now she does for Fehleen. She has left the room abruptly to stand at the edge of our small deck. Her posture is quite deliberate, as she seems to study the lapping of the tide's waves against the deck. Her posture is intended to tell me – and it succeeds – that I am not to intrude on her private grief.

My name is Michael Mulreney. As I begin to recount what I know of the events of 1991 when Lily went to Germany, it is important to me that you know my name.

Lily told me much of what happened then but I have known for all years since that there was more that remained untold.

I know for instance that the newly elected government of the recently reunified Germany rejected her property claim for the Fehleen shoe factory and I know that a German lawyer named Wolfgang Schmidt befriended Lily. As the years passed between then and now, the silence grew, the topics of property claims, of shoes and of the dead were, to my relief, finally relegated to the attic of our marriage.

But the Fehleen floods have washed away the covers and that past, which I only know partially, may threaten our stability again.

For a long time after Lily returned from Germany, she would wander the house like some nocturnal voyager, going nowhere, but ending up staring at the waves from our deck.

What I fear tonight, now, is that it will begin again – the ceaseless scrutinizing of the past, of the company kept with the ghosts.

Lily had left for Germany in May 1991 shortly after it became possible to travel to the former East Germany. She left a smiling, confident American woman. She returned less quick to smile, less confident.

Eleven years have passed since then, so my recollections may not be complete. But I remember feeling that Lily was not telling me everything that happened to her. Perhaps she felt I would not understand. In a certain sense I felt Lily was communicating with people – this is difficult to say to strangers – with people no longer alive.

After Lily returned from Germany, I remember that in the middle of the night, suddenly awakened out of sleep, I put together a list of questions that I needed to ask her in the morning. I would identify the task, place the items on the mind's shelf and go back to sleep, assured that in the morning I would remember the housekeeping of the night.

Morning can often betray memory, though, and so I would go about the next days struggling to reassemble the whole list of questions.

Lily spoke of those who died, and in her telling I knew that those long dead haunted her. She crossed an ocean on a journey into the past and came home with what had been for her an unknown history.

She also became one with the thousands from a particular era in Germany's history who are scattered around the world who know they are heirs to the sorrows of an earlier generation. They were born by chance to be young witnesses on whose minds, conscious or unconscious, are imprinted the crimes of the past which neither time nor its forward motion can erase. There are not too many left to remind us of this era, fewer every day.

It must be particularly disturbing at middle age to learn that you are not who you thought you were, but harsh to learn that the underpinnings of your life were fabricated to hide from the truth.

It was the collapse of the Berlin Wall and the reunification of what had been the Communist German Democratic Republic with the Federal Republic of Germany in late 1990 that changed our lives. We watched these events playing out on television as

3

most Americans did, amazed at so abrupt a change in world politics, at such sudden power shifts. Very few people understood how fragile the new union was and how subject it was to an uprising during its first few years. We were unaware of this risk until much later.

But there was nevertheless a difference in our reaction from that of most Americans who watched these events. First, Lily wondered whether old ethnic hatreds would emerge from under the cover of government-ordered harmony. The Communists had kept a tight grip over people's urge to act on old, remembered hatreds.

With new freedom came freedom to carry ancient hatreds into the present.

Lily's second thought was rather a question: would her mother's claim for property in what had been East Germany be honored?

The world in the west, immediately jittery at the possible menace posed by a unified, powerful Germany, was assured by West German Chancellor Helmut Kohl that the new Germany would be a peace-loving, honorable country.

But the disappearance of the Wall also removed the blinders from history, raising many of the same questions in 1990 and 1991, which had dominated days in West Germany after the defeat of the Nazis in 1945. Even as the Wall came down, the questions were coming up.

It has to be understood that in the swift shift at the end of World War II from Nazi to Communist control, neither the government nor the people of East Germany were ever required to address the roles they had played in implementing Nazi policies from 1933 to 1945.

As to those pesky questions about East Germany's role in past misdeeds against minorities, primarily Jews, during the Hitler era, Kohl assured the world it had nothing to worry about. Where settlements were needed, settlements would be made, and they would be honorable.

These were questions of rights and justice, which quickly irritated German bureaucrats, government officials, elected representatives, and very often the man on the street.

Lily Weitrek, my wife, added considerably to their irritation as she tried to hold the government to Kohl's promise. It was a promise that stretched in its reach backwards from the new, reunified Germany to the Communist era and to the Nazi era. Governments, ancient and modern both, move ahead, forgiving former enemies or making new ones, dragging an unwitting populace into new alliances or new wars.

Individuals, from the collective experience of the race, do not rush that quickly, particularly those who were damaged most by government policies.

Soon Lily and I at the time fashioned a common question: whether the German government, 1991, would really honor the claim which had been made by Theresa Weitrek, Lily's mother, as promised, or would instead turn shadow dancer to Hitler's 1933 policies of denial of human rights, including the right to own property.

Theresa. Her name evokes images instantly for me. Theresa Weitrek in 1981.

The events of that day in 1981, when this story began, are still as clear to me as if it were still that day twenty-one years ago. Those events surrounded our discovery that day of the official - looking letter from the U.S. State Department about Theresa's claim for property in what was still then the German Democratic Republic, an autonomous Communist country.

Theresa had not hidden the letter as much as she had discarded it under a stack of fragmented notes she had made to herself, old newspapers, which she enshrined, and unpaid bills. This stack, this pile, was on the kitchen table - Theresa's desk - which was sprinkled quite liberally with stray crumbs of English muffins and upon which also sat a half-empty cup of tea.

Whenever Lily had cause to survey her mother's work area, her eyebrows lifted. While mother and daughter were close, their approach to neatness was diametrically opposite; Theresa found neatness in conveniently ignored disarray. Lily thought otherwise.

Our visit that day to the Los Angeles house from our own in Imperial Beach was marked already for history by two major events. It was Inauguration Day for President Ronald Reagan, and it was also the day on which Iran released the American hostages it had held for 444 days. Almost no one remembers either, at least no one under forty. It was January 20, 1981.

But, as we later learned, neither of those events had any real effect on our lives, but the letter from the State Department did - a cataclysmic effect.

We stared at the crumbs on Theresa's work area, at the bills, at the letter from the State Department. Theresa tried quickly, even as we were entering the kitchen, to shuffle her discards together.

It was a stack too large and high to permit any but an awkward hug and kiss of greeting between daughter and mother.

The envelope, its upper left corner bespeaking its origin, edged out of the discard pile. Lily saw it, took it from the pile with a delicate excision of thumb and index finger.

"What's this?"

"Nothing. It is nothing important," Theresa replied.

And so it began, Lily's journey into the unknown.

With a little more prodding, Theresa agreed that we could read the letter.

It was from the Director of the U.S. Foreign Claims Commission, State Department. It was short and to the point. The letter informed a poor correspondent, Theresa, who had already had two years to complete the application for compensation for property in East Germany, that time was running out. Theresa, and presumably some number of others who were about to miss deadlines, had thirty days to complete the claim.

The postmark on the letter was one month old.

Theresa had been given one month; the postmark told us there were three days left. The "what ifs" of computer spreadsheet and modeling programs have brought special light to the tasks of planners of various kinds. But there is yet no program, nor, I think, will there ever be, to replace the "what ifs" of memory.

"The Road Not Taken," Robert Frost called it. That is a theme for meditation by almost everyone over ...I am not certain of the age.

In the remaining hours of the day, we had established with Theresa's concurrence, that she had initiated some form of property claim for property in East Germany, the German Democratic Republic, GDR. We heard small hints of hidden information from Theresa as we tried to elicit from her what the basis was for the claim, which she had initiated.

What became clear as we probed further was that Theresa had apparently buried her past deliberately when first she set foot on Ellis Island in 1940. She was carrying an infant, Lily, and a toddler, Lily's sister Emma, was, as I can see it, holding her mother's skirt.

Theresa was then alone in a new, not entirely welcoming land.

I reached a conclusion, perhaps possible for me to do because I was still somewhat new in the family, not as close.

I concluded that Theresa never looked back. She never listed what she had lost. She never referred to her native land. She never spoke her native tongue.

Most important, I heard from her brief, hurried, descant of recital, that she never would refer to the culture or the family she had lost.

Theresa kept her silence from 1940 to 1981. She broke the silence to us that day, when Ronald Reagan took office and the hostages started home.

Lily and Emma had grown up in that silence, which hurt each of them, I now know, in different ways. Ostracism, it is understood, imposes silence toward the one by the many. But, in effect, Theresa, for all the good reasons we learned, later reversed that definition: she imposed silence from the one on the many - her daughters, and on many others who might have known or should have known what she chose to hide.

These were the fragments of history that emerged.

Theresa had known a passion for music, even though Lily grew up in a house without music. Theresa spoke of a great, lost love, of a mother she loved very much, of a father, Georg Brodsky, who had died very young, and of property.

She spoke of property, which included a shoe factory in a small city, called Fehleen, in eastern Germany. She told us about a favorite aunt, Franziska, and her husband, Misha Sagal, a director of the shoe factory, and their crippled son, Ludwig.

She talked about two other uncles on her father's side of the family, one a newspaper publisher, the other, the director of the shoe factory's many retail stores.

We learned enough from Theresa to file the supplement to the claim, which was required.

But the price for Theresa, for looking back, for shedding the defenses of decades, for rediscovering the pain and anguish of her former life, was too high.

Frail to start with, she faded from interest as we watched. We brought her down to the beach to live with us, to care for her, to do everything we could to supply her with the will to live.

It was not enough.

Hour after hour Lily would hold her mother, grown so small, in her lap and rock her to the cadence of the lapping waves that came up on the deck. They seemed to become sculpts, artifacts – timeless – mother and child, child become mother.

Theresa's last request of Lily was a surprise.

"If it is possible, darling daughter, go to Weissensee Cemetery and put flowers on my mother's grave."

What archaeologists have learned and historians construe can never approach the certainty philosophers have found that each man and woman buried takes unrecoverable secrets to the grave.

Searching Theresa's few, carefully hidden papers, carried years before out of Germany, revealed what Theresa never had told. There were three tattered photos, yellow and brittle with age. One was the picture of a woman staring straight into the camera, seated formally, white lace collared blouse and dark skirt, hair swept up, the only jewelry a gold watch on a necklace. On the back of the photo was written the year 1905 next to the printed studio name, "Becker Berlin." Lily instantly said that the woman must be her grandmother.

The second photo was of a tall, lean man with deep-set eyes in a long angular face. He was good looking. I remember that at the time I knew that the man had to be Lily's father.

The last photo was of two little girls, one a baby in a carriage and the other a toddler, holding the side of the carriage and looking at the baby. On the back of this photo was written in what seems to be a shaky, masculine hand, "Children, 1940."

The only document was a tattered cemetery map. On it was the handwritten, German script words, "D-24: Emma Auerbach Brodsky." In the unsteady hand of a woman weakend in body but still strong in will Theresa had written her daughter a final directive, "Lily, go to my mother's grave."

We learned that Weissensee Cemetery, hidden behind the Berlin Wall for all those years, was a Jewish cemetery.

We understood that Theresa had taken into the next world the central truth about who she was.

She left a stunned daughter behind.

Ten years passed. We heard nothing from the U.S. Foreign Claims Commission.

I would call from time to time. Each time I was told that the East Germans wanted "most favored nation trade status" an unlikely concession from the anti-Soviet Reagan administration. Only then, apparently would the East Germans proceed to a settlement for those claims of losses in the past that the U.S. Foreign Claims Commission had verified and for which the U.S. government had commited itself to serving as a broker.

Theresa's claim was one of those.

Nothing happened in those ten years, until the Berlin Wall came down, and East Germany as a country imploded; until the two Germanys were reunited by a vote of all Germans in 1990. And Chancellor Helmut Kohl said, "We will honor the claims of those whose losses stem from the era of Nazi persecution."

The phone rang one day in early 1991. The call was completely unexpected.

At the other end of the static-filled line, a man identified himself as Otto Gesset, director of the shoe factory in Fehleen.

He asked if Theresa Weitrek would come to see him. She was the heir to the factory. Lily told him that Theresa had died, and that she was Theresa's daughter. He declared then that Lily was the heir, and that it was urgent that she then come. He needed to discuss the future of her family's business, now that the "command economy" was giving way to the "demand economy."

9

Lily went abroad alone. We might well have gone together. We needed only to arrange work schedules, house and dog sitting. But the truth, unexchanged between us, was that Lily had to learn what we both knew the trip might allow her to find.

She might find what her mother's history had been before Emma or Lily were born, before Theresa had constructed her life-disguise, the one she wore to her death.

So I say still, as earlier I did, that Lily seems unable, perhaps unwilling to relate to me completely what happened in Germany.

In that is a worry: has my wife, like her mother before her, adopted silence as a friend?

Perhaps if I approach Lily now, tonight, when the moon's rays shine on the waves' crests before they break, sit with her on the deck, hold her hand, and ask her, she will tell you her story.

## ONE: EAST BERLIN, MAY, 1991

The small, sputtering East German Trabi car blocked Schultz, the cab driver from stopping exactly at the midpoint of the hotel's revolving door. It had been his goal to make a good impression on his first American passenger by stopping just so. The dispatcher had it on the highest authority, he had told the cabdriver, that the passenger was definitely an American and, not quite so definitely, a big tipper. The tip would go into the pool to be divided at the end of the week, the dispatcher had reminded Schultz. Schultz needed no reminder.

Fuming, he got out and screamed insults at the occupant of the Trabi. The small Trabi had become the butt of jokes by the West Germans, a symbol of all they claimed was wrong with East German industry under the "commies."

Slow, ugly and headed for the scrap heap. That's where most of East Germany's industry and its workers belonged, brayed the West Germans just a few months after the euphoria of chipping away blocks of the old Berlin Wall had evaporated.

Galvanized by both random and some more precise insults about his Turkish parents, the owner of the Trabi finally got it to sputter and coasted down the hotel's circular driveway, allowing Schultz to pull his cab, just so, in front of the revolving doors.

Schultz flicked a handkerchief over the already clean dashboard. He was amazed that in just the few months since reunification he had moved from "communist" to "capitalist." The cab company was allowing him to buy his vehicle. Schultz marveled at the rapid change in his life - for years a maintenance worker for Interflug, the air carrier quickly pronounced obsolete by the "Wessies," whom he was developing doubts about. He had been "retrained" as a cab driver, now wandering the streets of Berlin in his new cab being bought under a government-subsidized loan.

Whenever Schultz looked at himself in the mirror of his small apartment in one of Berlin's large housing blocks, testimony to Soviet architecture, he would practice the slogans of capitalism:

"I'm going to be rich. Travel, do as I like. Everyone's on his own now."

He wasn't so sure of the last one, having spent his entire adult life under the old East German guidelines of mutual care and secured work.

Schultz straightened his tie as the revolving door turned and his passenger emerged.

Shit, he thought, do all Americans look so healthy? So confident? What do they know about life - about trouble?

Nerve, that's what it is. No self-respecting German woman would wear a beige jacket, slacks and boots at this time of the year. Not in May. June at the earliest, thought Schultz - until then custom called for dark colors.

He scrambled out to open the back door for her.

She barely nodded a thank you as she moved a small bouquet of flowers and the envelope to her left hand, keeping the right hand free for balance as she slid into the back seat, into its wonderful smell of new leather.

As he started the car, Schultz looked at his passenger in the rear-view mirror.

Definitely good-looking. Not quite as young as at first glance. Maybe mid-40s. But who could tell with all that makeup? In the East, makeup was frowned upon.

She was anxious, her fingers bent, tapping the envelope. Her grey-green eyes met his.

"Weissensee, please. I'd like to go to Weissensee."

Her voice was low, the German surprisingly clear, even if the accent was unpleasant to his ears.

Now why, thought Schultz, would anyone, much less the first American he had ever seen up close, want to go to so shabby a suburb of the former East Berlin? A big fare, he mused, and a good tip for so long a trip.

"You are from America, yes?" asked Schultz as he pulled away from the newly-renovated Metropol hotel, turning left into Friederichstrasse and quickly passing the old Friedrichstrasse train station, surrounded by scaffolding. Everywhere he looked buildings unpainted for decades were being ushered into new life. Just as he was.

The woman answered almost absently.

"Yes."

"From where?"

"California. San Diego."

"Is that in Los Angeles?"

"No. Further south."

"Americans don't come here to the old East," Schultz said, trying to establish some camaraderie for the long trip.

"They will. If for no other reason than to see where the Wall was."

That, thought Schultz, will help me buy my cab more quickly.

"The most famous checkpoint of the wall, Checkpoint Charlie, will be on your right in just a minute." Saying that, he waited for a reaction. She looked to her right but showed no particular interest at what was still, for him, a very strange sight in front of the checkpoint.

As long as he could remember, it had been a hated symbol of the West. After the Wall had come down, Schultz, a man in his 50s, had spent an afternoon with his mother on his arm, walking from one side of the old Wall to the other, trying to imprint it on his mind that the barrier to free movement from one side of Berlin to the other was gone. His mother, with tears running down her cheeks, had babbled on and on about the old days, the better days, and the great parades during the old days.

Sometimes in the middle of the night Schultz would wake up with sweat drenching his body, wondering if at his age he could suddenly become a successful capitalist. Rumors at the cab yard were that everyone's rent was going to triple. The subsidy he counted on, and had always had in the East, would be gone. Could he earn enough money? How would he take care of his mother?

His passenger's voice filtered through his thoughts. She looked at him as if she had asked the question several times.

"What are they selling?"

"Everything. Pieces of the Wall, old Soviet Army medals, East German flags - anything from before." Odd, thought Schultz, that souvenir was once my flag. I saluted it. Stood at attention. And now it's a souvenir.

He slowed the cab as they passed the small crowd in front of the makeshift tables draped with flags and covered with the remnants of his history.

"And tee-shirts," came the slow response.

"Yes." Even Schultz had to smile at that. "Always the tee-shirts."

He liked her better for noticing the tee-shirts and not commenting about his once-proud flag.

"Where in Weissensee would you like to go?" He realized she had not told him.

"Just to Weissensee."

"Madame, it's a suburb of Berlin, not big, but not that small."

"A suburb?" She seemed bewildered.

They had already left the center of Berlin and were traveling through shabbier and almost deserted neighborhoods as they reached the edge of the suburb.

Schultz pulled the cab to the next curb. He stopped, turned around to face the woman.

He spoke patiently. "I have to know where you wish to go. I do not want to drive you around in circles."

The answer was so low he almost missed it.

"To the cemetery."

He felt a sense of relief. For a moment he had wondered if she had any precise destination in mind at all.

"Which? Catholic? Lutheran?"

"No. Another one."

She's crazy, thought Schultz.

"There is no other one."

She opened the envelope she was holding, and took out a small map, frayed at the edges. She handed it up to him.

"Yes," she said, "there is another."

Just my luck, thought Schultz. The forsaken cemetery. It was said the government was setting aside some money to put it back in order.

Schultz felt his skin crawl.

"You want to go to the lost Jewish cemetery? Weissensee Cemetery?"

"Take me there," came the low voice from the back seat. He reluctantly took the map from her fingers to study it more closely. At the bottom he saw the designation "D-24." What could this blond woman want with D-24, so clearly a grave designation?

He drove as fast as he could until he found, and then began to circle the ten-foot-high crumbling outer wall of the cemetery, up and down Klement Gottwald Allee and Indira Ghandi Strasse, around Gurtel Strasse and Strasse 106. And back again.

He began to feel the damp under his arms soak his shirt as he wondered where the entrance was and whether he could find it. He promised himself he would never tell the other drivers where he had been.

He continued circling. He finally turned into Herbert Baum Strasse, a shabby side street, and found the secluded entrance.

The deserted small parking lot contained a single car.

Schultz kept his head averted as the woman got out of the cab and reached money toward him. The amount she counted out for the fare was correct. And then she added a 5 DM note.

"For your trouble, sir. Thank you," said the low, measured voice.

He desperately wanted to say something about how he had nothing to do with the past, but couldn't find any words. Out of the corner of his eye, he could see an umbrella of trees overhanging the cemetery. There really was nothing to say, he thought, as he turned the cab quickly and headed back to the center of Berlin.

# TWO

Lily hesitated as she began to push the cemetery's entry gate open. But it was unlocked; perhaps, it seemed, opened again only recently. And while she could see through the filigree into the cemetery proper, the veil of another world seemed to hang between the world in Weissensee Cemetery and the world she still stood within.

Inside the gates, past the veil, silence, a silence which was only emphasized when threatened by the rustling of leaves and birdsong.

Lily had tried to set before herself the widest path of imagined expectations she could fashion, because she knew as she set out from home on this quest that she didn't know what to expect.

Yet, as she registered what lay in front of her, awe formed slowly over and around her body. If anyone had been there with her, and looked at her, the awe in her face would have been frightening.

For fifty years, the leaves and branches of trees fell in Weissensee Cemetery unheard by the ears of the living. They descended, twirling in the wind, to add more cover to the 115,000 graves. They mingled upon landing with the vines and the earth itself, enveloping headstones until they toppled and fell.

The snow, sleet and rain of those fifty years made healthy soil for the vines, whose strengthened growth encircled the headstones, then eradicated the names of the long dead, sending them to eternal obscurity.

Thus the future could have no promise of remembrance for the dead; it would only be when a human being came with human grief that one obliterated individual name might have a moment of importance.

Such a human being was Lily Weitrek, though as she hesitantly considered entering the cemetery, she did not know that.

Her good sense, her practical wisdom wanted her to just turn and walk away.

Why in the world was she here? She knew. She just had to find the reason where she kept it in the corner of her mind.

She had promised.

She began to go through the few facts she had been able to accumulate about Weissensee, about this Jewish cemetery rediscovered only after East Berlin and West Berlin became just Berlin again. Allegedly locked up not long after one of the last permitted funerals there in the early '40s. The keys to its regal gates thrown God knows where. The final, untended resting place for 115,000 Jews. Men, women and children of the professional, artistic and industrious Jewish community so thoroughly assimilated into the cultural life of Germany that only in death did they return to final segregation.

Most of those who sleep in Weissensee Cemetery, she reiterated to herself from her self-instruction, came and went from earth before the Nazi rage of anti-Semitism.

What was before her as she moved farther into the cemetery was a half wagon- wheel of paths. The ends of none of the paths could be seen, they went so deep into the thickets of untrimmed vines, gnarling trees and the bed of leaves, which seemed everywhere.

As a camera does, her eyes began to focus on more precise things. Tombstones. But not the orderly, militarily precise look of most cemetery tombstones. These markers lay askew, on top of one another, an occasional undisturbed one seeming the exception in the rows.

And the mausoleums, small tributes to classical architecture intended for the burial of whole families. Some of these approached the appearance of venerable ruins, a pillar missing or tipped over, the geometry of the stone embroidered with the green and brown twists of vines.

She picked a path and took it. The path crossed rows. Rows intersected graves.

Row D is what she was supposed to find. What was there were ancient signs on the edge of the path on which she could barely make out the letters.

"I can't do this!" she said out loud, perhaps the first human sound to break the silence in many years.

She knew she must, she knew she couldn't turn back, not so much for the promise she had made her mother but because of who she was.

Quitting was not her way.

She pushed at a grave marker, trying to leverage it off the marker below it. Where was the row designation?

She said out loud again, "This is impossible."

And, continuing to talk as if to some unseen companion, "I can't do this; how am I supposed to find anything?" Lily wasn't looking more than ten yards ahead, even as she slowly made a circle with her feet as she tried to make some sense out of the rows and rows of barely distinguishable paths. She began at random to try to tear away the obstructing vines from the face of the grave nearest her.

Wolfgang Schmidt, a tall, slender middle-aged man was investigating his own way through the thicket of the cemetery, and he still hadn't seen her.

But he stopped short and lifted his head. He saw her. He knew she hadn't yet seen him, and his head and body movement seemed to suggest he might turn and leave before she did. He took a deep breath.

"Hallo! Hallo!" He called across rows of fallen headstones.

No answer.

In the best imitation of British gentry Wolfgang clipped off the ends of his words. This linguistic posture irritated many. More caring people understood that this mannerism was most pronounced when Wolfgang was upset or nervous.

As Wolfgang stared at the apparition in front of him, he recognized instantly that this mud-splattered woman had to be his American mail-order client. Americans, he thought ruefully, always ordering, commanding, insolent in their overbearing belief they can do no wrong.

The woman was oblivious to his presence, apparently lost in thought as she tore at the vines.

Why, Wolfgang questioned to himself, would anyone, even an American, wear a white suit to dig around old graves? It was his penchant to see all things as either black or white; shades of color in between were forced to flee to one extreme or the other. Thus in his general ignorance of women's fashion Wolfgang registered Lily Weitrek's beige suit only as white.

Another deep breath, followed this time by more of a shout mingled with a dose of frustration. He had made his way close to where Lily was standing.

"Are you Mrs. Weitrek?"

Lily's head weaved as she seemed to become conscious again of where she was and that someone was talking to her.

"Yes." She seemed totally caught up in pulling at vines.

"I'm Herr Schmidt, Wolfgang Schmidt." He almost clicked his heels together. But Lily did not so much as nod an acknowledgement.

"Your German attorney." He spoke as if he were explaining the fact to a child. "You wrote and asked me to meet you here in this cemetery, eh? You are Mrs. Lily Weitrek?"

"Yes. I am. I'm looking for someone. That's why I asked to meet you here. Someone somewhere in this area. I thought you could help me."

Lily finally looked at him.

"And that is why I am here, why I came here, even though the setting is quite different from a lawyer's normal environment. How can I help?" he asked.

"You can see what I am trying to do." She waved her hand in the general direction of the world. "Trying to clear some headway in this tangle of vines so I can see something. This is hard!"

"I'm a lawyer, not a gravedigger." He recognized quickly that his well-meant humor was unfortunate.

Lily's response was immediate and curt.

"I realize the $5,000 I sent you isn't much by lawyers' standards, but you did accept it. You did answer that you would help me during this short time I can be here. Help me do anything I need to have done."

Wolfgang drew himself up straight and said, as if peering down his nose,"Legal help, madame, not, I am afraid, physical help. Legal help in making a claim for property in what was East

Germany, property you report your family lost and has a right to. Not any kind of help, physical help...how would it look to have a German lawyer all covered with mud?"

Lily looked scornful, dismissive. She twisted around abruptly and started again to wrestle with vines that were enveloping a grave marker tipped at a 45-degree angle, prevented from reaching the ground by the halter-like net of the vines' branches. The effort seemed to loosen her hair, or in any event cause some twists of her hair to flop across her eyes.

She made an irritable-looking swipe at the locks, with little success. She exhaled forcefully, and strained to try to lift the headstone up now from its 45-degree tilt to see if she could read the inscription.

Wolfgang gathered his already tight-seeming body even closer to himself, affecting an uptight, almost prim countenance.

"Why," he said, "did you insist on meeting here? We should have met in my office."

"Look," Lily replied with exasperation, "pretend you're an American; pitch in. I need help."

"Of course," Wolfgang said, pursing his lips, "do Americans do that? 'pitch in?' and tear away at old graves?"

"Americans don't lose whole cemeteries, nor do they forget them."

"Mrs. Weitrek. If we are to continue at all together on this venture, you must listen. I know you think my firm assigned me to your case after you contacted us, but that's not correct. I want to help you regain the property your family lost. I want to give you the legal help you requested but exchanged insults over tombstones is not a very good beginning to our working relationship."

Lily snapped back in a most irritated fashion, emphasizing each word with a measured tug at a vine.

"My family did not `lose' the shoe factory. The Nazis seized it in 1933. My sister and I want it back now that it's possible. So help us get it back."

Wolfgang Schmidt was silent. Instead of talking, he began to wrestle himself with the vine thicket around the grave marker that had been the target of Lily's efforts. As he strained, his shoes

THE LAST CEMETERY IN BERLIN

began to sink into the soft earth through the vine cover on the ground. He paused and took a somewhat remorseful look at the shoe he had lifted out of the soil, the expensive looking Italian shoe.

"Is your sister here?"

"No." Lily avoided his intense scrutiny by tearing at the vine that was encircling her pant leg.

"Why not?"

She seemed to stop to think. She saw him staring.

"My sister couldn't come."

"But you decided to come even if she could not join you."

"I've come to look at the property. Get it back, or at least get some money for it. That's all."

"Well, what are we looking for?"

"A white headstone in Row D. But who can tell if this is Row D?" Her voice climbed up an octave as she pulled at a vine and almost fell when her hand slipped.

The exchanges between Wolfgang and Lily had kept their focus almost exclusively on the grave marker, one or both of them working away at it even as they talked.

So neither one took notice of a stooped and elderly man who had been moving slowly toward them starting about 50 yards away and up another path. As he was able to see more clearly that the two of them were twisting the vines ever more violently as they tried to free the grave marker, he hurried up until he reached them. Angrily, he shouted, adjusting his yarmulke with the two forefingers of his right hand as he did.

"Stop! Stop! You may not do this! You may not touch my graves! Young woman, step aside. Women should not struggle with stone.  And you, young man, where is your yarmulke?"

"I do not have one."

"No yarmulke?"

"Old man, this is Germany."

"Old Germany, new Germany. This is Weissensee Cemetery. I am its caretaker, and have been since the war ended. Here you must wear a yarmulke. Here. For five Deutschemark you rent a yarmulke." He thrust a gnarled hand holding a yarmulke at Wolfgang

"And I must wear it?"

"In my cemetery, the forgotten Jewish cemetery, for me, the last cemetery in Berlin, yes." The caretaker stared at the lawyer.

Wolfgang Schmidt was hardly gracious. He took a bill from his pocket, gave a dirty look to Lily, who looked as if she might laugh out loud at his discomfort, and handed the money to the caretaker.

"Your cemetery is a disgrace to the German government," Wolfgang said accusingly.

"The German government has been a disgrace to my cemetery."

"It is a mess."

"It is beautiful," the caretaker said calmly; "As God would have it. Now that it has been rediscovered, the German government is embarrassed. It will be `cleaned up.' My beautiful garden will be destroyed to make it pleasing to those who for years did not care about it, know about it. Put on your yarmulke!"

"It falls off," Wolfgang said, sounding querulous.

Wolfgang pushed the yarmulke back on his head, rotating it around as if trying to find a permanent position for it. He looked around the cemetery, and turned back to the caretaker.

"What happened here?"

"Nothing."

"Nothing?"

"Young man, young woman, the last funeral in Weissensee Cemetery was in 1942. As soon as that funeral was over, the Nazi storm troopers came. They destroyed what they wanted to, then locked the gates and took the keys away. Everyone forgot my cemetery. Almost no one ever came again, until a few months ago after reunification."

Wolfgang shook his head.

"This part of Berlin was totally destroyed by Allied bombs and by Soviet troops at the end of World War II. Nothing was left standing, not even the zoo."

"But God," said the caretaker, "kept the cemetery safe, and me. My family hid here when I was a child… all through the war… and I, I have never left. But now all the beautiful trees will be pruned and tidy rows will be made of all my fallen headstones."

"Is that not as it should be?" asked Wolfgang.

The caretaker took no notice of Wolfgang's question, but continued:

"All these years in winter only the falling snow has been heard. In spring and in summer only the songbirds in these trees. The dead have been comforted. I do not think the dead care much about being tidied up."

The caretaker began to pace a bit, moving slowly down the path, turning his head as if to inspect the rows, which radiated off the path on both sides. Wolfgang and Lily had no choice but to trail behind him. They realized they had lost him, at least for the while, because it was evident to both of them, without the need of any mutual confirmation, that the caretaker's look into his past had embarked him on reverie.

Following him up and down with their eyes as he paced, back and forth, seemed to provide them a sense of the cemetery's geography. The caretaker knew every path and every row - must, indeed. He had surveyed them for half a century.

Lily broke the silence after five or six minutes.

"Do you know where headstone Row D, number 24 is?"

"I know where every headstone is."

The caretaker then pointed to the headstone, which Lily and Wolfgang had been trying to loosen from the vines when the caretaker confronted them.

"That is old Ezekiel Abrahms. Died in 1922. His young wife came to the funeral, weeping and wailing. But all the time her eyes were on Martin Steiner, who was buried later in Row P, number 18, far from here."

He led them toward a mausoleum nearby, still largely intact. It was of rich proportion with a marble wing on each side of a centrally placed large tablet. The name "Aaronsohn" was etched above each of the three sides, still legible even though time had generally eroded the Greek-looking structure. He pointed to the central slab of marble, where the year 1930 appeared.

"That is proud Otto Aaronsohn. A prosperous citizen of Berlin. He thought he could predict the future, and left one side for each of his two sons, their wives and children. Too proud to leave, they all then died in Bergen Belsen, and Otto rests alone, waiting for them to come back to him."

He stopped.

"I know them all," he said. "For all these years I have studied them, made them my family. All of them wait for someone to come and mourn with them for all of those who are missing. Young man, your yarmulke."

Lily asked again, "Do you know Row D, number 24?"

"'The sweetest mother of them all.' I remember my father chiseling the scalloped edges. He worked on so many of these here. But that particular one - the daughter had insisted - had to be special. Pure white. Poor little girl. She wept and wept at that funeral. I was young. I had never witnessed sorrow like that till then."

"My mother?" Lily asked no one.

The caretaker looked shocked.

"Are you Row D, number 24? The granddaughter?"

"Yes."

"Imagine this. The granddaughter of Emma Auerbach Brodsky. You came back. But where is your mother? Why is she not here to say Kaddish?"

"She is dead. She died seven years ago."

"So you then will say Kaddish."

"I don't know how." She looked distinctly uncomfortable.

Again the caretaker looked shocked, even stricken.

"You do not know how?"

"No. My mother never spoke about the past. She never told us until just before she died that her mother was here in this cemetery."

The caretaker looked to the sky.

"What is this? What nonsense is this? Did your mother believe she could become someone else by pretending? By hiding who she was? And you? Who are you with no past?" He studied her intently.

Lily looked as if she had been chastised. It annoyed her. Her reply was almost curt.

"I am whoever I say I am. Right now, I'm here, keeping a promise I made to my mother."

Wolfgang, who had been only an audience to this unfolding dialogue, this developing biography, seemed to come alert when he heard Lily refer to a promise she had made her mother. That fact was the first bit of information he had been provided about the help he was supposed to supply this woman from America, who made appointments in cemeteries and made new acquaintances in a generally abrasive style. The caretaker's response would get Wolfgang's special attention.

"What was that promise?" the caretaker asked.

"I told my mother that if the time ever came when it was possible to visit her mother's grave, I would. If the cemetery even still existed, I cautioned her. And if I could find it, I would lay flowers on her mother's grave."

That recollection of latter-hour words spoken to her mother seemed to soften Lily's firm, but tense facade.

"Where is my grandmother?"

"Turn around. Look beyond the tree. Your grandmother is waiting behind you."

The caretaker's direction was exact. There was a tree one row away from where they had been standing ever since Wolfgang and Lily met, ever since the caretaker apprehended them struggling with a grave marker - the wrong one.

And just beyond that tree, framed somehow by the curl of some branches stood a scalloped, still mostly white headstone. It read "Emma Auerbach Brodsky," and beneath the name the inscription the caretaker had recited from memory: "The sweetest mother of them all."

A few vines traveled up from the ground around the headstone, like laurels for the inscription.

Lily took soft and slow steps to the graveside. She lowered herself and seemed insecure, as if she ought to genuflect, or even cross herself. She settled for spreading the flowers she took out of her bag in front of the grave. She bent her head.

Wolfgang had stepped to one side. He was uncomfortable. The emotion of this moment did not escape him, nor leave him untouched. He had to fight off involvement even more as the caretaker began Kaddish. Kaddish for a woman dead more than 50 years whose descendant did not know how to say the Hebrew verses for the dead. He expected the sky to darken, for a storm to appear. This meeting with Lily, this caretaker, this reunion in a cemetery all seemed suddenly unreal to him, not the working daily reality of an attorney-at-law.

Lily's voice, under the words of Kaddish, could almost not be heard:

"Well, little Theresa, I kept the promise. I am at your mother's grave in Weissensee Cemetery, East Berlin, 1991."

The caretaker finished and bowed his head. So did Lily and Wolfgang. For the fewest of minutes, only the songbirds in the trees were heard. The silence of the three at the graveside seemed to adjust the volume of the songs a little higher for just a while.

Then, just as it always seems to happen at gravesides, when the obsequies are complete, first one of those standing by, then the others, quicken pace, as if to show by motion that they are still among the living and returning to the course of life. In this case, it was the caretaker who moved first.

"You may as well meet the rest of the family, as long as you are here - the fighting Auerbachs and Brodskys. What a row there was at Great Aunt Marie's funeral!"

"Marie? Who was Marie?" Lily asked.

The caretaker, not answering, headed toward the cemetery's central path. Lily followed and Wolfgang fell in behind her. As they came closer to the back edge of the cemetery, they could see that the wall there was crumbling. Closer, they could also see that the wall, about eight feet high, was in fact made up of mausoleums whose backs were against the barrier wall that followed the perimeter of the cemetery.

The caretaker pointed to a section. There were nameplates there. They could see that it, too, was a mausoleum, though the elements had been less kind to the structure than they had been to the scalloped white headstone in Row D.

Their eyes scanned the names: Marie Auerbach 1932, Heinrich Auerbach 1928, Arthur Auerbach 1935, Elfried Auerbach 1931, Isador Auerbach 1936.

The caretaker explained.

"Marie was your grandmother's older sister. The two families, Auerbachs and Brodskys, met here one last time at her funeral. I was there with my father. The fight began as soon as the headstone had been placed."

\* \* \* \* \* \*

1932

Weissensee Cemetery in 1932 was a masterpiece of landscape architecture. In spite of the fact that it was a typical cold December day in Berlin, the art of the plantings served to keep the promise of verdure alive even through the days of sloppy, cold rain that dominated a Berlin winter.

German culture in the years between world wars, although centered on the hopeless dream of the Weimar Republic, hopeless at least as far as political reality was concerned, was nevertheless an outburst of sophisticated eclecticism.

Just as the society level of which the Auerbachs and Brodskys were part "sampled" the arts and letters of Central European, French, British and Italian cultures, so the landscape architecture adopted by the cultured Jewish community of Berlin for Weissensee Cemetery was eclectic.

There were Greek style mausoleums such as the Auerbachs', where this late afternoon, the Auerbach and Brodsky families stood circling a grave.

There were more Roman designs, and more French as well. Some of the larger ones were reminiscent of Sans Souci, that German dream of Frederick the Great outside Potsdam that vied in history now with the Sicilian Dream of an earlier Frederick.

The family that was there had remained by Marie Auerbach's gravesite after the Rabbi and the small group of friends had found their way down the many paths of the cemetery to the exit.

Uneasiness about their future safety in Germany pervaded all Jewish households throughout the country. There was a rumor that the Union of Orthodox Synagogue Communities in the anticipation of yet faceless future disasters was planning to send a petition to Adolph Hitler. The document, so the rumor said, would call on Hitler when he was elected Chancellor, as everyone expected him to be, to reveal whether or not it was his intent to destroy Jewry in Germany.

This cold touch of terror limited the attendance of even close friends at a Jewish funeral such as Marie Auerbach's.

The remaining women of the family stood on one side of the gravesite, the men on the other. Each person had torn black ribbons pinned to their clothes.

Theresa Brodksy, later to be Lily's mother, was 24. She was dressed as the other women were in a high-collared, white blouse and a severely tailored, long-skirted black suit. But her hat was different. Unlike the severe hats her mother and aunt wore, Theresa wore a daring French creation with a small black veil covering her face. Wisps of blond curls escaped the little hat and clustered below her ears. Theresa stood between her mother, Emma, whom Theresa often said was the sweetest mother in the world, and her only remaining aunt who had always been her favorite, Franziska Auerbach Sagal.

The only male member of the Brodsky side of the family at the service, Julius, was a large man in his mid-40s. He was a man whose posture and bearing suggested strongly he was accustomed to being listened to, and heard. He had been unable to contain the urgency of what he had to say even until the end of the service. The rest knew that, of course; knew what he was to say. After all, he had already infuriated the up and coming National Socialist Party by publishing an angry rebuttal to *Mein Kampf*, which the madman Adolph Hitler had written in jail. And Julius's acknowledged and very public Zionist sympathies had brought both the families to the attention of the new Anti-Semites, the Nazis.

Julius Brodsky was angry. The completely black attire he had assumed for the occasion, including the long waistcoat, suited his anger.

"I am saying to you all that you must leave. Leave Germany! Hitler will be elected next month, and whatever he needs to do next to be in total charge he will do. January, 1933 will begin the end of Germany as we have known it, helped make it, since the turn of the century."

Arthur Auerbach did not agree. His lawyer's habits of mind were more conciliatory, more willing to keep compromise open. He was more fastidious in manner than Julius, who kept a journalist's carelessness for complicated matters evident. Arthur too wore black, but the diamond stickpin in his cravat was a signal of his and the family's prosperity and success. Marriage had merged the Auerbachs and Brodskys, at least in part, but the marriages could not change the family differences.

The Auerbachs were old German Jewish money. While the family originated so far as their geneological efforts had been able to learn, in Pomerania, that left little room for further research. Pomerania had been a mixture of Polish and German families for more centuries than post-1600 Europe could bargain with.

The Brodskys were merchants. Successful merchants, to be sure, but the most recent forebears of this 1930s family had been, well, peddlers. At least that was the angry term flung in arguments, from Auerbachs against Brodskys.

That was an insult, of course, and meant to be. They were less peddlers now than what later history would call "manufacturers' representatives." They made shoes, and sold shoes. They had graduated from being leather merchants to being owners of the largest shoe factory in Europe.

The family differences were brought to the surface by disagreement, and disagree they did over the Zionist movement. Though both families were Jewish through and through, the Auerbach dream of assimilation had been realized - they thought for good - and the Brodsky dream still was part nightmare, nightmare of Jews in fear and trembling.

Arthur Auerbach answered his brother-in-law, Julius Brodsky.

"Julius, I say again that you Zionists are escorting destruction into both our families. All of us are now suspect because of your vituperation over that imbecile Hitler's book."

"But it is you, Arthur, who is insane, not I," Julius countered. "I see what is happening. You close your eyes. You must prepare to leave. If you do not, you will lose more by staying than whatever you would have to leave by getting away now."

The rest of the family members, it seemed, issued a collective sigh, as if it was happening all over again, and not for the second, third or even fifteenth time. Theresa and her mother, Emma, exchanged worried looks; Franziska fussed. Isador Auerbach, the tallest by several inches of all those gathered there, and, like Arthur, a lawyer, drew himself even taller. He spoke like the judges in whose courtrooms he had triumphed.

"The Brodskys are insane. Daniel Brodsky is about to testify against one of the highest-ranking Nazi officials in a slander case. You and he both attract too much attention from the press. This affects all of us. Court appearances for one and a Zionist newspaper for the other. You are quite right. If Hitler is elected, we all may be arrested, but you, Julius Brodsky, you certainly will be."

Tiny Theresa, five feet tall, pretty and lithe as a gentle bird, had to talk.

"Uncle Isador, they cannot just arrest Uncle Julius...."

"Theresa," Julius answered before Isador could, "try to understand what so few members of these two families seem to. The laws which will remove all Jews from businesses or professions, from any form of the society in which we have all grown up... laws have already been written. Yes, if Hitler is elected, these laws will take effect very quickly. That is why you must come with me to Palestine."

The rest of the family members appeared to have registered for the first time the simple truth as Julius had once more said it. They began to turn back and forth to each other, words covering words with general unintelligibility, just as in Greek tragedy, the chorus often mumbles truth collectively, even as the characters are blind to it. One of them here, Franziska, was mother of a handicapped young boy, a desperate fact that clouded the truth.

"Some of us cannot leave. My crippled son cannot simply be picked up and moved. We will, if we must, go to our house in the country until Hitler is gone."

Julius pressed. "But Franziska, it is precisely because of Ludwig that you must leave. The Nazis' new laws suggest all handicapped people should be killed, and may be."

Arthur re-entered the debate.

"You are so in love with the idea of a Jewish nation, you are blinded. We are Germans. We have friends. We live in fine neighborhoods surrounded by good and decent people."

"No, Arthur, it is you who are blind. Blinded by the belief that one can escape being a Jew but remain one. By the belief that old pogroms should teach us nothing. That Jews are forever free."

The family murmur rose again, quieting down, then rising again, almost to a cadence conducted by some unseen baton. It was a murmur of uncertainty, of wishful thinking, and of intuitions of things yet to come.

Emma spoke.

"We are here to remember our sister Marie who was just taken from us. We are here to pray for her, to recite psalms as is our tradition,"

Emma deflected Julius' attempt to resume his harrangue.

"Instead," she said, "we are too willing to quarrel with each other. That is all the family now meets to do. Julius, please stop this bickering!"

Isador broke in. "I think it would be better for all of us, Emma, if the Brodsky brothers kept a distance from us. We are Auerbachs, a highly respected, old German family, not Brodskys, and we have done nothing wrong."

"But Uncle Isador," said Theresa, "I'm a Brodsky and so is my mother."

"Your mother, dear niece, is a born Auerbach. She only married a Brodsky and she has been widowed almost 16 years. So she is not one of them. And you, without our permission, have married a Gentile, out of our history, our religion. A former

Prussian officer, no less. One who has become a favorite film director for the Nazis."

Theresa lifted the small veil of her hat. She bristled. "How dare you accuse my husband of being a Nazi. He is not a Nazi! How can you say that?"

Emma quickly reached out and placed her hands on her daughter's arm – to quiet her. "That is enough, daughter; we know that your husband is a good man."

"I did not mean to imply he *is* a Nazi," Isador responded defensively. "I merely am remarking that his quite remarkable ambition might cause him to overlook whom he serves."

"I know, I know," said Julius. "Isador might indeed apologize, but the great attorney may be right. I see great sadness for you, Theresa. Be careful. Try to convince your husband that he too should leave."

"All of you," he continued, "Emma, Arthur, Franziska, - Isador is right. Daniel and I may bring the Nazis' boots to your door. So I leave Germany soon. I will not be back."

Julius turned and walked quickly down the central path of Weissensee Cemetery. One by one the other Auerbach and Brodsky family members followed. Darkness had approached already in the late December afternoon, and soon nothing would remain visible there. Theresa turned around last as she neared the great exit gate. The caretaker's young son watched Theresa leave.


\*　\*　\*　\*　\*　\*　\*


1991


Lily shuddered at the story's end. "What happened to Julius?" she asked.

"Adolph Hitler became chancellor in 1933, as you know," said the caretaker, "and as Julius predicted. It is said Julius disappeared on his way to Palestine. The report was that he was running just ahead of the Gestapo. The Nazis took over the

Brodsky shoe factory. Daniel fought them, but lost. He committed suicide. His grave too is here in Weissensee Cemetery."

"And Franziska and Ludwig?"

"No one knows - at least not I. Neither she, her husband, Misha Sagal, nor their son Ludwig are here."

The caretaker's account of the last meeting of the two families had a sobering effect on both Lily and Wolfgang, neither of whom would claim their time together so far had been promising. It was colder now than it was supposed to be, they thought. Or was it really pathetic fallacy?

"I think the time has come to leave," Wolfgang said.

"Yes," said the caretaker, "I must lock up before dark. Darkness here still leaves nothing visible at all."

They headed down the same central path taken fifty-eight years before by the Brodsky and Auerbach families, leaving the same graves, the same mausoleum. The same enormous exit gate was still unlatched. A partially destroyed building lay off to one side. Lily was the last to turn around and look back.

"There was just my mother, my sister and I - for all those years. I came here to keep a promise, find one grave to lay flowers on. But now there is a whole family I never knew existed."

She stopped, looked at the caretaker.

"Do you know any more of what happened later?"

"I have told you all I know. If you look, you may find the rest yourself."

The caretaker looked at Wolfgang.

"Is he not here to help you?" he asked Lily.

"I'm here to find property. He's to help with that," she answered tersely.

"Some would say to find family is more important than to find property."

"This may have been part of mother's past, but not mine."

Lily walked quickly toward the gate. She stopped at a memorial plaque near the large gate. It was obviously new; it still shined. There were inscriptions on the plaque. Wolfgang and Lily went closer, the caretaker watching them. It read: Elfreda Roth - 16, presumed dead - Auschwitz, 1944.

The three had reached the edge of the cemetery. They stopped in front of the little shop just inside the cemetery gate. The caretaker reached into his pocket and extended a 5 Deutsche Mark note toward Wolfgang.

"Your money back, sir, for the yarmulke."

"I had forgotten I was wearing it. Keep the money."

The caretaker acknowledged the gift with a bow of his head. A kind of smile crossed his face.

"You wore the yarmulke well." He turned to Lily.

"And you, Madame, will never now be able to leave your family behind. They lay buried here, but will go with you."

Lily and Wolfgang passed through the gate, and the caretaker swung it shut. Gusts of wind blew, disturbing the branches of the overgrown trees. They sensed, they thought, a restlessness in the cemetery now, perhaps because they had come, had been there, as if the dead had been unnerved by the living.

# THREE

Lily and Wolfgang turned away from the cemetery after hearing the gate's lock click into place, Wolfgang's recently worn yarmulke shoved into the caretaker's jacket pocket. The old man, without another look at Lily or Wolfgang, walked out of their range of vision.

The rain that had threatened most of the afternoon began to fall in cold, large drops making a pit-patting sound on the ground, rustling the unswept leaves. Whatever had briefly bound Lily and Wolfgang together in the cemetery disappeared once they found themselves outside the gate with only Wolfgang's Mercedes to focus on in the otherwise deserted parking lot. Wolfgang painstakingly studied his expensive, soaked Italian shoes before shuffling them under the bed of leaves in disgust.

He cleared his throat as if to say something, but lapsed instead into staring at his car. Drops of rain gave way to a grey mist covering them and the cemetery in a shroud-like cocoon of silence. There was nothing to share, nothing to say.

"That's my car."

Wolfgang's voice startled Lily, shaking her into the present.

"Can I give you a ride?" he asked Lily; "taxis don't come out here and the trolley line is about a 20-minute walk."

Wolfgang opened the car door for her, leaving it up to Lily to either accept or reject his offer and got behind the wheel. Noting her hesitation, Wolfgang leaned across the passenger seat and called out, "Mrs. Weitrek, you can't stay here."

Whatever he felt for himself, the look in Lily's eyes made him uneasy.

"Mrs. Weitrek, please get in. Whatever happened to your family, it was long ago. They are not the reason you are here. You're here to make a property claim."

As she got into the car, Lily looked back for a last glance at the cemetery, now almost lost in the gloom. She wondered if anything would prompt her to return. She doubted anything could.

Leaving the narrow street of the cemetery, Wolfgang turned his car onto Hohenschonhauser Strasse, which would take them to Lenin Allee and back to the center of Berlin. He thought about the silly anger of East Germans as the West German government systematically removed what it considered "communistic" street names. New names would come from a sanitized list. Lenin Allee was headed for history's scrap pile.

He did not have to look at Lily to see the spasmodic tremors that shook her body. He could feel them. Hoping she was cold rather than suffering a delayed reaction, Wolfgang turned the car heater on as high as it would go. He floored the gas pedal, intending to put the cemetery quickly behind them.

"What a crazy arrangement," he thought, resentment beginning to build. "Why did I agree to meet a client I knew nothing about in a cemetery?" It had been impulse to write Lily and agree to her ridiculous request.

Wolfgang took enormous pride in his well-deserved reputation as his law firm's most systematic researcher. He knew that some of his colleagues made fun of him behind his back for being so predictable, so "anal," he'd overheard one lawyer say. But Wolfgang did not care what was said about him. His life philosophy could be summed up in one sentence: Wolfgang never wanted to be surprised by anything. A logical and systematic approach to all things, he felt, would protect him from the unexpected.

Having been conceived in 1942 during his father's war-time leave from the German army on the Russian front, Wolfgang was born nine months later to an hysterical mother convinced that at any minute she would become a war widow. Early in childhood Wolfgang had promised himself a life in which nothing spontaneous or unplanned would be allowed to happen.

He had followed that path to and through the study of law. And beyond. He had seen to it that both in his personal as well as his professional lives he constructed secure barriers against intrusion of the unexpected.

That included new shoes.

He had only worn his new, expensive Italian shoes to this meeting to break them in so that when he wore them to his law office the shoes would be comfortable, ready to go through the business day without causing an unwanted blister.

When Heinrich Gast, the senior partner of the law firm of Gast & Gast, had called a meeting of the entire firm, and waved a letter from an American looking for legal counsel in making a property claim for East German property, and asked for a volunteer, everyone had been shocked when Wolfgang offered to take the case.

Old Heinrich Gast had looked concerned, Wolfgang noted with secret satisfaction. It became a joke around the old, prestigious firm that Wolfgang, suffering a high fever — since nothing else would explain so atypical a move by the firm's notorious plodder — had taken the case of a demented American who required that the first meeting with her attorney be in a cemetery.

Nobody else wanted the case. Had Wolfgang not volunteered, Mr. Gast would have sent a polite letter stating the firm did not handle such matters.

Wolfgang suddenly realized that, lost in his own thoughts, he had left the main road and was on the back streets of shabby East Berlin. He had taken the wrong turn. The street sign said K. Lede Strasse, and the street jogged. Lily was speaking to him.

"I didn't know it would be so ..."Her voice trailed off. To his relief, she started again.

"I thought it would be simple. Once I learned the cemetery still existed, I thought I'd walk into a normal cemetery, rows neatly laid out, follow the map, find the grave and put flowers on it."

"What did you need me for if that's what you expected?" Wolfgang hadn't intended to be so querulous, but unexpectedly driving in circles somewhere in East Berlin irritated him. He had never spent an unnecessary moment in East Berlin. Like most "Wessies," he thought everything about it sub-standard.

He completed the U-turn, and headed back to the intersection where he would turn left onto Lenin Allee.

Lily hesitated, her fingers playing with the shoulder strap of her purse. "I wanted company."

Wolfgang was tempted to laugh. In the cemetery, Lily had been rude, brusque and quick to take offense. Revealing a personal need did not match the strong impression she had made on him of a woman who gave little and asked for less.

Changing the subject, he asked, "Where are you staying in Berlin?"

"At the Metropol Hotel on Friedrichstrasse."

This lady, he thought, is a bundle of contradictions. "Mrs. Weitrek, no one stays in the East Zone unless they have to."

"It's Ms., not Mrs. I wanted to stay at the Metropol." Lily caught his quizzical look. "Because of John Le Carre and Len Deighton."

"Are they friends of yours?" Wolfgang asked, not at all sure he was interested if they were or were not.

"They are writers — of spy novels." Catching his blank look, she continued. "You know — East-West spy novels, where spies from East Germany and the Soviet Union plot against spies from the West, usually English, sometimes American. Well, they all meet each other lurking around East Berlin at the Metropol Hotel and the Friedrichstrasse Train Station. So I wanted to stay there."

His laughter rang out so suddenly in the confined space of the car, the sound bounced off the interior. He laughed until tears ran down his face.

"You are an amazing woman, Ms. Weitrek. I really expected you to say something profound. Nothing about spy stories."

He started to laugh again. Lily, caught up in his laughter, joined in.

"It is a silly reason, isn't it? But the Metropol is also cheap."

Wolfgang looked at her in astonishment. "It is notoriously expensive — for us, at least 200-300 marks a night."

Lily was embarrassed for confessing to a love of spy novels, but felt a sense of vindication as she explained, "I'm a Citibank cardholder and, as such, the room is 50 percent discounted for me. With the discount, it's about $95 a night, and that was as cheap as I could find in Berlin. So I get it all — a cheap rate, a great room and I can wait for spies to show up."

With a twinkle in his eye Wolfgang dropped his voice to a conspiratorial whisper. "Your spy hotel may be open, but your spy train station looks closed."

For the first time it occurred to Lily that Wolfgang might not be as cold and distant as he appeared.

Resuming a normal voice, Wolfgang said, "The station was a border crossing controlled by East Germany. It was closed for repairs – short-term - immediately after reunification. The East Germans never repaired anything. The building and tracks were declared unsafe by my government."

"I'd like to see it anyway. It's just a block from the Metropol. Could we drive by?"

With a shrug of resignation, Wolfgang said, "You will not see much. But yes. If you want, we will even stop."

Using the light of the television tower in Alexanderplatz, visible even through the gloom as a beacon, Wolfgang turned the car onto the street, which would become Unter den Linden. East Berlin is totally depressing, he thought to himself. For the most part deserted of people and absent of cars, only an occasional passenger could be seen getting off a trolley car. The buildings they drove past were in various stages of decay. Paint and siding had peeled off long ago, with haphazard, mismatched colors reapplied. Broken windows were boarded up, front steps fallen in and never repaired.

"We will fix it. In a year it will all look different — except for those."

Following the direction of Wolfgang's gesturing hand, Lily realized he was pointing at a series of massive box-like structures that towered over surrounding neighborhoods.

"Soviet architecture. Housing for the masses." Contempt colored Wolfgang's words. "We will spend billions. Our tax rates will go even higher here in the West so we can spend all our money in the East Zone fixing roads and train tracks, modernizing the telephone system and cleaning up the lakes and rivers. But those ugly buildings will stay as a reminder of all the years the Soviets controlled part of Germany. All of us in the

West know our standard of living will go down to help our
`brothers' in the East."

The bitterness in his voice caused Lily to study him closely. "I
thought all Germans wanted the Wall down," Lily said.

Wolfgang picked his words carefully. He replied, "Yes, but
not the way it happened. So quickly. No time to plan, to study
how much of our money it would take to rebuild the East." He
added gloomily, "It is going to take billions, about 100 billion DM
a year for 10 years."

Wolfgang fell into a silent reverie. His silence allowed Lily to
pick out the different political eras of Germany reflected in the
buildings they were passing. Remains of buildings bombed out
during World War II and never rebuilt were more plentiful that
she had first realized. The rubble had been removed, but the
partial structures had been allowed to remain. Soviet architecture
was very easy to pick out with its oppressive size and lack of
design.

Wolfgang did not speak again until he turned the car onto
Friedrichstrasse. Lily's heart skipped a beat as she realized the
car was slowing down to pull up and actually stop at the train
station. Lily had arrived too late the night before from San Diego
to visit the station. As she looked at it, she was suddenly glad for
Wolfgang's company for the second time that day.

The station was built on both sides of Friedrichstrasse. One
side, Wolfgang told Lily, was for trains and train passengers. The
other side, the one closer to Alexanderplatz, was the S-Bahn
subway station.

Both sections were dark and deserted with yellow tape
glistening from the rain at the entrances.

Scaffolding ran along the entire length of both buildings,
which, Lily judged, were at least 40 feet high. In the gloom, the
deserted train station looked like a relic of another time, which
was being yanked against its will into a new era.

Small entrepreneurial efforts to enter the new free market
economy could already be seen in the small privately-owned shops
next to the station, which were undergoing quick facelifts.

Lily tried to remember what she knew about the station, built,
she thought, in the late 1800s. It was one of the most important

stations in Germany and, as such, had served passengers of all sorts during wars and between wars.

Trains and their stations were very much a part of German culture. The precision of the trains' operations was a hallmark of German organization, a point of national pride. Stations were little cultural centers where people dined, bought books, and met. And, in the last days of World War II in April 1945, Allied bombing added one more use to them: it drove German civilians into their tunnels, only to learn in terror that Hitler had ordered the flooding of his "cowardly" people. Even Hitler loyalists were reluctant to obey one of Hitler's last orders.

"What a strange, sad place," Lily said.

"Oh, it will re-open soon enough. For the first time since Germany was divided, the trains and subways will once again move freely between East and West," Wolfgang replied.

"By the way, what did your `spies' do here?"

"They pushed each other off the station platforms and under the wheels of oncoming trains after passing their military secrets." Lily smiled as she gave Wolfgang this brief synopsis.

"The wall coming down ruins this genre, does it not? No more spy novels for you to read. May I suggest, Ms. Weitrek, a little Goethe or Schiller?"

I bet he thinks I don't know these German authors, so here goes, Lily thought to herself.

"Mr. Schmidt." Lily pulled from memory, and, enunciating each word, said, "One ought every day at least, to hear a little song, read a good poem, see a fine picture, and, if it were possible, to speak a few reasonable words."

She congratulated herself on his bemused look.

"Goethe, correct? Not bad. Not bad at all, Ms. Weitrek, for an American from San Diego. Now let me get you to your beloved Metropol."

Approaching the circular drive of the hotel, Lily found herself unexpectedly saying, "Would you mind having dinner with me?" She sensed his hesitation, and quickly added, "We could discuss my claim and how to proceed."

Wolfgang was looking forward to going home, getting out of his soggy shoes and spending what remained of the evening with his two sons. They had been the unexpected in his life, his love for them a surprise in his orderly world. He wanted to say no to Lily, but the tenseness in her face had returned, he noticed, and she seemed sad.

"Well, if I catch the flu, I will add the doctor's bill to your account."

Lily looked relieved and said, "It's a deal. I promise I won't keep you long. And could you call me Lily, please. Ms. Weitrek is too formal for an American from San Diego." He nodded in assent.

"Then it is only right that you address me as Wolfgang," he replied, a small smile finding its way to his face.

# FOUR

The restaurant of the Metropol was a room off the mezzanine of the hotel. That morning, after a night sleep's trying to recover from the effects of the difference in time between San Diego and Berlin, Lily had breakfast in the same room. She discovered breakfast in Germany, apparently, was a meal she couldn't imagine anyone eating regularly without gaining weight.

The breakfast buffet covered at least 20 feet of the room, and was laden with every imaginable kind of meat, cheese, fish, fruit, pastry, bread, juice, cereal and yogurt available. Lily tried not to stare openly at the mounds of food that the hotel guests were piling on their plates and then actually ate.

"That's a real difference between Americans and Germans," she thought, watching people eat everything on their plates. "Americans take more than they plan to eat and just waste the food, but here they take everything and intend to eat it all."

The hotel guests were mostly middle-aged men in suits and ties looking exactly what they were: bureaucrats. Scattered around the room were small groups of foreigners. "Potential investors in East Germany," thought Lily, observing a group of Japanese men at one table, an apparent Indian trade delegation at another. On the Lufthansa Airlines flight she had taken from Los Angeles, a pamphlet was passed out describing the investment opportunities that were now available in what had been East Germany.

She was, Lily noted, the only single woman in the room and the only American. It also registered quickly with Lily that it was not the custom for people to look up from their plates or newspapers as someone entered the dining room to establish eye contact long enough to nod a neutral recognition that someone was sharing the same territory. Besides a perfunctory "Guten Tag" from the hostess who showed Lily to a table, there was no reason to say another word to anyone. "Very un-American," Lily thought to herself.

Here now with Wolfgang at night, Lily noticed the difference in the ambience from the utilitarian character of breakfast time.

The darkness and the carefully planned lighting changed the vast room to a collection of smaller spaces seemingly attached to each other by passageways. The eyes of the guests were drawn to the textures, which defined the draperies, the upholstery in the banquettes, the use of deep color in the linen tablecloths and napkins.

What had been a cafeteria, albeit an elegant one in the morning, had been transformed by nightfall into a plush and private assembly of dining areas, suitable, Lily thought, for the many spy exchanges which had taken place there, and which she found in fancy, even now, going through her mind.

And, as busy as the morning traffic in the restaurant had been, this evening patronage was slow. Lily had taken note of only two other tables with diners.

A tuxedoed maitre d' had shown Lily and Wolfgang to a candlelit table at which Lily had indicated she'd like to sit. In response to Wolfgang's question about her choice, she replied that, sitting there, she could see the train station and darkness of East Berlin on one side and, in the distance in the other direction, the sparkling lights of West Berlin.

"We're sitting here between two worlds in a period of history that will never be again — it's a moment in time that will quickly be forgotten."

The waiter issued from the shadows of the kitchen to their table, asking whether they were prepared to order.

Neither Lily nor Wolfgang had even touched the heavy, red leather menus, which the maitre d' had placed on the table with a flourish.

"No," said Wolfgang for both of them, "not yet."

The waiter retreated.

"Did you know that the annex of your train station was called `The Palace of Tears?'" asked Wolfgang.

"No. Why? Why was it called that?"

"After the Wall itself, no other symbol of the separation of the two Berlins was as hated as that annex, which made people who waited in that glass cage, shuffling along from one VOPO to the other with guards and guns, feel so helpless, wondering if they'd be arrested either going into the East or trying to get back to the West after a visit with family. The tears came from the relatives, who had to stay in the East Zone, crying as they said goodbye at the station. It was a horrible, frightening hour or more each time, shuffling along under the bright lights, cameras watching every movement, being moved from one small interrogation cell to another."

Wolfgang's voice faded, but the fear in his eyes did not. Almost as an afterthought Wolfgang added, "My grandmother lived in Rostock — in the East. She died in 1984. I never crossed again after her death."

"I'm sorry," Lily finally said, feeling that her response was inadequate to his remembered fear.

The waiter approached the table again, prompting both Lily and Wolfgang, as children do, familiar with parental chastisement over too much time taken coming in for dinner after being called from play, hastily to pick up their menus.

They looked at each other briefly and quickly, each seeing the other's same quick motion, and smiled at their recognition of a childish reaction to the waiter's approach.

"Shall I order for both of us?" Wolfgang asked helpfully, noting Lily's somewhat confused look at the menu.

"Yes, please."

"Meat, poultry or fish?" he asked as he looked up and down the extensive menu.

"Fish."

"Fresh or saltwater?"

"Saltwater."

"Good."

Wolfgang looked up to the waiter.

"Two egg-broth soup, to begin. Two langusten with asparagus and spaghetti and...," looking at Lily, "Would you like wine?"

"No, coffee, please, with dinner."

"And two coffees."

The waiter, his need for efficiency satisfied, nodded a "Danke," and marched off.

"I have learned much today in one trip to the cemetery about Lily Weitrek," Wolfgang said. "But there is more to know, more I need to know to represent you properly. San Diego, California. What do you do in San Diego?"

"I work for the San Diego Convention Center serving as translator for foreign trade delegations. I live south of San Diego, actually, in a beach town called Imperial Beach, with my husband and two dogs and a cat. Michael, my husband, who was a philosophy professor, is publisher of the town newspaper. We live in a small beach house in a quiet little town."

Providing Wolfgang these pieces of autobiography sent images of home, Michael, and animals across her imagination. She felt suddenly misplaced, out of place, unexpectedly lost.

"It's only been one day," she said to herself.

The soup arrived. The waiter bore it high over his shoulder on a huge platter, and lowered it as he placed the soup in front of each of them.

They ate silently for a while, Lily trying to determine, given the difference in time, what Michael would be doing. She realized he would still be asleep, one dog on one side, the other in her place.

"And you? Do you have family? I know you are a lawyer, but that's of course all I know."

"I am married. I have two sons, one 12, one nine. We live in Charlottenburg, and my office is near the Ku'damm."

"Ku'damm as in Kufurstendamm, right?"

He smiled. "Yes."

Lily had tried out her German and was pleased Wolfgang showed no problem with her pronunciation.

The entrees arrived. An assistant removed the first-course dishes to make it possible for the waiter to serve them their dinner.

The waiter asked them if there would be anything else; Wolfgang, first checking Lily's eyes, told him no.

As they began to eat, Lily paused to say, "There's something about the station beyond what I said about spies." Lily hesitated, not sure herself where she was going. "Something about my family, about…"

She shook her head, puzzled at some glimmer of the past she could not get hold of but had first sensed long ago in a Len Deighton novel in which the train station was described. "Strange, isn't it, having a sense of something familiar and not knowing why? But the air - I had completely forgotten the smell of the air - until I arrived last night. It was totally familiar, like a forgotten childhood memory, buried, which comes out so unexpectedly it's rather frightening. You almost ask yourself about what else is buried in your memory."

Wolfgang had listened with a sense of growing confusion. "Why would the air here be familiar - the famous smell we all hate of burning brown coal?"

When Lily didn't answer right away, he fumbled in his mind for what might explain her odd statement.

"Have you visited here before now?"

"Not really."

Somewhat impatiently Wolfgang said, "What does that mean - `not really'?"

"I was born here in Berlin."

"I thought you were American - a real American."

"Wolfgang, I am a 'real American.' Just as real as any other."

"I meant, I thought you were born in the U.S." Wolfgang seemed exasperated.

"No, I was born here in Berlin - during the Hitler era."

Wolfgang looked at Lily so intently she finally turned her head to look out the window, feeling decidedly uncomfortable.

If she'd been born in the Hitler era, Lily had to be older than she looked. Wolfgang wryly thought of all the jokes made about Americans' frantic quests to always look young, to be healthy and thin. He finally asked, "Was your sister born in America?"

"No, she's two years older than I am. She was born here also."

Lily had been conducting the food on her plate around its circle, eating little. She stopped even that activity.

Wolfgang looked at her over the rim of his coffee cup. He didn't want the coffee as much as he needed the time to cover up his confusion. To take the case of an American whose mother had made a claim for property before her death was one thing, since

Lily would only be a second-generation heir and foreigner in his government's opinion. Would having a client who was by right and birth a German national and very possibly a direct victim of Hitler's policies make a difference? He shifted uncomfortably in his chair, realizing that Lily was watching him.

"When did you leave Germany?" he asked.

"1940."

"The borders were sealed. It was almost impossible to obtain a visa to get out."

Lily, he noticed, was tapping her spoon rhythmically on the tablecloth and had resumed her study of the train station. "Why is she not looking at me?" he wondered.

"After my father died here of a heart attack - I was six months old - some of his friends - my mother said from the film industry - helped my mother, my sister and me leave. My mother said she had to leave because she was a widow and a well-known Communist."

Lily's eyes roamed around the room, avoiding Wolfgang's gaze before continuing.

"Of course, we both know that wasn't the reason, particularly after learning that all of her family - well, almost all - are buried in a Jewish cemetery. When my mother asked me to go to the cemetery she never mentioned anyone else in her family being buried there. She just mentioned her mother."

Lily's face, Wolfgang realized, had turned chalk-white, but her tone was one of distance, disinterest.

Wolfgang's stomach began to churn. "Film industry?"

"Yes." Lily's reply was a monotone.

"Weitrek. It is a very unusual name. Are you related to the film director Franz Weitrek?"

The answer seemed dragged out by Lily. "Yes. He was my father."

Wolfgang's surprised look irritated Lily.

"I know you're going to say he was a Nazi film maker. Please don't! I already know it."

"What are you talking about?" Wolfgang's surprise had turned to shock.

48

"My mother said he was a Nazi. He made Nazi films and it was something we could never talk or think about."

Wolfgang looked puzzled.

"I do not understand. Your father was a highly respected film director whose films are still occasionally shown in the art houses in film retrospectives."

Wolfgang struggled to remember what the bios handed out before the screenings said about Lily's father. Speaking aloud, Wolfgang began to run through the few facts he could remember. "Franz Weitrek gained his reputation in the pre-Hitler era with a trio of psychological films, introducing a new genre to German cinema. He continued making films until he..."

Wolfgang's voice trailed off. "Did you say he died of a heart attack in Berlin?"

"Yes."

"But he didn't. At least that's not what's written. The bios say he disappeared on the German-Swiss border in 1940."

It was Lily's turn to look puzzled and then angry. Her voice took on a sharpness Wolfgang had not heard before.

"My mother was very clear about his Nazi affiliation and his heart attack."

Wolfgang tried to get an image of Lily's mother. What could she have been like? A woman who denies her heritage, doesn't tell her daughters who she or they are and calls her husband a Nazi? On the other hand, he realized the bios he had seen contained no information about a Jewish wife or two daughters. It's a mutual washing away of the truth, of personal history, he thought. But as he looked at Lily's tense face he realized he better not say.

Instead he asked, "Could there still be someone in Germany who knew both your parents?"

Lily thought for a moment before answering. "My mother once mentioned a woman who lived here in the East who somehow helped when we left Germany. I think maybe she was our `nanny'." Lily mentally counted off the decades that had passed since then. "If she is still alive she'd be quite old."

"Do you remember her name?" Wolfgang asked.

"Her first name - I remember it because it was so unusual - it was Hanine."

"And her last name?"

Lily looked perplexed. "Something - an opera - *Tales of Hoffmann*," Lily looked relieved. "Yes. Hoffmann. Hanine Hoffman"

"Maybe you should try to find her - this person might be able to tell you more about your father."

The waiter, who had some time ago cleared the dishes from their table, hovered over it now, his earlier charm turning to barely concealed hostility as his feet swelled in his new shoes as these two customers - one a hated Wessie and the other a dreaded American - kept the waiter from going home. The few customers in the restaurant had left long ago. All the waiter's colleagues were gone except the maitre d', who stood at his podium and drummed a pen on his reservation pad. The waiter and the maitre d' conferred in hushed tones from time to time. The maitre d', very much more important than the waiter, illustrated his superiority by pointing out to the waiter, understandable from the gestures to one watching, that the restaurant was technically open for another hour, until 11 p.m., and so the waiter would do his job and politely attend the table. The waiter muttered that under the old system people were only allowed to occupy a table for a limited and reasonable amount of time, which the two foreigners had far exceeded. In the waiter's opinion, a "Wessie" was also a foreigner.

The maitre d' did not want the waiter to know that he was enjoying his private speculation about Lily and Wolfgang.

Who were they, he wondered?

The tall blond woman, he noted when he pulled out the chair for her, had a quick smile. She looked up at him, the grey-green eyes locked momentarily with his. The look was more open and friendly than he was accustomed to receiving or giving. Clearly an American, with that natural casualness no European could imitate. Her short blond hair framed her face. Her high cheekbones dominated her image.

Attractive - perhaps not beautiful, but very attractive, he thought.

Her boots, however, were another story. Maybe they had been walking around one of Berlin's many lakes, or through a forest, because the man's shoes were mud-stained also. From where he was standing, because the tablecloth did not reach the floor, he could see both pairs of muddy shoes.

Who was the man with the chiseled face, he wondered? It suggested a man of determination.

Of the two, the maitre'd, whose name was Dieter Kruse, thought he preferred the woman.

Whatever was being said had made her unhappy. She had eaten the soup as if starved, but, since then, only played with her food. At one point Kruse thought she was about to get up and leave. What could they be talking about?

From the formality between them, it was clear to Kruse that they were not old friends. But then he had seen so many people in strange circumstances over the years at the Metropol: parents, children, friends, lovers, separated by the Wall, some waiting for the first reunion in years with families living in the West, some waiting for friends to celebrate a special occasion, some old and frail saying goodbye for the last time to sons and daughters on the other side of the Wall.

He tapped his pen on the reservation pad and absent-mindedly looked out at Friedrichstrasse. The rain had almost stopped. But few cars passed.

What would he do if the rumor turned out to be true and the Metropol was sold to private investors? Would the new owners fire the staff? Fire him? Kruse almost groaned aloud at the thought of leaving his beloved hotel.

His grandfather told stories of an elegant Berlin in the old days, before the bombing and before the Wall, stories of the hotels, cafes and cabarets surrounding Friedrichstrasse and Unter den Linden with the Palace, the theaters and opera house just minutes away. In his wildest imaginings Kruse never thought the Wall would come down and the two Germanys be reunited. Everything was changing under his eyes. Once the train station was reopened, Friedrichstrasse and Unter den Linden would once again be the very heart of Berlin. His restaurant would be full every night.

The thought made him smile, but just as quickly the worry returned: would the new owners fire him?

He tapped impatiently on his reservation pad as he contemplated his uncertain future.

The maitre d's order to the waiter to be polite when he served Lily and Wolfgang was irrelevant since they weren't ordering anything, just sitting. Therefore the waiter felt justified in shooting dirty glances and resting one pained foot over the other.

"I don't think he likes me," said Lily, catching one of the dirty looks.

"He thinks you are an American devil. If he knew you are here to claim property in his country - the East Zone - he might just poison you."

Wolfgang laughed, relieved to get away from any more conversation about Lily's father. Wolfgang had been surprised by Lily's lukewarm response to his suggestion that she try to locate the old woman who had known both of her parents. However lukewarm to the idea, Lily did not refuse outright Wolfgang's offer to undertake the search for Hanine Hoffman, possibly her childhood nanny.

"Let's get back to why you are here," he said. "Tell me how this property claim came about."

Lily was also relieved to change the conversation. She had had years to consider her mother's property claim, now her sister's and hers. At first she had thought about it often, but hearing nothing for almost 10 years, she'd almost forgotten the claim until the Wall fell and the telephone call had come from East Germany from the director of the shoe factory. She'd even had trouble finding the claim folder, having stuck it in a suitcase and stored it in a commercial unit south of San Diego. Lily had a sudden image again of her oceanfront home, her desk at the office and felt a division of time and place so strong she wondered if she was turning into someone else.

Wolfgang repeated, "How did this claim come about?"

"In 1981. Do you know what the State Department is?"

"The U.S. State Department? Yes."

Lily hesitated, unsure of Wolfgang's interest or patience. She tried quickly to marshal her thoughts.

"Well, go ahead," Wolfgang urged.

"Have you ever heard of the American War Claims Act of 1948?" she asked.

"I cannot say that I have."

Lily closed her eyes, as if to shut out the restaurant and to focus instead on a short narrative.

"Back then, after World War II, the American Congress set up the War Claims and International Claims commissions to help Americans born in the U.S. or naturalized citizens to get property back that had once belonged to them or their families, property that had been taken by force by another government or as a consequence of war. Are you with me?" Lily asked.

"So far," he said.

Lily suddenly opened her eyes and said, "Did you know that under American law the illegal taking of the property of a U.S. citizen anywhere in the world is considered an injury to the United States?"

"That's a basic principle of international law." Wolfgang immediately saw that Lily's claim to property in Germany might have more muscle behind it than he had first thought. Every day the newspapers were full of claims stories. But all of them dealt with West Germans filing for properties in East Germany, properties or businesses or land West Germans suddenly remembered "Onkle" had owned in the East before the Soviets in 1951 annexed, confiscated and nationalized these properties. The government in Bonn sourly predicted it would drown under the millions of pieces of paper of hundreds of thousands of West German claims.

"What a mess it all is," Wolfgang thought, unaware that there were more than a few West German bureaucrats saying the same thing every hour of every day. The property claims mess was the least expected by-product of the reunification of the two Germanys. It instantly pitted German against German as those from the West rushed to the poverty-stricken East Zone, crowing at the current occupants of an apartment house or farmland, "It's my family's and I'll get it back."

East German newspapers, free of censorship, ran countless cartoons of the fat West Germans, smoking fat cigars, descending in their fat new Mercedes on unsuspecting East Germans in their homes or on their land. Fistfights over property were a daily occurrence. Nobody really knew who owned what and it would take a long time to sort out.

Lily registered Wolfgang's sour look, thinking it was directed at her.

"Perhaps we should continue this tomorrow."

"No, no, Lily. Please go on."

"Over the years, the U.S. Foreign Claims Commission became responsible for addressing the losses of U.S. citizens in 39 different claims programs for losses in countries such as Vietnam, China, Japan, Czechoslovakia, Poland and, in 1977, Congress authorized the State Department to create a program for Communist East Germany, the German Democratic Republic. The commission finalized its work on East Germany in 1981."

"With what result?"

"Accepting 1,200 claims out of close to 3,000 filed by Americans for property or businesses in East Germany which had been illegally seized by the Communists. My mother's claim to the shoe factory in Fehleen and a small house were accepted as legitimate claims."

"So it has nothing to do with the Nazi era - just the Communist regime after 1951."

That flat statement was rebuked by Lily's response.

"Not quite," she said. "The Commission wrote in its final report to the U.S. Congress that it found itself in the unusual position of having to unravel a half century of political turmoil and persecution. The Commission was forced to go back to prior to the creation of East Germany in 1951 to the Nazi era - back to 1933, to unravel the history of the properties and to establish when they were first taken."

"Americans are famous for not knowing their own country's history. I wonder why they think they can unravel my country's."

THE LAST CEMETERY IN BERLIN

*A Post-Holocaust Love Story in the Ruins of the Berlin Wall*

Wolfgang realized he sounded childishly defensive. He had nothing to hide. After the war ended, the existence of the concentration camps had been revealed, and when his father was home again, Wolfgang had asked, as all children had, "What did you do in the war, Pappi?"

His father had answered, "Nothing."

Wolfgang was comforted that his "good Catholic family had nothing to do with the atrocities." That conclusion had come from his mother, who went to church two times a day, in the morning for Mass and, in the evening, for devotions.

Lily continued, "By using a field office in West Berlin and through inquiries of the American Consulate here, it was established that the factory in Fehleen still existed in 1981, had actually stayed open throughout the war right through the Soviet occupation, and is still open and standing. A business has to still exist to get it back or get money, 'compensation' for it. Anyway, the research showed the Nazis first seized it in 1933."

"Who seized it? How `seized'?"

"I don't know," Lily answered.

Wolfgang shook his head. It wasn't the first time that day he had wondered what kind of bizarre situation he found himself in as a result of offering unexpectedly to take a case no other lawyer in his firm wanted.

"Let me see if I understand this. Your mother put in a claim for property through the U.S. Government program and her claim was recognized. It stemmed from a Nazi taking in 1933. What was the reason the Nazis seized the factory?" Wolfgang asked.

"My mother never said."

Wolfgang studied Lily's unhappy face.

Gently he asked, "What do you think?"

Lily put the spoon she had been fiddling with down on the tablecloth, lining it up carefully outside the unused knife.

She took a deep breath.

"Even the final report the U.S. Foreign Claims Commission submitted to Congress left the question open. Of the 1,200 claims accepted as valid, about one-half were based on racial persecution. Others, like ITT, Woolworth and Ford Motor Co., were based on government seizure. I finally understood after my mother died the nature of her claim. I looked up Weissensee Cemetery and learned that it was Jewish. After today, it is very obvious my mother at best misled my sister and me our whole lives. Her family is in a Jewish cemetery. Maybe she was a Communist, too, but I don't think that has anything to do with the claim. My mother's mother was born an Auerbach and she married a Brodsky. According to the cemetery caretaker all the Auerbachs except Franziska are there. And a brother of her father, a Brodsky, is also there. Logic therefore says that my mother's claim is based on persecution that stems from 1933. Why couldn't she have told us the truth?"

Lily's eyes begged Wolfgang for an answer.

"Lily, she must have had her reasons."

"Do you understand that, if it were not for this claim, I still would not know anything about my mother or her family?"

Wolfgang wanted to change the conversation. "So what has happened since 1981?"

"Nothing. I called the State Department a few times. All I was told was that American and East German officials were meeting occasionally and eventually some agreement would be reached and some money would be paid. But by then Ronald Reagan was president and everyone knew he'd never give East Germany 'most favored nation' trade status, which is what the East Germans wanted. So it was an impasse. Then my mother became very ill. And I forgot the whole thing pretty much."

"We will have trouble with 1933 as the year of the property seizure."

"Why?"

In his mind Wolfgang ran through what his school textbooks covered so briefly, and he answered, "It was 1935 when the anti-Jewish laws - the Nuremberg Laws - were implemented. That is the year my government recognizes. Lily, why did you not question your mother more closely about who she was?"

Lily offered a small, resigned shrug. "You didn't know her. I tried a few times when I was growing up, but she refused to answer. But there was something else, too."

Wolfgang was struck by the candor in her eyes as she suddenly looked directly at him.

"Wolfgang, if you were a young child and told your father was a Nazi, and your mother wouldn't tell you who she was, would you want to look, really look, at who your parents were or who you might be?"

Her question rang a bell that resounded in Wolfgang's very nerve center. He reached over and patted her hand lying on the tablecloth.

"Probably not," he said.

Lily smiled for the first time since the discussion about the claim had started.  She said, "I finally heard from the Claims Commission as all claimants did after the Wall fell, just before the vote on German reunification in October, 1990. It was a hasty letter saying more or less that we were all on our own since the changes in Germany were so abrupt. The letter suggested we all register our claims with the West German government in Bonn. I think we had about a month's notice. There were probably others like me - people who had given up in the nine years during which no one heard anything and couldn't remember where the documents were." She shrugged, turning the shrug almost into a shudder.

"I did find the documents and I filed with your government just under the deadline. My claim must have gotten - or been forwarded - to the factory. In late January, four months ago, the phone rang. It was the factory director calling from Fehleen - a man named Gesset asking me if I'd come. He needed to talk to me, he said, about the future of the factory. That's when I wrote to your firm. You answered, and here we are in the Metropol."

Lily tried to smile, but failed. "I couldn't get here any quicker."

Wolfgang stretched, realizing that tension had turned every muscle to stone. His feet, soggy, damp dry now in the ruined shoes, reminded him that he and Lily had had anything but a quick dinner. The waiter, totally forgotten until now, looked apoplectic. Seeing Wolfgang signal for the check, the waiter released a long, audible sigh of relief.

Lily reached for the check saying, "It's on me. It was my invitation." As she signed her room number on the bill, adding a large tip, the waiter looked mollified.

Delaying until the waiter was out of earshot, Wolfgang said, "When I got your fax stating your arrival date, I made an appointment for tomorrow morning with the section head for leather and textile factories at the Treuhandanstalt. It will be up to them to decide what validity your claim has for the factory. An American-issued judgment, even by your State Department, may not be enough. We will have to wait and see."

Lily almost yelped in disbelief. "But the claims result has to mean something. It's the only reason that I'm here."

"Maybe. Maybe not."

Wolfgang looked uncomfortable. "I think you may find some obstacles put in your way"

"Why?"

"Because the Treuhandanstalt is now the trustee for all of East Germany's properties, factories and industries, something like your Resolution Trust Corporation, only much, much bigger. The Treuhand, as it is referred to, is the largest agency in the world, responsible for 8.5 million workers and 40,000 businesses of all kinds. It plans to close every outmoded or environmentally dangerous business of any kind from steel to coal to shoe factories to China plates, and find buyers for what's left. Yours - the factory, if it is yours - I learned recently was scheduled to be closed very quickly, within weeks."

Shocked, Lily sat back in her chair. "Can I stop the closure?"

"You already have. Simply by claiming the factory, it has to stay open until your claim is ruled on. So you've made the Treuhand angry. But there's something else."

"What?"

Wolfgang seemed momentarily unwilling to reply. Then he said, "Yours will be viewed as a Jewish claim. I think it is the first of its kind to come to the Treuhand. With it you raise the ghosts from a past we would like to forget and your claim makes us look at again. And again. It is the worst by-product of the Wall coming down. The world was ready to forget the past. And now, you're here and with you, the past."

As if suddenly very uncomfortable, Wolfgang looked at his watch. He got up quickly and said, "Forgive me, Lily, I really must leave, it is almost 11 o'clock. Tomorrow I will pick you up in the lobby at 8 a.m. Try to get a good night's sleep."

He bowed over Lily's extended hand, then turned and left the restaurant.

The waiter, maitre 'd and Lily all looked at his retreating back.

As he drove home in rain beating down on his car, Wolfgang felt an embarrassment about his quick departure, and was not really looking forward to getting home either. He knew no warmth would greet his arrival at the elegant Charlottenburg apartment unless his sons were awake and came barreling to the door as they heard his key in the lock. That was highly unlikely because they should have been in bed hours ago. The housekeeper would have made sure of that, Wolfgang thought. He smiled as he thought of 12-year-old Klaus and 9-year-old Peter. Greta, his wife, had chosen the names saying, "What could be more German than Klaus Schmidt," and later, when Peter was born, "Peter Schmidt?" Indeed, what could be more German?

"What is it to be German?" Wolfgang asked himself. "What combination of amnesia, impatience with the past, arrogance about the future, defines us?"

Wolfgang worried from time to time about what he might say to his sons when they were older and raised questions about the past. He had faced the question when, unexpectedly, it came into his thoughts as he held his eldest son, Klaus, in his arms for the first time minutes after the child's birth. The thought was totally unwelcome as he held the tiny baby in his hands. How would he explain the past to his sons? Or would he, could he ignore it?

Greta satisfied herself with the answer that "it was long, long ago and has nothing to do with us." A respected children's doctor, Greta had answers for everything. Things that displeased her were eliminated from conversation. The past was such a topic. Early in their marriage Greta had made it clear that in her father's house no discussion of the Nazi era was allowed, a tradition she intended to continue in her own home. The school

59

textbooks, said Greta, handled the past adequately. She and Wolfgang had gone to school in cities far apart, but each had studied the Hitler era in the same three paragraphs and the "Holocaust," never called that, in a scant few lines. His children would get the same textbooks. "Was that enough?" he asked himself.

A recent survey Wolfgang had read about in the newspaper revealed that only Germans over 40 years old had any passion for the Wall being torn down and Germany being reunified. The younger generation thought the Wall should be torn down but that East Germany was a different country and could remain that way. On the topic of Hitler, nobody under 30 years of age felt responsibility for any of his policies or the Nazi death camps for Jews, Gypsies, gays or the disabled. Another survey had a somewhat more telling result. Overwhelmingly, the answers to the survey revealed that 60 percent of the respondents harbored anti-Semitic feelings, and many blamed the Jews for allowing themselves to be killed in concentration camps.

"Where does the past end and the future begin?" Wolfgang wondered. "Am I the only person left who cares?" he thought to himself. What was it that so troubled him? Within the large law firm he had never heard any mention made of the past. On his next birthday, his father-in-law would be 72. Ticking the years off in his head, Wolfgang pondered the question of what the revered Mr. Gast was doing between 1940 and 1945. In the military? Definitely. What were the old man's thoughts on the past?

The prestigious law firm was founded in 1947. It achieved instant success and some notoriety when the two Gast brothers defended dozens of German industrialists in the economic war trials of Nuremberg. And got most of them off with fines. The world knew about the trials against humanity at Nuremberg, but little attention was paid to the subsequent trials. Those industrialists or their heirs were still among the firm's clients. Who is Gast? Who was my father? What had his father's one word response of "nothing" meant? The questions crisscrossed Wolfgang's mind.

Feeling a headache coming on, Wolfgang tried to banish the questions without success. Instead, larger questions about his government crept into his thoughts. He realized that Chancellor Kohl's government embarrassed him. First, the instance with U.S. President Ronald Reagan over the memorial service at the concentration camp at Bitburg a few years ago. Kohl's speech ignored the murder of the Jews there in favor of praising the Nazis who had died in battle. Was it to test the world's reaction? If so, Kohl had succeeded. After vacillating, even Reagan had not protested. Reagan had been warned by his advisors not to go to Bitburg in the first place, but Kohl had forced Reagan into attendance at the ceremony by threatening to veto more American missiles being placed on West German soil.

And then there was Kurt Waldheim. Wolfgang realized he had never questioned Kohl's friendly endorsement of Waldheim's election as President of Austria before. Waldheim, former Secretary General of the United Nations, had been tied firmly to a Nazi past by the Americans after leaving the U.N., so firmly that Waldheim was barred for life from entering the United States. In Kohl's warm reception to Waldheim was Kohl throwing down the gauntlet to the Americans? Daring them to object to the political choices of the strongest West European nation?

Wolfgang could not shake a feeling of dread. How radically would Lily's case change his life? His comfort zone of avoiding the hidden demons of his life? "If no one cares, why should I? It must be a sign of age," he said to himself. "Only people my age — in their late 40s or older — can remember fathers and brothers coming home from the war just as the world learned of the camps."

Wolfgang felt an unexpected surge of contempt for his father's generation. "They took everything from my generation, but most of all a belief that we were decent people."

A more immediate worry made its way into Wolfgang's mind, a worry that grew directly out of his dark thoughts about his father and father-in-law. The Treuhand meeting in the morning. He quickly sifted through what he knew about the Treuhand. The newspapers were full of innuendos about shady dealings, wholesale closures of East Zone businesses or businesses sold to friends of friends at small, suspiciously small, prices. The press was having little success in penetrating the Treuhand's inner secrets. "Now if this was America, the press would be all over the Treuhand," thought Wolfgang. "We don't really have the same kind of openness. We just pretend."

Wolfgang shrugged off the thought, but found himself back to worrying about the meeting.

"The heads of all sections are men. The executive board is made up of men, also. What else have I read?" he asked himself. Wolfgang wished he had paid more attention or taken the time to do what he was known for in approaching other cases — research. "Why did I think this was a simple case?" he asked himself. The Treuhand was recruiting lawyers and economic specialists from businesses throughout western Germany and out of retirement. Wolfgang felt a ball of tension wrap itself around his stomach. After the assassination a few months ago of the Treuhand's chief, a man named Detlef Karsten Rohwedder, a woman, Birgit Bruel, had been named to fill the post. Wolfgang knew little about her since her appointment was so recent. It was the older men that troubled him. They had all been appointed by Kohl.

Wolfgang remembered some words he had read.

"When Germany sleeps, the ghosts come out and deface property with the slogan, `All foreigners and Jews out of Germany.' And Kohl is the father of the ghosts."

"What am I into here?" Wolfgang muttered to himself as he turned into his street. He parked his car in front of his apartment. The beautiful neighborhood even after all the years never failed to surprise him.

Growing up in the post war years, living in a burned out building in Berlin with his parents, begging for food from the American GIs in their zone of occupied Berlin and all during the airlift that marked the beginning of the Cold War with the Soviets, Wolfgang was aware of his family's fight toward stability, toward normalization. It had left indelible scars. "Stability" was the one word Wolfgang used struggling toward a law degree later. "I just want stability."

Greta had offered that. As a young medical student at the same university, she had laughed often at Wolfgang's vision of a safe world in which nothing unexpected would happen. She would shake her long blond hair in his face, and say, "I can offer stability, but what can you offer?"

Wolfgang was an exceptional student. Even before he graduated, his professors recognized Wolfgang's research abilities. Discussing students at the home of Heinrich Gast during dinner, an invitation much sought after by the professors, the name of Wolfgang Schmidt came up often.

So that was what he could offer and Heinrich Gast, head of Gast & Gast, prestigious law firm, approved the marriage of his only daughter to the promising young attorney, and took Wolfgang into his law firm. The elegant apartment in Charlottenburg was the father's wedding gift to the young couple.

After he parked his car, Wolfgang looked up at the scrolled balconies that decorated the exterior of the 10-room apartment and hesitated. If Greta were awake she would ask him if he had been with a client. If he said yes, she might ask what the client's case was about. She rarely asked because he was almost never late getting home. Wolfgang said a small prayer that his wife would be asleep. He knew he could not tell her about Lily or Lily's claim. Greta felt very strongly that German soil belonged to Germans. No foreigners need apply. Jews were foreigners.

Wolfgang put his key into the door lock, turned it and quietly entered. The apartment was silent. Everybody was asleep. Wolfgang felt a sense of relief. As he lay down in his bedroom, one occupied by Wolfgang alone since the birth of his youngest son, Wolfgang suddenly thought of Lily's father. "Franz Weitrek. I'll have to do some research." His head touched the pillow and he was asleep.

# FIVE

Lily was right on time, standing outside the hotel entrance, five minutes early, in fact. Wolfgang saw her as he drove up the hotel driveway. He stopped the car and reached across the seat to open the door on the passenger side.

Lily got in.

After the briefest of small-talk exchanges, Wolfgang began to instruct Lily, so to speak, about what she should expect, what she should say and do.

She bristled.

"Look," she said, "I'm nervous enough. I filed a claim. I believe I am due something, preferably the shoe factory property. Please."

Wolfgang did not look chastened, but he did nod, and dropped any further attempt at conversation.

The ride to their destination took only 15 minutes. The drive took them through one of the more unkempt sections of the former East Berlin. The streets taken were narrow canyons flanked by coal-grey buildings, mostly five floors.

Lily's eyes followed their route with an interest somewhat below that of the committed traveler but with, nevertheless, a certain anxiety. They were, after all, fast approaching the focus destination of her trip to Germany, the authority which now held the keys to the factory, her family's properties and, to an extent, the future. Suddenly Wolfgang turned right and into an intersection on the far side of which, and on both sides of the 90-degree angle of the intersecting streets, was the huge structure about which Wolfgang could say, "This is the Treuhandanstalt."

The street sign identified where they stopped as the intersection of Leipzigerstrasse and Otto Grotewohlstrasse.

Parking in Berlin surrendered nothing to the worst congestion of New York. The difference, Lily learned as Wolfgang pulled his car up on the sidewalk, was that enforcement in Berlin was far less important than accommodating drivers.

"This is satisfactory," Wolfgang said, as if in reply to the question about where he was parking which Lily certainly had formed.

The Treuhand occupied the building that had housed the government of the GDR East Germany. The building, which was huge, many thousands of square meters, had been built by the Nazis to house the bureaucracy of the Luftwaffe and its chief, Marshall Hermann Goering.

Whatever architectural intent the building might express was impossible to perceive. Although there were several vacant dirt lots in the adjoining block, no doubt sites of cleared but still unrebuilt war damage, none could have provided the distance needed to view the structure as a whole.

It may be a high point in the ironies of history that the post-reunification bureaucracy established to deal with private property seized by prior governments occupied a structure whose only two previous tenants were tyrants.

Lily and Wolfgang found a sign at what had appeared to be the main entry door where the two wings of the building came together at the corner. It told them they had to walk down one of the streets to the end for "authorized entry" through a revolving door.

Inside the main door was an enormous lobby. It was broken into sections, but by what seemed non-structural walls. A sign gave directions about what to do.

There were several displays also which were designed to provide illustrations of Treuhand success stories: one showed a hotel obviously benefited from rehabilitation and projecting a welcoming sight; the other was of a building surrounded by scaffolding.

Wolfgang and Lily needed to go to their right and take a place in a short line behind others who were conducting their business across a counter with several clerks.

The men - there were only a few women - lined up to secure entry - were an international scene in themselves. Presumably, all of them were there on business, some form of claim for restitution, more likely there to explore acquisition of one of the auctionable former East German, state-owned enterprises.

The man in front of Wolfgang and Lily in the line that they had joined was clearly German, West German, it appeared. As the clerk handed him a paper, he nodded stiffly and turned toward the entry door to the inside of the building at the back of the lobby. Wolfgang stepped to the counter.

"We have an appointment at 8:30 with Herr Laudermit," he said. "I am Wolfgang Schmidt and this is Ms. Lily Weitrek."

The woman to whom he spoke gave no evidence of having heard him.

"Your passports, please," she said.

Lily produced hers readily. Wolfgang showed the clerk his German passport.

Without speaking, she copied information from the documents into a ledger, one in which it seemed a list was kept of who came to the Treuhand and who was admitted.

She then prepared what might be called name-tags, except they were much larger, and carried the information about the time of their admittance. They also were inscribed with the name of the official they were admitted to meet with, Lautermit, and where in this vast building he was, 5th floor, room 3568.

"If there is no one in the room," the clerk ordered, "you will wait inside for Herr Laudermit to come."

The clerk also explained to Wolfgang and Lily that they must not lose the tags. They needed them to be allowed to leave. Lily wondered what fate awaited those who lost their tags.

They passed through an entry door where their tags were examined carefully by the guard. Once through the door, they were in the middle of a long corridor, which seemed to extend indefinitely in both directions.

In front of them and a little to their right was a sweeping set of steps, the right side going up, the left side going down. A large numeral "1" was painted on the wall just above where the steps on both sides met level with the floor on which they stood.

"Too many steps, "Wolfgang declared, "we'll take the lift."

Wolfgang's quick turn to his right was followed by Lily's eyes.

Her eyes widened when she saw it. The "lift" was a paternoster, a device she had never seen before. She simply gaped.

A paternoster, so named sardonically to suggest that before using a paternoster one say a prayer for safety - an "Our Father," "Pater Noster" in Latin.

A paternoster is a very simple device, a very primitive elevator.

Two shafts extend from the top of the building to the bottom. In one shaft people go up, and in another they go down.

It is how and on what they go up and down that warrants the prayer.

The platforms that carry passengers are attached to a cable on pulleys. The platform headed down reaches the bottom of its shaft and is rotated across to the other shaft and begins to be pulled up as the platform headed up.

The platforms are in continuous travel. They do not stop for passengers floor by floor; passengers must step onto them, judging just when the upcoming or downgoing platform will reach the fixed level where they are standing.

"No, thank you," said Lily. She looked as terrified as one might suddenly confronted by a fierce predator.

"You can ride this, of course, if you choose to," Wolfgang replied. "The alternative is four long sets of stairs."

"I will see you on the fifth floor," Lily said, having turned back to the staircase.

Wolfgang was waiting at the top of the stairs when, more than a little breathless, Lily arrived. "I'm in better shape than I thought," she said to herself, "but I'll get my breath before I talk."

Wolfgang was courteous; he said nothing that would require a response from her. Instead, he pointed wordlessly down the left corridor; since there was no indication anywhere as to what room numbers were where, Wolfgang, she reasoned, must have used the time waiting for her to climb stairs quite well.

Having found the room after numerous missteps down the long corridors that diverged in every direction, Wolfgang had finally located 3568. The designation puzzled Lily unless it had to do with the height of the building, which was, she thought, five stories above ground and who knew how many stories the former Luftwaffe building had below ground.

Every wall in the building glistened with fresh paint; newly-installed windows sparkled. The furniture she'd peeked at through doorways and now in the room they waited in looked as if it had just been delivered.

As the clerk had foreseen, the room was empty, and, as they were told to, they entered.

The smell of the fresh paint tickled Lily's nose. A remnant of the newly-laid carpet was rolled up against the wall nearest the door, apparently forgotten by the work crew.

Lily spent the time waiting for the Treuhand's head of the Textile & Leather Division to appear studying the large room. Wolfgang, increasingly irritated at the lack of punctuality, had left the large conference table with its dozen carefully placed chairs to pace the room, finally landing at the sole window overlooking remnants of the graffiti-sprayed Berlin Wall immediately adjacent to the Treuhand building. Every few minutes Wolfgang looked angrily at his watch.

"This is very rude. The appointment was precisely arranged for 8:30. If no one shows up by 9:30, we will leave."

Now that, thought Lily, will accomplish nothing. Lily doodled on the yellow pad she'd brought along to take notes. Having given up small talk after a few minutes of entering the empty room, Lily began to worry whether her knowledge of German would be good enough to follow everything the head of textiles and leather might say. Having studied German in high school and college over her mother's objections, Lily had continued to learn on her own in subsequent years. She thought she was fluent, but that assumption was finally going to be tested.

Almost everyone she'd talked to even casually, first at the Frankfurt Airport and certainly at the hotel, spoke English. Lily resented that most people ignored the fact she was speaking German and addressed her in English. It's probably my hideous accent, she thought. Lily knew that the American accent, with its unmistakable twang, gave her identity away in the first few words. In the East Zone kids in school, Lily had read, were taught German, Russian and sometimes Polish. There were still some signs in Russian by the Metropol's elevators, quickly being replaced by English. It was doubtful that the people in Fehleen had already added English to their linguistic arsenal. She'd have to ask Wolfgang when he was in a better mood what he thought of her German. She looked at him again glowering at the remainder of the Wall. Lily hoped somebody would show up before Wolfgang decided they'd been insulted enough by being kept waiting so long.

The door suddenly opened inward and three men entered the room, causing Wolfgang to jump away from the window, his scowl turned toward the first man through the door.

"Herr Schmidt," said the lead man, extending his hand, "forgive our tardiness. Our prior meeting took longer than anticipated."

Lily could not catch any of the names rattled off as she stood to be introduced. Seating themselves across the wide table from Lily and Wolfgang, who quickly sat down next to Lily, the men pulled out nameplates and placed them on the table. They read: "Dr. Johannes Lautermit, Director Textile & Leather; Dr. Luther Haftig, Consulting Legal Counsel; Joachim Kurz," with no other designation.

Lautermit spoke almost as soon as he was seated. A tall, angular man in his 60s, impeccably dressed with a silk cravat at his throat, his teeth were too long for his mouth. His voice was that of a man used to ordering people around. He tapped the thick folder in front of him from time to time to emphasize a point.

"Mrs. Weitrek, Mr. Schmidt, I am Dr. Johannes Lautermit, the head of the Textile & Leather Division for the Treuhand. I am a very busy man implementing the closing of outmoded factories in the five new states — the old East Zone. I have a very successful law practice in West Germany from which I have taken a leave of absence to help my country accommodate the many recent changes that have taken place so suddenly. It is a very big challenge for all of us here and we have very little time to waste. So please tell me why you are here and what you want from us."

Lily froze into her chair. Whatever she had expected, Lautermit's officious speech wasn't it. She noticed that the man named Kurz never looked up from the table, and even when she had shaken his hand had not looked at her. The lawyer Haftig on the other hand stared at her with curiosity. Younger than either Lautermit or Kurz, Haftig had, unusual for a German, red hair, freckles and blue eyes. He, too, was well dressed, but in a casual tweed jacket with leather patches at the elbows and a tie that he had already pulled away from his throat. Kurz was the real puzzle, Lily thought. He was a grey man with a grey twinge to his skin, dressed in a poorly-fitting grey suit. His face registered nothing, neither curiosity about her nor approval or disapproval at Lautermit's speech. Lily realized that Wolfgang was speaking and having difficulty keeping his temper under control.

"Herr Dr. Lautermit, my client and I are here in good faith. You agreed to this meeting and I ask you to give us the time necessary to cover the information we have about my client's claim to the factory in Fehleen."

"A miserable place, Mr. Schmidt," Lautermit said patronizingly. "Do proceed. But I ask you to be brief. You don't have to cover information I already have, by the way."

Wolfgang looked surprised and tried not to show it.

"We can save time then, Dr. Lautermit, if you tell me what you have."

"I have your client's filing of a claim with the Bonn government last October. It was not only sent to Gesset, the director of the factory, but also to my office."

Lily was having no problem understanding what was being said or the hostility between the two men. Wolfgang carefully picked his way toward what he hoped was going to be a neutralizing presentation of the facts.

"Then you know the original claim for family property was filed by my client's mother with the American government. And accepted."

70

Dr. Lautermit, Lily noted, jotted down two words. She guessed they were "American government." He then tapped the note pad with his pen in a dismissive fashion.

"What proof do you have, Mr. Schmidt?"

"Proof of what? My client has the documents from her government."

"Mr. Schmidt, I too have them. I sent for a copy after her claim was forwarded to this office. These things are public record in the U.S. and easy to get."

Wolfgang felt his face flush and sweat break out on his body.

"Well then, Dr. Lautermit, you know the Americans stand behind their findings."

Lautermit, his lips pulling back to expose his large teeth, chuckled. The sound made Lily's hands, hidden in her lap, shake.

"Amateurs, Mr. Schmidt."

He threw back his head and studied the newly-painted ceiling as his face settled into a frown.

"Child's play. Amateurs. The Americans had a single field office here in West Berlin. They sent a man to the East Zone to make inquiries in Fehleen as to whether anyone knew of this woman's family. It turned out that people did, but whether the family still owned the factory in 1935 is in doubt. They sold it, probably for a good price, got their money and left Germany. A typical story of those times."

Lily suddenly wondered what Lautermit's family was doing in 1935.

"1933," Lily heard herself saying. "The year was 1933 — the year of the taking."

"The anti-Jewish laws — the Nuremberg Laws — were in 1935, Mrs. Weitrek."

Lautermit studied Lily as if seen from a great distance, a person in his way and not of great interest.

"My mother said the seizure of the factory by the Nazis was 1933."

Lily, having found her voice, realized that she was no longer afraid of Lautermit. If he was the voice of the new German order, then both Germany and the world were going to have a troubled future.

"Mrs. Weitrek, you would have to find absolute proof that the sale of the factory in 1933 was a forced sale."

"It's Ms. Weitrek, not Mrs."

"How American. A modern American woman. How nice."

And you, thought Lily, are detestable.

"And if my client finds the proof, Dr. Lautermit, what then?"

Wolfgang had no idea at the moment how he or Lily could find a contradiction to the universally held belief that the Jewish persecution did not start before 1935, a year he also had noted in his memory, thinking it was absolute fact.

"What then, Mr. Schmidt?"

Lautermit pondered the ceiling again.

"In this amateur sleuthing by the Americans there are other problems."

"Such as?" asked Wolfgang.

"Property deeds, Mr. Schmidt. The Americans did not require proof." Lautermit emphasized the word "proof."

"Property deeds from then, showing what it was the family owned and which members owned what. And who their heirs are. Not only personal property deeds, but also business property deeds, and stock records for the company known as PrinzLine Shoes. You will have to find out what was property personally owned and property owned by the company. You will have to find all these things, Mr. Schmidt. And birth and death records, Wills, if there were any. And when you have found all these things, you will let me know."

Wolfgang's nervousness had given way to white anger. Suddenly standing up, his voice escalating with each word, Wolfgang shouted at Lautermit, "This is an outrage! An insult to this woman, to the American government and to me as a German. I will call the American press — The New York Times office here in Berlin — and tell them this story. Is this how you handle legitimate claims that come to your office?"

He sat down abruptly. Lily studied her yellow pad of paper. Lautermit tapped his pen. Kurz continued to stare into space, and

Haftig ran his hand through his red, curly hair. The silence lengthened.

"I would like to ask about the factory, if I may?"

Lily kept her voice steady. Recognizing that the meeting would quickly be over if she didn't do something, Lily realized nobody had brought up what she saw as the real focus of the meeting — the factory and its future.

Speaking more loudly, she said, "Please tell me about the Treuhand's plan for the factory."

Haftig cleared his throat and shot Lily a relieved look.

"Yes, of course, Ms. Weitrek. There are plans to close the factory. You see, the building is over 100 years old. The equipment, the machinery, was perhaps up to date, let us say in the 70s, but now, well, quite behind the times, not like Western technology."

Lautermit broke in. "The Treuhand spends money every month it is open to keep the workers on. Nobody wants — there is no market for these shoes, these boots."

Kurz, Lily noticed, shifted uncomfortably in his chair.

Haftig, ignoring Lautermit, continued. "The factory sent its shoes to the Eastern Bloc countries — Russia, Poland, Yugoslavia. Now these old Iron Curtain countries have nothing to trade, like oil as in the old days or hard currency, so that market has collapsed."

"And nobody in the West will buy the shoes. They are old-fashioned," Lautermit interrupted again.

"There is a great deal of competition even for our West German shoemakers in a flooded market from Taiwan, from China, from countries where the labor costs are so much lower," Haftig said in his reasonable tone.

"We in the West must protect what we have built over so many years," snapped Lautermit. "We cannot afford to keep the factory open. It's throwing money down a hole."

Kurz suddenly spoke. His voice low and measured, his deep baritone rang out angrily in the room. Pointing at Lautermit he said, "You lied. You lied to all of us so we'd vote for reunification of my country with yours, but you lied." He got up and walked to the window and pointed to the remnants of the Wall. "It wasn't all so bad — my country. We had jobs, guaranteed for life. We had, under socialism, a caring for each other. We had housing, guaranteed. We had medical care. And now what do we have? You are closing all our factories, all our industries, all our little shops — 40,000 business in all with their 8.5 million workers. The unemployment rate in my country is already at 40 percent. All so we could join you in your sickening chase for power and money in which people count for nothing. You lied."

Lautermit turned to Kurz and said in a tone of dismissal already familiar to Lily, "You are a fool. Everything we are doing is for your own good. You'll thank us before it's over."

"You conquered us. You do not share our sense of responsibility for others. You are only interested in power and money — not people."

Saying that, Kurz sat down across from Lily and smiled.

"Go to Fehleen, Ms. Wietrek. Generation after generation has worked in the factory. People did not move much in my country. They stayed where they were born and then raised their families. Under my system people knew where they belonged and where they were taken care of."

Lautermit's superior tone challenged Kurz's statements. "You mean they weren't allowed to move."

"Go to Fehleen, Ms. Weitrek. You may not find everything you need, but you will find a great deal." Saying that, Kurz resumed a study of the conference table's shiny top.

"Thank you Mr. Kurz," Lily said with a smile to the grey man. "I'm going tomorrow and I'm looking forward to seeing the factory and meeting the director."

"Mr. Gesset is a fool full of pipe dreams that you will not only be declared the heir but that you also have money — a lot of money — to invest. Do you have a lot of money, Ms. Weitrek?" Lautermit gave an expressive shrug. "I assume you don't."

Haftig slid in smoothly before Lily could retort to Lautermit's demeaning statement. "There is another road, Ms. Weitrek. If you could find investors to modernize the factory and the equipment, it is possible that, while we establish the legitimacy of your claim, you could put a financial and business plan together to present to us."

Kurz broke in. "What is meant, Ms. Weitrek, is that, heir or not, if you bring several million dollars with you, you could in effect buy back what you say was once taken from your family."

Lily could feel Wolfgang fuming next to her. "It's an outrage," he said. "Sell her her own business. It's corrupt."

"Not really, Mr. Schmidt." Lautermit responded in a tone that suggested he was enjoying the cat-and-mouse game. "We have to sell those businesses we can. Privatize them. Those that have no buyers we will close."

"The Wessies do not see that an unrestrained free market only encourages inequality. They believe that the power of money is absolute, forgetting that the economy should be at the service of the people. Not the other way around." Kurz addressed Lily directly before turning away to study a space directly above her head.

"Is it true you are planning to close the factory?" Lily asked Haftig.

"As long as it is open, the workers have to be paid. As long as they are paid, they expect a miracle — like you or investors or contracts for shoes from retailers in the West. It will never happen. It's a hopeless situation," he replied.

"We would like your agreement to close the factory," he added. Lautermit, Lily felt, was deliberately provoking her. Taking a deep breath, she counted to 10, afraid that, like Wolfgang, she'd start shouting at Lautermit.

"Why would I agree to that? I haven't even seen the place."

"Because, Ms. Weitrek, if you agree, we can save millions of our Deutschemark. And then, if we find you are the heir, some settlement will be made to you."

Lautermit's snide tone so irritated Lily she clenched her hands in her lap to keep herself from pounding the table.

Haftig said softly, "It's called `Stilleliquidation.'"

"What's that?"

"Silent liquidation."

"What does it mean?"

"It means," said Wolfgang angrily, "that your claim is delaying — only delaying — what they will do anyway." Turning to look at her, he said, "But if you agree to the closing, then they will be able to blame you in the press as the person who took jobs away from the factory workers in Fehleen."

Lily looked around the room, totally confused by the choices presented.

"If you agree now, Ms. Weitrek," Lautermit said smoothly, "we can spare you a trip to Fehleen."

"Thank you, but I really don't want to be spared, Mr. Lautermit."

Lautermit stood up and looked at his watch. He smiled benignly at Lily.

"Think it over."

He picked up the thick folder from the table, walked to the door, and looked back briefly at Lily.

"There's one more thing, Ms. Weitrek. Were we to decide that your claim is frivolous, German law allows us to take you to court to recover the money spent on keeping the factory open. But I'm sure your attorney, the fine Mr. Schmidt, has already told you that."

He did not offer to shake hands before he abruptly left the room. Mr. Haftig extended his hand to Wolfgang, then to Lily, and followed Lautermit.

Kurz slowly got up and looked at Lily.

"I'm sorry," he said. "The West is in a great hurry to rebuild my country to look like theirs. There will be many mistakes made which will be overlooked, forgotten when they succeed. You and your factory may simply be sacrificed to the ambitions of these men. Be very, very careful."

"May I call you after I've been to Fehleen?" Lily asked.

"No. I won't be here. Today is my last day. It was agreed after reunification that those of us from the East Zone would be part of the decision on which businesses are to be closed. But now we are judged incompetent. I have been fired."

He looked at Lily for a long moment before saying, "You may have a legitimate claim, but the price to you may be very high to pursue it. You should consider going home, Ms. Weitrek."

INTERLOG:
IMPERIAL BEACH, CALIFORNIA

The period of time Lily was in Germany was very short. She allotted herself only the minimum amount because, as she said over and over again as the time for her departure drew closer, she was going to pursue the property claim, not for nostalgia.

Our plan for communicating with each other, giving us a sense of security as we planned it, was that Lily would call me at 10 p.m. German time, 7 a.m. West Coast time. And, while she might indeed call every day, since at seven each morning I would be scanning the daily newspaper, we had agreed she would call at least every other day.

It was only after she arrived in what had been East Germany that she discovered the phone lines to the United States were poor in East Berlin and almost non-existent the farther east she went. The phone system at her hotel was still part of the antiquated trunk lines, and every call was delayed.

Someone once told me that the difficulty with ear trumpets, those strange, musical instrument-like looking devices from years ago with the mouthpieces designed for the ear to help hearing, was that, with the increase in volume came also an increase in information, the latter more than the person whose waning hearing was accustomed to. The problems created by Lily's phone calls to me did not relate to deafness. The problems related to what she was discovering, to what she had been seeing and learning, and to hours spent trying to get a call through to California.

But what I heard in every telephone conversation with her traveled to me just as if it entered the wide span of an ear trumpet's bell and stuffed itself down through the narrow cone of the earpiece.

I had not been of much help to her as I worried about the voice at the other end of the line, a voice that spoke uncertainty in all it said.

After one of these calls, which the technical problems reduced in frequency, I would find myself in a true quandary. It was clear that Lily's idea and mine of presenting her claim to a balanced and friendly government agency was far off the mark. It became clear also, to me, that she was being absorbed into a needed level of family research, which neither of us had anticipated. I had no idea about how she might proceed with that task or knowledge of whose help she might solicit.

When two people who are close, and together much of the time, are apart, as Lily and I were then, she in what had been East Germany and I still at home, the conversations between them by telephone are generally versions of conversations they would otherwise have face to face.

But Lily had encountered and was still discovering a world she had not known existed.

Everything she reported to me by phone was detail for a new geography, people for a new history, or people from an old history.

After her phone calls I would feel as if I were watching a film which I had walked in on in the middle.

That is the way Lily's reports to me seemed.

She reported there was some worry that the determination by the U.S. Foreign Claims Commission would play no role in the German government's approach to restitution or compensation. The German officials whom she encountered had conceded nothing to the past in the present.

It looked as if time, just as the thirty days in early 1981 were all we had to justify Theresa's claim, might so constrain Lily in what she had to do that she could probably not meet all the requirements set forth to her by the Treuhand.

We had tried in the weeks before the day of Lily's departure to learn as much as we could about where she was going.

It is one thing to go on tour, guided by someone not only knowledgeable but also reliable. It is quite another for someone to set out alone - and yes, the times notwithstanding - especially a woman, to try to recover locations she had never heard of.

In particular, of course, what we had to learn most about was East Germany. In 1991, tour books were yet to be updated. If they had been re-published since reunification, it was fortunate to find a few added pages about the five new states, as the West Germans named what had been East Germany, and little that was there was useful.

The Iron Curtain had not been just a passive barrier between the two Germanys. It represented an ongoing and continuous force for disjunction. If phone connections plagued both of us, figuring out and coordinating train connections plagued Lily.

Every train transfer between the two countries, the few that were allowed when there were still two countries, had been just a few months before a border crossing. Moreover, the train schedules in East Germany had not yet been synchronized with those in West Germany. And while in 1991 a transfer was no longer from one German country to another an international event, the cultural contrast between a railroad station in the East and the West was startling.

So soon after reunification, Germany was still two countries in the minds and attitudes of Germans. Each had its own philosophical identity, each an image of itself, often at war with the other.

Lily was contending with them both: the country that had conquered and the one, which felt it, had been conquered with the disappearance of the Wall.

Germany's status as a nation in its own right was quite recent, at least as historians view it.

In fact, I realized as I pondered Lily's apparent plight in Germany, and mine at home, the reunification of Germany that had made her trip abroad possible and necessary had hardly been the restoration of a longstanding national geographic unity.

Germany, I remembered, had spent the quest of centuries seeking unity, sometimes finding it, then losing it again.

Germany had until recently no real status in the so-called modern world. The Renaissance had passed the culture by. In fact, the culture had been on the receiving end of the thought and art of the other European nations, including England, well into the 18th century.

The great age of German thought and culture began with Goethe, and probably also ended with Goethe's death in 1832. This onset of cultural greatness, which began with the publication of his *Sorrows of Young Werther*, and which extended to art, music and philosophy as well as literature, happened in spite of the political and economic weakness of the nation.

It had been barely sixty years before Hitler's rise to power that Bismarck had manufactured the New German Reich in 1870 under William I, accomplishing in reverse, so to speak, the much earlier unification efforts of Otto I in the late 10th century called *Drang Nach Osten* (Drive to the East). My mind marveled at the irony.

Had the reunification process encountered once again the German penchant for political centrifuge? I remembered, again suddenly, how at the end of the Thirty Years' War in 1648 Germany was left with virtually no central government, certainly one devoid of effectiveness, but instead with some 300 virtually sovereign states, plunged back into Merovingian disarray.

Almost any person who does historical research would say that there are periodic points in the course of that work where the cliché is true which says there are times "when one cannot see the forest for the trees." And the East was where Lily labored, less successful I had to infer both from what she said and what she chose not to say, than we had hoped.

I realized that I considered Lily, whom I loved very dearly, an unusual if not a strange woman. When we first met at the research center in Colorado– that was when I was still a philosopher – or rather a man trying to teach philosophy – I was struck by her energy. Every single task of the day was an effort she addressed with total focus. Other issues the day asked for received no answer, at least right away.

The time we spent together increased each day, making it possible, though not my intention to do so, to measure more readily and more this infusion of her energy into the task.

The research project that had brought us both to this retreat-like setting in Colorado was scheduled to last a month. The month's program was designed to place professionals in the fields of ethics and theory of knowledge together with professionals whose work involved broad communication, such as Lily in her field, public relations. By the beginning of the second week, it was implicit in my mind, and I know also it was in hers, that a month for us to be together would never be enough. Once that silent if mutual understanding became overt, expressed, fretted about, it was this focus of her total energy that set about to see whether a month's love could be permanent.

It was.

But then early in our stabilizing time together, about a year later, a problem that Lily had expected loomed over each day. It was Lily's mother. Theresa. Her condition, growing worse, frightening us daily more and more, took the full attention of us both. But it was Lily who plotted the larger plan, and explored it.

That was when we moved Theresa down to Imperial Beach to be with us, at first on her own next door to the beach house that we were still completing, followed by a move to a larger apartment that could accommodate a caregiver, and finally to a guarded facility.

Lily and I saw to it that Theresa was seldom alone in her last days; when neither of us was available or when we both seemed too worn out to go, we were fortunate in that Concha, the woman who kept house for us, would step in to visit Theresa and stay with her.

It happened that we both were with Theresa at the end. Her last words were much more cogent than her idle and barely periphrastic utterances had become. Theresa repeated her simple request that Lily, if she could, find her grandmother's grave and place a flower on it. But she added an observation she had never made before: that she hoped Lily might find, not only her grandmother, but also some family.

These are stages in the discovery of detail, facts, minutiae even, where the larger pattern into which they are to fit all but disappears. The mind is overcome with detail; today the state is often referred to as "information overload."

Of such a nature was the task that had become mine as I tried to assemble the flurry of information from Lily's calls to me into images of sufficient dimensionality so that I could imagine, as I simply had to, what a film of her day or days would be like.

But the images jumped like some early Edison crank projector's film. The details I had, or remembered, were all the stuffing for the imagined images I had.

The result was that I had no coherent image of Lily in Germany, in fact, an image that was more disappearing than growing.

All in all, I left each of our more and more sporadic telephone conversations having heard a different Lily than the Lily I heard when we last talked. Her hopes of success seemed to be fading, even as her irritation grew. But, I could tell, so had her fear.

I no longer could guess what might be expected.

# SIX

Lily leaned her head against the train window and watched Berlin slip by. She closed her eyes, grateful that she had bought a first-class rail pass, and that the compartment was empty except for herself. After the disastrous Treuhand meeting, a shaken Wolfgang had abruptly suggested that they part ways.

"You really should take a tour of your 'birth city,' Lily. With so many requirements put on us by the Treuhand for documents, you may not get another chance to see Berlin."

"What are you going to do?" she had asked, surprised by his suggestion.

He walked them hurriedly to his car, parked willy-nilly on the sidewalk. The day had turned warm, and Lily had trouble keeping up with him without gasping in the soot-filled air.

"I am going to the civil records hall — first in Charlottenburg. Depending on where that leads me, I could end up going to every district office in Berlin."

"Why Charlottenburg?"

He leaned against the side of the car before answering.

"Fortunately you brought your birth certificate. You were born in Charlottenburg, so I will go there to search civil records to see if I can find records about your grandfather. He was a Brodsky, and it is the Brodskys we have to trace."

Lily felt as if the ground was shifting under her feet as she contemplated the enormity of the Treuhand's requirements.

"What if you can't find the Brodskys?"

Deep lines of worry creased his forehead. "We have two Brodsky names — Daniel, the factory director and Julius, the writer. I assume these were the brothers of your grandfather."

Looking at Lily, he felt he needed to be more reassuring. "It should be possible to find the birth certificates of all three. Each will carry his parents' names. That should establish the family connection. If we find the documents, we will be able to support your claim as a direct descendant. We both understand that there are probably others. But for now if we can find what we need, you will serve to stand in for them until they can join your claim."

What he did not say worried him more than he wanted to admit. He would also have to find the birth and marriage certificates of the original founder of the factory — Benjamin Brodsky. If Benjamin Brodsky had been born in one of East Europe's small Jewish stetls behind what had later become the Iron Curtain, the records might have been destroyed or lost. If they still existed, it could take years to get certified copies.

Wolfgang unconsciously shook his head in so depressed a manner Lily felt she had to offer to go with him on his search.

"No, Lily. Thank you. I think it will go faster if I go alone."

Opening the car door for her, he said, "Take the tour. It will be good for you to see Berlin."

As she got into the car she asked, "How far back do my family records have to go? Truthfully."

Wolfgang wondered what his expression had unintentionally revealed. Quickly counting back three generations, he said, "Possibly to the mid-1800s."

"You mean you might be able to trace my family back to my great-grandparents?"

The idea that she, like most people, had a family that could be discovered through records had never occurred to her before. She remembered once, long ago, being invited to a classmate's family reunion and marveling that so many people could count each other as belonging to a family: parents, children, their children, nieces, nephews, cousins, grandparents, great aunts and uncles. She remembered later that night lying in bed and crying for want of some larger group than just her mother and sister to belong to.

"What if the documents can't be found?" she finally asked as Wolfgang backed his car off the sidewalk before entering the flow of traffic. Wolfgang took his car quickly into Berlin's infamous bumper-to-bumper traffic, and pounded the steering wheel in frustration as he came to a halt.

"There is a backup. The yearly stock report. If the PrinzLine issued stock shares, which it surely did, those reports, which go back to the early 1900s, will be in the archives of the library."

"How will that help?"

The car sped up and immediately had to stop again as another car edged in front of Wolfgang.

"Damn it," he cursed under his breath. "The report will tell us how many stock issues existed in 1932-33. The value of the properties owned can be gotten generally from their insured value, which is always listed, the production level, gross and net income for the business. The report will also contain the names of the directors."

"Isn't that enough?" Lily asked.

"It will help to arrive at a value of the business if you cannot get the property back and agree to compensation — to money."

"But?" She knew there was a qualifier in his statement.

He thought before answering. "What is not listed, because it has always been considered privileged information, is who owned the stocks and how much stock each person owned."

"Wouldn't the people - the Nazis who took the factory in 1933 - know that?"

He looked at Lily in astonishment. "Of course," he thought, "if we can find out who they were and if their heirs are still alive. We could subpoena the records."

He did not want to raise her hopes, so he limited his response to saying, "If we can find who that was, that is another approach. The best outcome, Lily, is to trace you directly back to the founder of PrinzLine through Brodsky birth and marriage records."

After finally arriving at the Metropol, Wolfgang rushed through the revolving door. He had a short conversation with the hotel clerk and, as Lily watched from the car, both Wolfgang and the clerk looked at the clock above the registration desk. Getting back into the car, Wolfgang quickly pulled away, saying, "We are in luck. A full city tour leaves in ten minutes from Hotel Stadt Berlin, just around the corner from here."

On the way to the tour bus stop, Wolfgang hurriedly gave Lily the train information for her trip to Fehleen the next morning, reminding her that she had to go into West Berlin to catch the train.

"I am sorry I have a meeting early in the morning; otherwise we could drive to Fehleen together. As soon as my meeting is over, I will leave. If we are lucky, I will be in Fehleen in time to pick you up at the station since you have to change trains in Magdeburg. But, if I am delayed, at least you will not be late to your appointment with the factory director."

Lily was grateful that she did not have to drive to Fehleen with Wolfgang, who drove as most Germans - with a total disregard for life or limb. Even on the short ride from the cemetery to the Metropol last night, Wolfgang's driving had caused Lily to practically sit on her hands to keep from grabbing the steering wheel. She knew that on the autobahn the average speed was over 110 miles an hour.

The tour bus was just pulling out as Wolfgang slammed on the brakes, got out of the car quickly and ran to flag it down. Wolfgang gestured at Lily to hurry and ushered her onto the bus when she caught up to him, cheerfully waving at her as the bus pulled away.

Lily wondered as she turned to wave back at him whether he even noticed the dark-skinned woman with the baby in her arms lying on a frayed mat on the sidewalk. The baby's body lay limp against its mother, its head rolled back. The bus pulled away so Lily could not see whether Wolfgang put any money into the hand the woman stretched out to him.

Lily had been shocked at the number of women with tiny, underfed babies she had seen begging in the streets of East Berlin. They did not fit into her picture of Europe's most prosperous country. Passers-by, she had noticed, seemed to be unconcerned.

Lily sank into a seat in the half-empty bus, knees shaking with fatigue. She realized there were only eight days left to find her family and establish her claim successfully before leaving for home. Home, she thought wearily. Where is home from here? In her mind's eye images arose of San Diego's sparkling bay under a blanket of sunshine and walking through Horton Plaza holding Michael's hand or playing with her dogs on Imperial Beach's sandy shore. She tried to concentrate on what the tour guide was saying.

The tour was exhausting. The first stop was the observation globe above the Alexanderplatz, that bleak, open, grey plaza in East Berlin with the huge department store with few goods in it so shortly after reunification. Even on this May day, the wind howled through the open space.

The tour guide did not mention that Gestapo headquarters had also once been on the same strip of land before being bombed to the ground during World War II, the place where thousands of political prisoners and Jews had been interrogated and tortured.

There was also no mention of the nearby Hitler's Fuhrenbunker, also bombed out of existence in April 1945 after Adolph Hitler and his bride of one day, Eva Braun, committed suicide to avoid capture by the allied forces.

Next was Potsdamer Platz, a bleak, open area.

The guide did not mention that just a few months earlier it had tall viewing platforms from which West Germans could look at the mined no-man's land the East Germans had built on their side of the Wall, a no-man's land on which fleeing East Germans had been killed.

The tour went by East Berlin's opera house. In 1933, tens of thousands of books and paintings by Jewish authors and painters were consumed in a bonfire in front of the famed opera house.

The bus traveled past the Tiergarten. The guide pointed out that a 15-minute air raid on Nov. 22, 1943, destroyed 100 years of work. She did not say "Allied raid." By April 1945, only 91 animals out of thousands survived as the Soviet Front ran through the zoo.

The tour went next to the Schoenberg district to view the Berlin Airlift Memorial, commemorating that major supply effort into Berlin by the Western Allies in 1948-49 when the Soviets erected a land and water blockade intending to starve West Berliners and drive the Allies out of Berlin. The blockade started on June 25, 1948. The Americans, British and French responded with 277,264 flights to Berlin, delivering 1.8 million tons of food and other essential supplies. The Soviets lifted the blockade on May 12, 1949.

No mention was made that on one of the nearby side streets the Jewish Bureau of the notorious SS was headquartered under the icy leadership of Adolph Eichmann, who personally implemented 'The final solution to the Jewish problem,' which led to the deaths by gassing of six million Jewish children, men and women.

The guide made several references to West Berlin's 'Big Sister,' the Spandau district. All of them referred to Spandau as West Berlin's largest industrial center. The guide made no mention of Spandau Prison, no mention of its history: a German military prison in the 1880s for political prisoners and Jews. And, after the 1947 Nuremberg trials, at which just twenty-two Nazi officials were charged with crimes against humanity, crimes with 50 million dead as a final count, twenty-one of these were actually imprisoned in Spandau, guards rotating every month among the Allied occupying forces.

Not long after the first and most public trials for crimes against humanity took place in Nuremberg, the United States military government's denazification program fell apart. There were over 4 million hearings set to find those Nazis guilty of the most serious crimes. But it was impossible to find enough "clean" Germans to make up the hearing panels. In 1948, President Harry Truman withdrew American financial support for the Nuremberg trials. The U.S. government, tired of hunting Nazis, turned its attention to the more serious threat posed by an increasingly belligerent Soviet Union.

In the pragmatic political order, the U.S. decided rebuilding a strong West Germany tied to American apron strings, which would serve as a buffer between the U.S. and the Soviet Union, was more important than pursuing the tedious and unsuccessful denazification of Germany.

The United States, otherwise preoccupied, did not even murmur when in subsequent trials or hearings German industrialists who had seized Jewish businesses or used slave labor for Hitler's war machine were quickly declared rehabilitated in the late 1940s. The Americans had lost interest in establishing Nazi guilt.

Lily did not join the other tourists in their unabashed expressions of admiration when the tour guide proudly listed as hallmarks of German efficiency and productivity the top German conglomerates, whose names stood out in neon lights on glittering, sparkling, expensive Kurfurstendamm, Berlin's answer to Paris' Champs Elysees. Some of those companies reportedly had used slave labor from the concentration camps and from countries conquered by Hitler's troops. The average tourist was being introduced to a thriving, prosperous, prideful Germany.

Lily felt entirely isolated by seeing in her mind's eye another Germany. The tour guide smoothly slid over references to the past. Lily thought she was probably the only tourist who noticed that not a single statue existed to commemorate those killed by Hitler's racial policies.

The tour left her drained. She entered her hotel room after returning from the trip, intending to lie down for a short nap.

She did. Her last thought was of Lautermit and his expression of disdain about the U.S. Foreign Claims Commission's findings about her mother's claim. "Worthless" was the word that went through Lily's mind as she fell asleep.

Early the next morning a hotel maid knocking on her door shocked Lily out of a restless sleep. Looking at the maid, who cheerfully informed Lily she needed to make up the room since Lily, according to the front desk, was checking out, Lily realized she had slept straight through the night and would have to scramble to catch the morning train to Fehleen.

A scratchy throat and aching muscles added to Lily's disoriented sense of being lost in an unfamiliar place. She practically threw her clothes and cosmetics into her suitcase, dragged it to the lobby, checked out while reconfirming she would be back in two days, panicked at the delayed arrival of a cab, gasped "Zoo-Bahnhof" at the driver and closed her eyes as he zig-zagged in Berlin's stupefying morning rush hour.

As the train left the Zoo Station and entered East Berlin, she wondered if the scaffolding seen on so many buildings had twins farther into the East Zone or if it was only in the showcase of

89

reunited Germany, the city of Berlin, that the push was being made to obliterate decades of neglect.

Her eyes closed, and her body sunk gratefully into the overstuffed train seat. She slept.

The lurching of the train woke Lily. Looking out the window, she could see they were on the outskirts of a large city with cathedral spires in the distance. The reason for the train's sudden stop was unclear.

Turning from the window, Lily realized two people must have entered the compartment so silently that she had not been awakened at any of the train's stops. A man was in the seat furthest from Lily and next to the door. He was reading a newspaper, snapping the pages; he showed no interest in the abrupt halt. A middle-aged woman sat across from Lily and looked at Lily with some curiosity as she knitted a baby bootie. The woman was dressed in a much-ironed blouse, and a grey cardigan shirt. She wore "sensible" shoes.

"Please, where are we?" Lily asked.

"Outside Magdeburg."

Lily was pleased the woman understood her German and responded. She asked past her scratchy throat.

"Why did we stop?"

"There is a political rally today in Magdeburg," said the man from behind his newspaper. "It says here that Chancellor Kohl is making a speech today." He lowered the paper somewhat, and looked suddenly at his watch. "Right now, in fact, to the workers - over 20,000 are expected - to explain why unemployment is so high." Dryly he added, folding the paper neatly, "And why it will still go higher. But of course he will not say that."

The man turned back to his newspaper.

"Both my sons have lost their jobs and one has a wife expecting their first child. It is very difficult," the woman said, as her needle clicked off another row of the baby bootie.

The train picked up speed, but stopped suddenly again at the outer edge of the depot. Lily opened the window to stick her head out. It looked to her as if the train station itself was less than a mile away. The train was stopped at the edge of an open field with an impromptu speaker's stand clearly visible from Lily's compartment. The woman joined Lily at the window.

A tall, heavy-set man was speaking into a microphone. The static distorted his words, but the angry tone was clear. The catcalls and booing from the large crowd overrode the speaker. The fringes of the crowd spilled almost to the rails heading into the train station. Only a fence divided the train from the surly crowd.

"That is Chancellor Kohl," said the woman, pointing to the speaker, whose face seemed to have a purple hue even from a distance.

"What is he saying?" Lily asked.

The woman struggled to make out the few words audible between the boos of the crowd. "He is saying this is a transitional period, a period of unrest, but things will get better. To be patient."

A disturbance caused the crowd midway between the train and the speaker's platform to move and give way. The crowd turned away from the speaker toward two men with shaved heads who suddenly emerged at the outer edge of the crowd closest to the train. They were dragging a slender, dark-skinned man between them. His clothing identified him as a non-German, a foreigner – black shirt, pants, and a cap, a fez-like cap on his head. Lily clearly heard one man say to the other, "Shall we toss him?"

"Yes, toss them all out."

One man grabbed the arms, the other the legs of their victim and began to swing him higher and higher as if they would let him go to sail over and into the crowd and to fall in the crowd's midst.

A smattering of applause broke out at the edge of the crowd. A voice yelled, "Get rid of the foreigners!" Followed by another, "They take our jobs." Another said, "And our housing." A woman's voice yelled out, "You pigs! You Nazi pigs. Leave him alone!"

Arms reached out to pull the terrified dark-skinned man from his assailants, only to be beaten off by other hands. Police whistles rang out from the lips of two very large, uniformed *polizei* - Lily thought in a belated fashion - causing the two thugs to drop the man on the ground and run alongside the train tracks in the opposite direction from the train station. The policemen reached the man lying on the ground and picked him up.

Once standing, the man shrugged off any other assistance and walked slowly away, carefully staying on the outskirts of the crowd before crossing the open field to what looked to Lily like a public housing project in the distance.

Shaken, Lily sat down. The woman resumed her knitting and said, "Foreigners should not see things like that, particularly Americans. You are American, yes?"

"Yes."

"These are difficult times. Things happen to those who should not be here."

"What do you mean?"

Lily knew she should have kept her mouth shut. Her questions could only make the situation worse. The woman looked at her steadily for a minute, enough time for Lily to read the resentment in the woman's eyes. The train began to move again. The woman shrugged and apparently decided not to say anything more about the attack they had witnessed, folded her knitting and put it in her large purse.

"We will be in the station in a few minutes. Will you be staying in Magdeburg?"

"No, I'm changing trains here...to go to Fehleen."

The woman made no attempt to hide her surprise.

"Fehleen? What an unlikely tourist spot. Let me wish you a safe journey."

The train pulled into the station and quickly offloaded its few passengers at the almost deserted train station. Lily struggled to get her large suitcase off the train quickly enough before the train pulled out, headed for Hannover.

She found herself avoiding the curious glances of her fellow passengers. "Conspicuous consumption," she thought with self-contempt. "I look like some ugly American who owns too much and doesn't know how to pack."

She found herself alone on the platform, neither a porter nor a cart in sight. Deserted trains stood on several of the eight tracks she could see, but no one was around to ask for directions. She had no idea where to find the train to Fehleen.

"Hobson's choice," Lily thought to herself. "I can leave my baggage and go find someone, or I can spend the last years of my life in this drafty place. What I can't do is drag this suitcase down the steps to the main part of the station to get directions."

Bewildered, she started looking around, and spotted a skinny, gangling young man leaning against a pole at the far end of the platform on which she was standing. Hesitantly, she waved an arm to catch his attention. After considering a minute, he began to amble toward Lily, a quizzical look on his face. As he got closer, Lily could see his acne-pocked skin and the dilated pupils of a drug user.

A broad smile broke through as he contemplated the large piece of luggage and Lily's predicament.

"You own too much," he said. "Less is better." He added, scratching the stubble on his chin, "Of course, too much of less is nothing. It is not good to have nothing."

Lily didn't know whether she was going to laugh or cry.

"I am a philosopher, as you have no doubt guessed," he said. "In these troubled times, times of such great change when some of us are little corks in a choppy sea, it is important to sit in the park, or in a tunnel, and take the time to think, to make sense of things."

He waited for a response from Lily, who just stood and stared at him.

"You look hungry. Have you eaten lately?" she finally blurted out.

He smiled again, saying, "I am a spiritual person and require little food. You, I can see, eat well. Why did you wave at me?"

Lily looked at his skinny body, then down at her heavy suitcase and moved to pick it up.

Reaching out, he stopped her and said, "I can do that. I am very strong. Now where are you going? Downstairs to the main part of the station to catch a taxi or to another train?"

The wind had picked up and whistled through the platform, causing Lily to shiver. She was again reminded of her poor choice of Southern California clothing, which was inadequate for formal meetings or travel in Germany.

"Fehleen. I need to find the train to Fehleen," she replied.

"Fehleen? What a lovely spot in our beautiful country to visit," he said sarcastically. He picked up her suitcase and started to walk down the long platform toward a train, which had "out of service" signs hanging on each car.

"Do you know where the Fehleen train is?" she asked, trying to keep up with his long strides.

"It is on a side track, which you cannot see yet. It will be an experience for you taking the train to Fehleen."

He passed the out-of-service train, and led Lily across the tracks. Lily's mouth fell open as she looked at what he indicated was the train to Fehleen. The young man put down the suitcase and watched her reaction with laughter in his eyes.

"Madame, your train."

Lily looked at the World War II relic with dread. Rusted sides and cracked windows lent to the impression that the three-car train had been dragged out of a graveyard of old trains and called unexpectedly into service.

The few passengers waiting to get on pretended not to look at her, but she could see their eyeballs move toward her and then away only to come back to her.

"Well, are you going to get on or not?" the young man asked.

"Yes."

If there had been any other way Lily knew of to get to Fehleen, she would have said, "No."

The young man swung her suitcase easily up the rusted steps, trailed by Lily, and he put her luggage on the floor of the first row of wooden benches, which contained seating for four on each side of the aisle.

She sat down and fished in her purse for a tip, so rattled that she reached a handful of German mark notes toward the young man. Considering the pile of bills, he gingerly picked through them before disengaging a 10-mark note from the others.

"This is very generous, so I will take it, but no more. 'More' would be too much. Today I will have a hot meal, maybe even tomorrow, so I thank you."

He watched Lily stuff the remaining bills back into her purse. He said, with concern in his voice, "You must be careful. These are hard times for us." He looked around at the few passengers scattered throughout the car, all studying Lily and her luggage surreptitiously, and said, "Do not be afraid of them. They will not hurt you. You are an American and your luggage is safe since Germans never steal. Have a good journey."

As Lily watched, he swung his lanky body down the steps and disappeared from view. The train pulled away. For the hour it took to get to Fehleen, she kept her eyes glued to the outside to avoid looking at the other passengers.

Wolfgang was pacing impatiently on the platform when the train pulled into the small Fehleen station. The station had only one platform, and it was old. The station house was closed; it was obvious that no tickets were sold there. Lily could see a kind of parking area around in front of the station. She headed there. As she dragged her suitcase down the rusted train steps, she dropped it on the platform, the clatter catching Wolfgang's attention as he waited at the front of the train.

He turned, walked to Lily and was taken aback as she threw her arms around him.

"I'm glad to see you."

"Now, now," he said, awkwardly patting her shoulder. "It is all right. It is all right."

Disengaging himself, he said, "Congratulations. You are Lily Brodsky Weitrek, the great-granddaughter of the founder of the factory, Benjamin Brodsky."

# SEVEN

"How am I related to Benjamin Brodsky?"

Wolfgang was carrying, more, rather, dragging Lily's cumbersome suitcase across the narrow, bricked walkway across the train tracks. It was not a simple effort; he was breathing quite hard.

"I will give you the answer," he said, "as soon as we are in my car and I can breathe again."

There was no one around to hear their conversation, so far as Lily could see, but Wolfgang's voice dropped to a whisper.

"Just be patient, please."

Lily contained her excitement as they approached the place where his Mercedes was parked. She watched Wolfgang pull and tug the large suitcase into the back seat of his parked car.

As soon as they both were seated in the front seat, and as soon as Wolfgang pulled the door to the driver's seat shut, she began.

"Please now, tell me everything."

Wolfgang thought that she looked happier than she had at any time since they first met.

"I found the pertinent documents, not in Charlottenburg, but in Wilmersdorf."

He held his hand up in the "stop" position to preempt Lily's obvious intent to interrupt.

"Let me explain. Wilmersdorf, like Charlottenburg, is one of the boroughs of Berlin. It is, fortunately, also in West Berlin. The records from former old East Berlin are being boxed for transfer from their centralized location under the Communists back to the various cities from which they originally came that were behind the Wall. It will be up to a year before they are accessible once the transfer has been completed. So we were lucky."

"Wolfgang. Just tell me what you found. Skip the details," she said impatiently.

"Very well. But it is important that you be told about the differences in the manner in which records were kept in the old Communist regime. Other demands for documents that may be made on us will require that we pursue finding them accordingly.

I said we were lucky because the documents I found could just as easily not have been there."

Lily nodded, apprised of the importance of what he had said, but no less impatient for the results of his quest.

"I started with the copy of your birth certificate which you had given me and worked backwards. I went from the time of your birth to that of your mother's, then, in turn, to her mother's - your grandmother's."

Lily wanted to shake Wolfgang, to dislodge the words he had yet to speak, the ones she wanted most to hear, to accelerate the pedantic pace at which he was unrolling information.

"How did you do that?" she asked, forcing herself to sound cooperative.

"It states on your birth certificate that you were born in Charlottenburg. It gives your parents' address when you were born as Wilmersdorf. That is when, as you Americans say, I 'hit the jackpot'."

Lily almost laughed at what by now she recognized as Wolfgang's atypical use of an American colloquialism. "Jackpot?"

"Yes. Your mother was born in Wilmersdorf. Her birth certificate had her parents' names and addresses."

Lily's need to interrupt could not be stopped this time.

"What was my grandfather's name? We know now my grandmother's name was Emma, what was my grandfather's?"

"Georg Moishe Brodsky."

Lily wrinkled her nose.

"Moishe?"

Wolfgang was surprised at her evident distaste.

"I am sorry, Lily, but that was his name. He died, by the way, when your mother was five years old, in 1913."

All this exchange had taken place while they were still parked in the small lot outside the small Fehleen train station.

Lily turned away. She looked out at the grimy building, the station. She lost Wolfgang, instead lapsing into a brown study.

What was life like for her mother as a five year old trying to understand the meaning of death as it had visited her father, and stayed with her family?

"Why do you suppose my grandfather isn't buried next to my grandmother in Weissensee Cemetery?"

Wolfgang hesitated. "Perhaps there is a Brodsky plot, or mausoleum which we did not know to look for," he said, "but that is how I found the 'jackpot.'"

"What's the jackpot?"

"Their marriage certificate."

Wolfgang smiled with a kind of self-satisfaction. Lily looked confused again.

"Whose marriage certificate?" she asked.

"Your grandparents, of course. Emma Auerbach married Georg Moishe Brodsky on August 14, 1898. "I also found a birth certificate for a son, Ernst, who was born before your mother. He died, another document tells us, when he was two. Did your mother ever tell you that she had a brother who died?"

Lily's snapped, "It seems my mother never told me anything."

Wolfgang's look of consternation arrested her.

"I'm sorry. Go on with your big secret."

Wolfgang was clearly taken aback, even a bit offended.

"This is your story, Lily, not mine."

"I am sorry again. You're right. Please. Go on."

Wolfgang nodded. But he inserted the key into the ignition and started the car. He drove out of the train station parking lot, out on to the cobblestone street in front of the train station, Bahnhofstrasse, a street name Lily recognized from Theresa's claim, the street on which there was a house very important to her mother, and one which, if it still existed, she intended to see herself."

"It was there," Wolfgang said; "what we need for the Treuhand on your grandparents marriage certificate."

"What was there - exactly?"

Wolfgang's look was triumphant. What he would say next was the end of the account of his research that Lily had wanted to hear immediately. But he, as a research-oriented lawyer, wanted to pursue all the unfolding steps that led to the knowledge.

"The witnesses to the marriage. Your grandparents. They all signed their names, giving their relationships to the bridegroom, your grandfather, Georg Moishe. Can you guess who signed?"

Lily's heart had begun to pound.

"His brothers?"

"Yes. Daniel and Julius Brodsky, as brothers. And one other, Lily. Can you guess?"

"I don't think so," Lily said. "I can't."

"His father, Lily, Georg's father."

Wolfgang hit the steering wheel of the car with his free hand. While the struggle to keep the car steady on the uneven cobblestones kept him from looking across at Lily, the punctuation was sufficient.

"Benjamin Brodsky, founder of the shoe factory."

He almost beamed as he looked at her.

"So there you are, Benjamin Brodsky's great-granddaughter."

His smile disappeared. He suddenly looked much more serious.

"An official document which even the Treuhand cannot dispute."

Wolfgang thought to himself that the acquisition of these documents was a fine first step toward locating all the needed documents. His experience as a lawyer had reminded him that these documents were only a few of many which they would need to authenticate Lily's claim.

Lily had been talking to him, he suddenly realized.

"Do you have my grandparents' marriage certificate here-with you?"

"No. I ordered copies of it and of your mother's birth certificate and a few others, which we may need. They will be ready for us to pick up by the time you get back to Berlin."

"What others?"

"None as important at all as those which I have told you about. Just papers to fill out the file."

"Oh."

Lily fell silent. Wolfgang was grateful. This was not the time to tell Lily about her parents' divorce, ordered by the Nazi German government in order to separate an Aryan husband from a Jewish wife. To anyone's eyes, even those of an experienced lawyer, the swastikas that framed the divorce decree were a shocking display on a legal document. He had never seen one before. He was dismayed that the history of so much multiple harm perpetrated on so many people went unrecorded. The paragraphs in history books about the Nazi era in Germany, few or many, did scant justice to what actually happened.

Wolfgang promised himself that he would find the time and place to show Lily all the documents, particularly those whose information he had shielded from her, but, for now, he was content that he had been able to bring her some good news.

Lily gasped when Wolfgang pulled his car to the curb across from the entrance to the factory. How thoroughly the factory dominated the economic health of the city could still be seen in its vast size. Not even the soft-coal grime of decades or broken windows could obliterate the importance of the massive structure, which in a convoluted way covered acres and acres of city land.

The soft-coal burning stoves throughout Fehleen on this still-chilly spring day cast a pall so thick that the sun was barely visible as a bright red ball seen eerily through the pollution. The acrid smell made Lily's eyes water and she could barely breathe through the weight on her lungs.

As Lily looked at the massive structure, she was, surprising herself, frightened by the sheer enormity of the claim she had been so sure she was right to pursue. The factory director had said in a vague way that Lily's claim covered the large, main five-story building and many smaller buildings.

She suddenly understood Wolfgang's warning that the government might fight her. But even he had not understood the size of the property claim until he stood next to Lily and looked up at the buildings. Or understood the role of the factory as the major employer in the city across two centuries. "The economic well-being of the city is directly tied to this factory," Lily thought unhappily to herself.

She felt an unwanted anger at her mother for so misleading her. "Why, Theresa, did you pretend this claim was just a simple claim? Why didn't you remember the factory's size if you spent part of your childhood here with Aunt Franziska, Uncle Misha and Cousin Ludwig?" Lily remembered her repeated attempts to get her mother to describe the factory, only to get vague answers. Lily had imagined up to the moment of arrival a modest, small building.

Wolfgang had been right about the warm welcome, the quick recognition by the factory's management team that waited at the entrance to greet her. The "heiress" had come back, it was rumored, to rebuild the factory, to modernize it and to introduce a new shoe line within six months to present at the yearly shoe convention in Italy, the most important in Europe.

The "chief" and his staff all waited to greet her as she and Wolfgang walked past the small factory plaza up a short flight of broken brick steps and through the large front doors of the main building. Through the grimy double doors Lily could see the outlines of art deco reliefs on the inside wall.

There was the chief, Otto Gesset, a man in his early 50s with a pale complexion. In addition to the chief and his assistant, the attorney, the raw materials buyer, and a secretary were present as Lily and Wolfgang entered Gesset's office, at the end of a long, dark hall. Once inside the office, Gesset introduced them all, bowing formally as he spoke each name.

Charming and quickly solicitous of Lily's chattering teeth in the freezing building, Gesset ordered his assistant to make hot coffee for the "heiress." Gesset explained that the cost of heating the building was such that he had to shut it off. Lily estimated the temperature at about 40 degrees.

Except for this small group in Gesset's office, the entire factory was apparently deserted. Lily bit back her disappointment at not being able to see any of the operations of the factory. Gesset explained that all the workers were on "kurzarbeit" - "short work," a term Lily had never heard before.

"What's short work?" she asked.

"When we have no contracts, workers are sent home. When we get a contract, such as the one we are waiting for from Salamander — a large West German retail chain — for 30,000 boots, the workers are called back. When the contract is finished, the workers are let go again."

Gesset's staff mustered not only coffee but small sandwiches for the assembled group. Gesset quickly rattled off his plans for the factory in this new era of moving from Communist, state-controlled and subsidized shoe production into the free market economy. And his plans for Lily to contribute "her property," so his plans would succeed. Gesset without any modesty proclaimed himself a premiere shoemaker. Never once was a reference made to former Jewish owners. Just former owners. Lily wondered at this omission, but quietly realized it was exactly what she was doing herself, omitting, as she was beginning to understand it, a central fact of her life and the factory's.

"His enthusiasm is catching," thought Lily, "but there's a giant step missing. The German government has to recognize my claim first."

She did not want to remind Gesset of that fact. But she was puzzled. Gesset's demeanor toward her made her realize that in the world she grew up in and now lived in, no one had ever treated her as an heiress. She found she rather enjoyed this new sense of importance, even if, she told herself, it was only temporary.

Wolfgang had listened patiently for as long as he could to Gesset's pie-in-the-sky plans. "Mr. Gesset," he jumped in as Gesset finally took a breath. "My client and I would like a tour of the factory."

Following Gesset's lead, they all rose from the conference table and moved into the darkened corridor. "No heat and every other light bulb unscrewed," thought Lily. Lily almost groaned aloud when Gesset stated matter of factly that the elevator was broken and they would be walking the five flights of stairs.

Two hours later and totally winded, Lily and Wolfgang, led by Gesset, had seen countless large empty rooms, hundreds of idle sewing machines, storage areas in vast, drafty halls containing a few remaining rolls of silk and a small number of piles of remnant hides. Next they saw an odd assortment of minor buildings added by the East German government over decades to house equipment. Each asbestos-laden, stated Gesset. They had also toured the old horse stables, which housed one brand-new black Mercedes Benz.

Gesset, in response to Lily's surprised and Wolfgang's scornful look said, "As head of the factory I have to represent well, like the `Wessies.' A good car is important. I can't be expected to drive around in a Trabi now that we're one country."

Lily gave Wolfgang a warning look that clearly said, "Don't you dare say anything." He didn't.

The rest of the day had been a blur of actual, shoe models in small sizes, held high by an enthusiastic Gesset, who lovingly explained the different materials used and future shoe lines already in the design process. Page after page of photos of shoes and boots in the planning stages were handed to Lily for her admiration. "This is one of life's great ironies," thought Lily. "I can go barefoot most of the time at home, hate wearing shoes, and I'm sitting here an instant expert on what shoes might sell to other women."

Wolfgang, thoroughly irritated with Gesset and his pompous plans for Lily, picked up one of the new shoe designs, studied it for a fraction of a second and said, "They're old-fashioned, FabrikDirektor Gesset. No woman in the West would wear these."

Smoothly, before Lily could interrupt, Gesset responded, "We will change them so they are marketable in America. Lily will find markets for us in the U.S."

Lily and Otto Gesset had agreed earlier in the day to skip the usual German formality of addressing each other by title or last name. But Wolfgang insisted on using Gesset's formal title, "FabrikDirektor Gesset," and consistently put a sarcastic spin on the title as he let it slowly roll off his tongue.

"You are being a perfect pig," Lily thought as she studied Wolfgang. "You've insulted the man, his factory, the grime on the bricks, pointed out each broken window, how old the machinery is and now you've moved on to breaking his heart — you've attacked the shoes and his designs."

Lily watched the two men as they eyed each other. "Their dislike for each other is pretty clear," thought Lily, "but I'm going to need you both in facing off with the German government."

As if to smooth over Wolfgang's words, she said, "I'm sure Otto with his years of experience can create shoes anyone would want to buy. We just need to help him by researching the American market, which I will do when I get home." Otto shot her a look of gratitude. Wolfgang's face shut down and for the rest of the day he refused to say anything except, "Goodbye, FabrikDirektor Gesset," again with that unmistakable spin.

As they stood at the end of the afternoon once again on the broken brick steps, Gesset asked Lily to come back the next day for a private visit. She agreed.

Wolfgang was obviously irritated that Lily had agreed so readily to return to the factory the next day. He announced that he himself would drive the next day to the town of Barby, some 25 miles away. He hoped, he said, to find the original deeds to the factory land in the Land Registry there.

Providing authentic documentation, he reminded Lily needlessly, was one of the requirements the government had imposed on Lily to prove that her ancestors were actually recorded as the owners at the time of the Nazi takeover in 1933.

From Barby, Wolfgang said, he would return to Berlin.

Lily was relieved she'd have the next day alone in Fehleen. She would visit with Gesset. And be rid of Wolfgang.

Wolfgang had urged her to take advantage of the visit to the factory to try to learn everything Gesset knew about the takeover in 1933.

He also directed her to go the Land Registry office in Fehleen to find, if she could, the records of personal family property in the city.

But in her heart more important than any documents was locating the family house her mother had spoken of so fondly, the one Misha and Franziska Sagal had lived in with their young son, Ludwig, and where Theresa had spent summers as a child.

Wolfgang dropped Lily off, at her request, on the street leading up to Fehleen's small Jewish cemetery. Lily had been surprised when Otto told her that the little city had its own Jewish cemetery, however small. He had never heard of anyone going there, probably since World War II. The gates, he had warned her, were probably locked and rusted.

"And here I am — in front of another cemetery. Shoes and cemeteries, big dreams and lost dead people — relatives I never knew I had." Impressions of the last three days scuttled across Lily's mind. The cemetery gate had clearly been locked for years. Lily studied the cemetery wall closest to her. "It's low enough to climb over," she observed to herself.

# EIGHT

The tiny Fehleen Cemetery had none of the imposing grandeur of Weissensee Cemetery in Berlin. Off a side street, it was forgettable and forgotten. Its original design reflected no lofty illusions that Fehleen would ever be a center of Jewish life.

A short wall enclosed the small area on three sides. Peering through the locked gate on the fourth side, Lily could make out about two dozen headstones, as if the Jewish community, in the main, expected to die and be buried elsewhere.

Maybe, thought Lily, whatever was true about my mother's aunt and uncle, they were important to the town but not really of it. Lily could not know how profound an impact her family had had on the city of Fehleen.

For it was here in 1883 that Benjamin Brodsky had bought a small shoe business from a famous shoemaker, Hans Prinz. Prinz had gained a reputation for his handmade shoes, much sought after by the wealthy women of Berlin. These elegant ladies arrived with their servants, the ladies fluttering handkerchiefs as they got off at the small Fehleen train station, dusting the train's soot off their clothes. Complaining. Complaining about either the heat or the cold, the soot, the inconvenience of coming to so backwater a place. Hans Prinz personally picked them up in his carriage, and nodded sympathetically. His ladies' discomfort disappeared under his personal attentions and Frau Prinz's coffee and delicacies. Since there was no hotel, the elegant women stayed just long enough to be fitted for hightop shoes or boots of brown, black or grey leather. Prinz introduced the color grey into the shoe business and became famous for it.

Benjamin Brodsky, a Polish Jew, a peddler in shoe leather, was the only leather supplier from whom Prinz bought leather. Prinz tested Brodsky again and again in the early years of their business dealings to produce a finer and more subtle leather. Through a tanning process Brodsky developed, he finally achieved a soft, pliable hide. Following Prinz's lead, by the early 1880s, competitive shoemakers across Germany were relying on Brodsky to supply their leather.

Brodsky often studied the much older Prinz while watching the shoemaker's painstaking personal attention to each shoe. Bowed over with a permanent hunch, Prinz would work the nails in the sole of the shoe and pull and stretch the leather of the upper part of the shoe over a clay mold of his customer's foot. While Brodsky watched the shoemaker, Prinz educated the younger man about the history of shoemaking and the passion needed to create a beautiful shoe. Prinz marveled at how progressive shoemaking had become from the peaked shoes of the 15th century with the toe so long walking was almost impossible to the Elizabethan duckbill shoe with its legal limit of no more than 5 1/2 inches toe-width. More breakthroughs in shoe technology had occurred since the 1850s, Prinz declared, than in all the centuries before.

Prinz remembered too well that when he started his line of shoes there was no difference between a right and left shoe since all shoes were made on undifferentiated foot-molds. To break in a shoe so that it would mold to a right or left foot was both a serious and always a difficult and painful task. Prinz recalled that to break in a shoe it was necessary to pour water into the two shoes and than to slosh around as long as it was necessary for the leather to break down and form around each foot, resulting in a right and a left shoe.

Boots, well, boots needed urine, not water. Horse urine was particularly potent. Prinz roared with laughter as he remembered chasing horses around a field, boots slung over his shoulder as he tried to catch up to a urinating horse.

Prinz took great pride in making each shoe carefully and by hand.

But that made no sense to Brodsky. He knew there had to be a quicker, better way. Made by hand, no two shoes were ever the same. Brodsky knew from hearing his wife's complaints that, however elegantly shod, one shoe always hurt, pinched. Brodsky had learned recently that the English had invented an automatic nailing machine for attaching the soles of shoes. Even more recently, the Americans had invented a shoe "last" machine, a "last" being a mold on which the bottom of the shoe is formed, allowing the "upper" part to be shaped around the "last," the bottom. Set at precise sizes, the "lasts" allowed the production of about a hundred pairs of shoe bottoms a day. Brodsky dreamed of a machine that could turn out hundreds of shoes, not in a day, but an hour. It was a revolutionary concept, the idea that all feet, even children's, could be sized.

Brodsky was so intrigued that he ordered an American "last" machine and stored it in the basement of his modest Berlin home. Night after night he improved on it, using old foot molds from Prinz to create full sizes and then half sizes. Brodsky's ambition was to build the first mass-produced shoe factory and the largest one in Germany, preferably in all of Europe.

When he knew he was ready, he offered the aging Prinz a partnership in the new company he planned to start. Prinz preferred, he said, to sell. He said he preferred money to throwing in with such a wild idea as every woman's feet fitting into a specific size.

"Madness," said Prinz.

Good friends, they agreed to disagree. And Prinz was grateful to face his last years not hunched over a piece of leather, smelling horse glue. He sold his business, client list and reputation to Brodsky.

Two years later, in 1883, Brodsky set himself up in business with an old friend, Alfred Baum, a financier. Pooling their resources, they bought Prinz's leather shop and the 35 acres of empty land around it. In 1885, for 1.5 million German mark, they built the first building and installed the steam-driven machinery that would by 1932 produce 2 million pairs of shoes a year and deliver them to the 140 retail stores, carrying the PrinzLine name to every major city in Germany and well beyond, to the main capitals of Europe.

Brodsky personally designed the three factory flags which were flown daily from the day the first building was dedicated to the last day, on May 31, 1933, when the Nazi crowd tore the flags to shreds.

Between 1885 and 1932, the shoe factory dominated the city's employment history, providing work to generations of townspeople. Health plans and vacation villas were part of employment under Brodsky because his company was progressive. When he died in 1929, Benjamin Brodsky had built his dream and lived it.

At his death, which followed his friend Alfred Baum's by a year, and whose interest he had bought out, Brodsky left his eldest son, Daniel, and to a lesser extent, his younger, flamboyant Zionist son Julius, responsibility for the huge firm. Brodsky worried about Julius, but was content with his protege, Misha Sagal, a cousin whom he had brought into the firm when finally incorporating in 1911. Sagal was factory director in charge of production in Fehleen. Daniel and Julius, located in Berlin, were managers of the retail network.

Benjamin died in the main content and without having paid much attention to a group calling themselves Nazis. He could not know that, in 1933, the group would overwhelm Germany, his shoe factory and his family.

Brodsky's last thought was that if one were to lay out all the leather used in his shoes, it would stretch one meter wide from Berlin, to Cologne, to Frankfurt am Main to Basel, Switzerland.

He died smiling.

Contemplating the low cemetery wall, Lily told herself no one would see her since no one was around. "I wonder if the Germans would arrest an American for breaking into a deserted Jewish cemetery?" Lily muttered to herself. Shrugging off her doubts, Lily moved to the low wall, swung herself over and with a quick dusting off of her pants, was inside the cemetery. A pungent smell almost as of old fires filled her nostrils as she stood in front of the burnt out synagogue. "How can anything smell after so many years? Surely," she thought, "the fire was long ago."

Moving from headstone to headstone, looking for Aunt Franziska and Uncle Misha, she realized that not a single headstone had a name or date on it. Time and the elements had erased memory of the entire, small, rural Jewish community. Or perhaps people had, she thought.

The voice coming from behind her was that of an old man. "There are easier ways to get into a cemetery." Shock turned

Lily's knees to water. The face of the man was badly scarred on one side and he leaned heavily on a stick. One leg was bent so the foot was at an unnatural angle to his body. His high sweater collar almost covered the scars around his throat. But above the collar Lily could see tendrils of raised welts of a dark purple hue.

"He isn't that old. The strangled voice isn't because of age but rather some damage to his vocal cord," thought Lily.

He peered at Lily intently. "I said there are easier ways to get into a cemetery."

"I'm sorry," Lily said, trying to keep her voice from trembling.

"I forgive you," replied the man, never taking his eyes from Lily's face. "Actually, since it's not my cemetery, but rather the illustrious City of Fehleen's, I don't care. But since I saw you jump the wall from my garden shed next door I was curious as to why anyone would want to come here after so many years. Are you looking for something? Someone?"

"I wish you would stop staring at me," went through Lily's mind. Her answer sounded as confused as she felt.

"Yes — well, no. Anyway, I don't see any names so perhaps I should just leave."

The man lifted his stick and tapped the nameless headstone closest to them. "Sandstone. They used sandstone instead of marble, so the years wiped away the names. Just as we wiped away their people." Each word was punctuated with the tap, tap, tap of his stick on the headstone. His tone was flat, devoid of any interpretation. "We did, as the world knows, a very thorough, precise job of it. Only a few escaped."

He waited for Lily to respond. She stood frozen. Waves of repulsion swept through her.

The man lifted his stick and, pointing it at Lily, asked, "What names are you looking for?"

The words felt dragged out of her throat.

"The Sagals — Misha, Franziska and Ludwig, their son."

His response surprised Lily. "They are not here. Never were. My father said they were good people. Mr.Sagal was the factory director before — before." The man's voice faded on the last words, as if he could not bring himself to identify the era.

Lily held her breath as she asked, "You knew them?" She could feel her heart beating in irregular skips as she waited for his answer.

The man looked up at the sky as if searching for a blessing. He smiled suddenly with the unscarred side of his face to Lily and stuck out his hand toward her.

"Mauer. Walter Mauer. And you are?"

"Lily Weitrek."

Their hands met above the headstone. "My father knew the Sagals quite well," he said. "Almost everybody in Fehleen had family working at the factory. My father delivered the flowers that Mrs. Sagal had ordered every Monday and extra ones for parties."

"What happened to the Sagals?"

Mauer turned away from Lily to study an outer wall. His answer, when it came, was so low that Lily had to strain to hear it.

"My father said they stayed until 1938, until the Jews all over Germany were registered — city by city, town by town, street by street, house by house. Until they had all been found. Could be identified for later. The Sagals stayed even after the factory had been taken over by the Nazis, until the last moment, because of the boy. He was a cripple. No country would let a cripple in. And then, suddenly, they left — were suddenly gone. Disappeared. Poof! Into the air."

Lily had been so intent on his words she didn't realize until he stopped that he had dropped his stick and was wringing his hands.

"Do you know where they went?" she asked.

"We were told so and so had gone to America, Argentina, South Africa, China. China was a jumping-off point to other places for those who couldn't get to America. The Sagals went to Berlin to try to hide. A big city is easier, people thought, to hide in."

Mauer began to circle the headstone in a strange, limping dance.

"We heard they went whoosh, whoosh, whoosh to America. But maybe it was their niece who went to America."

Lily thought to herself, "I have to stay calm, learn what I can from this man." But her body felt chilled to the bone as she asked, "Did your father know her, the niece?"

Mauer's voice registered impatience with so stupid a question. "Everyone knew the stories about her because she always ran around barefoot in the summer when she came for vacations. People laughed at the picture of her family owning a shoe factory and the niece refusing to wear shoes. When she grew up, we heard later, she married a famous film director."

Lily felt faint. She had met someone who could actually place her mother as a child in this small East German city. She turned away to hide the tears that suddenly blinded her; she found herself facing the burnt-out synagogue.

"Was the building bombed?" she asked.

Lily felt Mauer's eyes at the back of her neck. She shivered at the sound of his high-pitched laughter.

"Bombed? No — we had no bombs in Fehleen. If the Allies had known the factory here produced the boots Hitler's army marched in — to France, Poland, Czechoslovakia — two million pairs a year, we would have had bombs everywhere — whoosh-whoosh-whoosh."

She forced herself to turn to look at Mauer. She had to grab the top of the nearest headstone to keep her knees from giving out. Mauer was waving his arms like the wings of an airplane and muttering "whoosh-whoosh-whoosh," eyes rolled back in his head.

Forcing herself to speak very calmly, she used as matter-of-fact a tone as she could muster.

"The factory here?"

Picking up Lily's measured words, Mauer answered in a monotone, arms dropping to his side. "The owners were by then a Nazi family producing big, black shiny boots made of excellent leather, strong soles. The men were gone to war so the pretty ladies were brought from conquered countries to make the good boots."

"Women?" Lily could not keep her shock under control, her voice breaking as she said "women."

"Young and old," answered Mauer. "Some fat, but not for long. Someone had to make the boots to march in."

"What happened to the building?" Lily had turned back to the burnt-out structure, not wanting Mauer to see the pain in her eyes.

The strange laughter made her shrink against the door. She ran her hands over the metal bar of the front door. The wood still contained the smell of an old fire. Lily leaned her head against the door, wishing it would open so she could hide in the gutted remains of the building that had been used for religious celebration long ago. Mauer's voice filtered through her thoughts.

"I was standing over there — by the gate of my father's garden when I heard people running — lots of people running. Run. Run. Run. We could hear the cannons in the distance. It was April 1945. We knew the war was lost. The Russians were closing in on Fehleen. The Allies stopped on the other side of the river to let the Soviets overrun us."


FEHLEEN
APRIL 1945


Panic gripped the city as news of the impending attack by Soviet frontline troops swept from house to house and even into the factory, where the women slave laborers were locked up. They, too, were afraid of the Soviets. The aged town mayor ordered the Nazi flags removed from all official buildings, rounding up anyone who could walk to destroy any evidence that Fehleen had been devotedly Nazi, had been so proud since 1933 of being the site of the first takeover of a big Jewish business by a family loyal to the Nazi cause.

The noose the Red Army had already thrown around Berlin, just 60 miles away, left no doubt that the entire city of Fehleen would join Berlin in being punished for the two million Russian men, women and children who had died in the defense of Stalingrad. News was filtering through that the women and children of Berlin were hiding in cellars and subways. As the

Soviets found them, they were raping women, old and young alike, before killing them. Three million Berliners huddled as Soviet artillery and tanks pounded Berlin. The only ones to escape were those hiding above ground level. It was said for years after the war that the Red Army's march through Berlin was marked by the troops' fear of being exposed to any of Hitler's fanatical followers, even children who might be hiding up a stairwell or in a bombed-out building above ground level.

If the Russians' hatred of the Germans came from the Nazi invasion of Mother Russia and the millions dead as a consequence, the German fear of the Soviets came from the troops' relentless rape and murder of those hiding in the cellars of Berlin as the war came to an end in 1945.

All day long the sound of Soviet tanks and artillery could be heard in the distance. The women and those few old or wounded men in Fehleen studied their homes and shops for telltale signs of Nazi loyalty. They stripped windows of once proudly displayed pictures of dead sons, brothers and husbands, and some buried pictures and war medals in back yards. Others joined the massive bonfire the mayor had started in front of the town hall. Into it went the mementos of the 1,000-year Reich, especially pictures, newspapers and magazines extolling Adolph Hitler.

As dusk fell, bonfires sprang up all over Fehleen, but with the sound of gunfire drawer closer, there just was not time, the mayor realized, to burn everything. He waded through a particularly large mountain of uniforms and Nazi flags still waiting to be burned and ordered them taken to the small Fehleen Jewish cemetery.

"Hide these in the Jewish cemetery. The Russians will not look there. Get rid of these things - now!" Hundreds of pairs of hands grabbed whatever was nearest and the sound of feet running through Fehleen to the background of artillery were the only sounds heard.

The boy, Mauer, stood watching at his father's gate as townspeople ran frantically up the hill and crashed through the cemetery gates, their arms laden with banners, flags and uniforms. It was the sound of the running feet that had brought him out of his mother's kitchen. He had been sitting on the floor making a bridge of cooking utensils and talking to his mother. Since her husband's death in the invasion of France, she had become very quiet, even more so after someone had seen her give the last Jewish woman to leave Fehleen a piece of bread. The woman had been hungry and terrified, dressed in rags. She said she was walking to Berlin to find family.

Since then, the neighbors shunned Mauer's mother and him. "Jew-lovers" were eradicated from the town's life by being ignored, never spoken to. The fact that Mauer's father had died for the Fatherland kept them from doing worse things.

Mauer didn't mind much not having anyone to play with since most boys, as soon as they were old enough, picked up wooden guns to play with and then, a little older, joined the Hitler Youth. Mauer didn't like guns — or the boys who teased him in their brown shirts and black shorts, teased him when his mother wasn't watching.

The rush of people entering the cemetery trampled over the few tombstones, knocking some down. Because the cemetery had been deserted for years, Mauer at first thought there was going to be some sort of Jewish celebration. Even as young as he was, Mauer realized that wasn't possible. As the people threw open the doors to the small cemetery building, he watched in amazement as Nazi banners, floating in the air momentarily, were quickly bundled up and thrown inside. He watched in astonishment as wounded men stripped off their uniforms down to their underwear, threw them into the building and then fought their way through the press of people coming into the cemetery and staggered back down the street.

When the building was filled and not one more picture, uniform, flag or newspaper would fit, the doors were slammed shut, the heavy bolt dragged across door and the people ran back down the small street and disappeared into the darkness.

Silence. Mauer marveled at the sudden silence. The cannons had stopped in the distance. The sound of running feet had stopped. He knew his mother would be worried if he did not go back to the house, but he wanted to take just one look through the window of the building.

The big hand coming from nowhere grabbed him by the throat, lifting him like a chicken into the air. Mauer, walking into the cemetery, facing the building, had not heard the first of the Soviet frontline troops silently enter the cemetery behind him. War weary, red-eyed and hungry, the dozen men, unwashed, unshaven, entered, guns drawn, ready to shoot anything that moved.

"Look what I have," said the soldier dangling Mauer. "A little Nazi."

Mauer could feel the soldier's foul, warm breath on his face. He squirmed to get free.

"Not so fast. I'm going to kill you for all those you pigs killed in my family."

Mauer felt himself fainting, and the soldier slung Mauer across his shoulder to keep the boy from falling.

The soldiers surrounded the cemetery building quickly but, after opening the doors, hesitated at the sight in front of them.

"Burn it! Burn everything Nazi off the face of the earth!"

Torches were fashioned and lighted, and the soldiers threw them inside and watched as the Nazi treasures caught fire. Mauer could feel the heat from the flames sear his face.

"I'd almost forgotten you, little Nazi. You'll burn well."

As the soldier said that, he lowered Mauer to get a better grip to launch him head-first into the flames. At that moment another soldier waved one of his torches at his comrade saying, "Igor, take this. It won't smell as bad." Igor dropped Mauer and, having grabbed the torch, threw it. Sparks flew wildly, some landing on Mauer's sweater, short pants and in his hair. As Igor turned away, Mauer, his clothes smoldering, scuttled on his stomach to his father's gate. It opened and his mother's hands reached out to drag him through. As he fainted, he could smell his flesh burning.

**1991**

Mauer sat on the ground, sobbing into his hands. Lily had the sense that he had never spoken to anyone about these memories of his childhood. What happens in a country where no one ever talks about the past? Lily sat down next to him and put her arms around the broken man.

"I'm sorry about what happened to you," she whispered against his hair.

"And I about what was done to your people," he replied.

They knelt together in the waning day in the burnt-out structure. Lily felt rather than saw Mauer bow his head, the unscarred side of his face toward her. In repose she could see the man who might have been.

Lily wondered if he believed in God. Very unexpectedly, memories of a horrible day with her mother came into Lily's mind. She cowered trying to escape the images, which emerged from her childhood, crystal clear. She could feel her mother's eyes on her, her cheeks with bright red spots of choleric anger beating down on her, sitting in a child's chair. The thunderous anger that had followed Lily's question, "Do you believe in God, mama?" had so frightened Lily she tipped over the untippable chair and ran crying from the room.

"God," her mother had screamed, "has no place in our lives. Never look to God for help."

What was it if not faith that sustained others? Lily asked herself for the hundredth time. Over years of taking care of her sister, and her mother's death, the question had haunted Lily. What replaces God, central to human hope?

Clearly her mother's slowly emerging real history was tied directly to this country's theft of home, family, language and culture which so many millions had suffered.

Was belief in God the final theft?

Where had God been during those terrible years? Absent? Indifferent? Out of a despair deeper than any Lily had ever felt, she slowly began to mouth an answer. Without thinking, she spoke the words aloud, spilling them over the dusty film of ashes of long ago burnt Nazi banners, uniforms on a Jewish altar.

"The question is wrong. God wasn't absent. Human evil was present in unparalleled fashion. It had nothing to do with God."

She felt Mauer looking at her, exposing both sides of his face to her.

"Of course God exists," he said. "It is we who fail God. God does not fail us."

He reached over to put one of her hands over his and placed her remaining hand underneath his until, like children do, their hands were layered.

"Why don't we pray together?" Mauer said.

# NINE

Night had fallen before Lily arrived at the Hotel Stadt Fehleen to check in. Wolfgang had warned her that it might be impossible to find a cab near the cemetery. "It isn't too far to walk from there to the hotel," he had said.

Trying to be helpful, Wolfgang had given her a map with detailed instructions that only confused Lily.

"I wish I'd paid more attention," she thought tiredly, pausing to read the map again.

The streets were dark, the ancient street lamps throwing more shadow than light on the tiny map. She stopped several times to ask for directions from the few people she passed. They looked at her with poorly concealed suspicion, the question "What is an American woman doing here?" clearer than their hasty directions in a dialect Lily could barely understand.

Gesset had told Lily he held an interview - actually demanded an interview - with the local newspaper shortly after the Wall fell and East and West Germans voted for reunification. His purpose, he proudly told Lily, was to announce his discovery of an American heiress who would work with him personally to find world markets for Gesset's beloved shoes.

The article, when it was published, Gesset reported, did not refer to the past. There was no mention of the Nazi era or of a forced sale of the factory in 1933. Lily realized that the article would have appeared several months before her arrival in Fehleen. She hoped none of the people she had asked for directions to the hotel knew she was the "heiress" referred to by Gesset.

Whatever optimism Lily had felt during the flight from Los Angeles to Frankfurt Airport and then on to Berlin by train was disappearing. Lily forced herself as she walked to observe the dismal, shabby small city wrenched so suddenly from the physical neglect of disintegrating Communist control, now waiting to be reborn as a democratic hotbed of freedom, civil liberty and human rights. And the free-for-all known as capitalism.

The anger of the factory workers in Fehleen at the closing of East Germany's industries and wholesale layoffs of workers by the West Germans mirrored the simmering fury throughout the five new states that had once been East Germany. Gesset had pounded his fist on his desk, growing increasingly angry as he railed against the broken promise of the "Wessies" that East Germans' jobs would still be guaranteed for life after reunification of the two countries.

It was that promise and the promises of continued housing subsidies, free medical and child care and equality for women that led to the East German vote for reunification. That done, the Wessies broke one promise after the other, screamed Gesset. Wolfgang had watched Gesset's "tantrum," as he later described it to Lily, with contempt.

Thinking about Wolfgang only darkened Lily's mood. She was relieved he had gone alone to Barby. She desperately needed time alone to sort out her feelings. "I'm drifting between the past and present, being pushed farther away from what's familiar into a tunnel of darkness, of sorrow. Do I really want to know what happened or should I run away - go home?"

Lily shivered, partly from the cold, partly from the question that emerged, so unwelcome in its clarity. "Who am I?" She remembered her flippant response to the caretaker at Weissensee Cemetery: "I am whoever I say I am." That was no longer true. Lily was afraid.

Lily forced herself to refocus on the buildings she passed. Scaffolding appeared skeletal-like out of the gloom on a few buildings. Other structures were completely caved in. But along the way were early signs of a new era. A small store tucked between larger decaying buildings proudly displayed a hand-painted sign: "Bakery — open for business 5 a.m." The flowers inside the window caught her attention, reminding her of the startling abundance of flowers in every back yard seen from the train out of Frankfurt to Berlin as it entered what had been East Germany. The landscape, denuded of trees after years of deforesting by the East German government, had offered up flowers in every back yard. For mile after mile, as the train clacked along, Lily observed the polluted sky, lakes and streams destroyed years ago by chemical runoff from East Germany's industry, killing all fish and waterfowl. The contrast had been so striking as the train entered East Germany that Lily wondered if the Berlin Wall could have been much more of a symbol of division between the two Germanys than the incredible destruction of the environment by one of them.

"Love of nature has always been part of the tortured German soul." Lily remembered reading that somewhere, probably explaining, she thought, the abundance of flowers everywhere, nurtured in the otherwise barren, treeless, foul-aired landscape.

It was the Soviet officer standing on a street corner that caused Lily to stop and stare. He stood next to a lamp post, not moving, in full military uniform with the telltale Red Army star on his officer's hat. The long coat almost touched the tip of his highly-polished boots, with a toe sticking out of one of them.

A man with no country that wanted him, or tens of thousands like him, back. No country that would take him in, welcome him. Tall, erect in a uniform once worn proudly, he had become a prisoner of change.

Lily had asked Wolfgang about the row after row of bleak housing they had passed on the outskirts of Fehleen when they drove from the small train station into the city. Barbed wire running the length of the grounds suggested it was a prison; shattered windows covered inadequately with cardboard suggested a camp left to decay.

"What is that?" she asked Wolfgang, pointing out the car window.

"Those are the barracks of the Soviet Army. They were trapped here when the Wall fell. We have locked them up. The officers are allowed out a few hours a day."

"Why are they locked up?"

Lily could sense as well as see his anger. Wolfgang's jaw moved as if he were grinding his teeth.

"The Soviets killed my brother. He was just a boy - 17 years old."

Everything you touch in this country, every question you ask, leads to the past, Lily thought to herself. Maybe the soldiers are locked up to protect them from Wolfgang and more like him, who still grieve for brothers. Wolfgang took a deep breath and went on matter-of-factly.

"We do not want them - thousands of Soviet soldiers asking for political asylum - staying here for us to feed. The Soviet government does not want them either, cannot afford them. Russia is on the brink of revolution. So we wait."

With a resigned shrug he said, "We will end up paying the Soviets to take them back. We will pay to get them out of our country, out of Germany. Kohl will give Gorbachev - or Yeltsin, whoever is in control - a bear hug and a portfolio of monetary aid to prop up that miserable country. We will pay the people who killed my brother to go home. Governments, Lily, do what they want. People like you or me have nothing to do with it. What we feel or remember about the past is swept under the rug of history."

They had been silent for the rest of the trip into Fehleen, Lily's questions about Wolfgang's brother unasked.

As Lily passed the lone man, the officer called out to her, "Amerikanski?"

Lily responded, "Da."

Their eyes met briefly. He smiled and said in broken English, "President Reagan, I was his bad dream, yes?"

"We were each other's bad dream." Lily could not keep from smiling as she passed him. The officer smiled again and saluted Lily as she walked by.

By the time Lily reached the small empty plaza leading to the Hotel Stadt Fehleen, every bone in her body ached. Narrow cobblestone streets ran along each side of the plaza creating an island on which the shabby three-story hotel stood.

Wolfgang had dropped off Lily's heavy suitcase in the lobby before he left Fehleen and it stood exactly where he had left it next to the unattended, utilitarian hotel desk, made of wood with a formica top. A hand-penciled sign indicated ringing the bell could get service.

Nobody responded to Lily's tapping the bell. She stood uncertain as to what to do next. Exposed heavy keys with wooden knobs hanging on the wall indicated none of the rooms were taken. Three keys with "W.C." on the knobs made Lily's stomach tighten. She desperately wanted a bath and looking at the prominent keys told her the bathroom was going to be down one of the halls.

Across from the hotel desk were two large central doors. Unwilling to keep waiting for someone to appear, Lily opened the doors to find herself in the hotel dining room, deserted except for one couple. A young woman came out of what Lily guessed was the kitchen carrying a tray of food, which the waitress placed in front of the waiting couple.

Seeing Lily, she called over her shoulder, "Oh, there you are Mrs. Weitrek. Mr. Schmidt registered for you, but if you want anything to eat, it must be now. We will close the kitchen in half an hour. So please sit down."

Lily sat at a table by the window, the carefully tended rows of flowers outlining the perimeter of the square. The waitress approached her and said, "We have no menu since our customers are few. But you have a choice of beef goulash or baked chicken. Each comes with noodles and apfel strudel for dessert. Which one would you like?"

"The chicken, please," responded Lily. "May I ask what room I'm in and whether there is a private bath?"

"You are on the second floor and, no, there is only a bathroom at the end of each hall."

She scurried away toward the kitchen, leaving Lily to contemplate the signs in Russian on the wall. Unable to make them out, she returned her attention to the foot of the plaza, which was beginning to fill up with young people on motorcycles. The sound of the bike riders chasing each other up the street on one side of the hotel and down the other, stopping momentarily at the foot of the plaza, began to fill the dining room. Trabi cars, famous for their noisy two-cylinder engines, pulled up to join the bike riders, and one after the other, the bikes and cars began a continuous large circle around the hotel.

More young people arrived on foot and began to drift from side streets toward the plaza carrying net shopping bags filled with beer which they placed in the flower beds, allowing bike riders to grab a drink as they continued to circle the hotel.

The waitress placed Lily's dinner in front of her saying, "We had to put you on the second floor because we close next week and all the furniture has been taken out of the lower rooms."

Lily gestured toward the growing crowd across from them outside, and asked, "What are they doing?"

"They have nothing to do now - many have lost their jobs or training positions, so they come here at night, drink and ride around in circles. Sometimes they start small fires or get into fights."

"What about the police?" asked Lily.

"What police? They either quit because they were not being paid or quit because, once the investigations start to identify those who were members of the Stasi, they know they will be charged as criminals. So we have no police. You are a foreigner. You cannot understand what is going on here."

Whatever appetite Lily thought she had was completely gone, and once again she was pushing her food around. The waitress watched her for a minute and said, "I have to go wash the dishes, but a piece of advice. Do not go out again tonight. They are just kids, really, but once in a while they look for foreigners or people who they know do not belong in Fehleen. So lock your door and go to sleep."

The room Lily finally entered after dragging her suitcase up the long flight of stairs was the most Spartan she had seen since her dorm room at college. The bed, thank God, had a goose down comforter, so things could be worse, she said to herself as she lay down on it fully-clothed and fell asleep.

She dreamt of a Soviet soldier with a hole in his boot chasing her down the empty rooms of the shoe factory. Somewhere in the background a woman was crying.

# TEN

There was no welcoming committee waiting to greet Lily as she returned to the factory the next day. The three flags outside the main building hung limply on their poles with faded imprints on which she could still read, "The People's Shoes."

Since Gesset had asked her to come back, she pushed open the unlocked entrance door and found herself in the darkened hallway. Lily remembered from the day before where Gesset's office was. After knocking twice and getting no answer, she walked into his outer office. The secretary from the day before wasn't there. In response to her knock on Gesset's inner door, a voice bellowed, "Come in!"

Gesset sat alone at the end of the long conference table, shoe models dotting its length, with a bottle of aquavit at his elbow.

"Ah, Ms. Weitrek — Lily. How good of you to come."

Dark shadows underlined his eyes, yesterday's skin sheen replaced by two red circles on his cheeks.

"I'm sorry," he mumbled, getting up with difficulty to shake her hand. "I've been drinking."

He fell back into his chair at the head of the table, where, until Lily's arrival, he had been lost in a drunken daydream. He had imagined the table lined on either side by his admirers, people praising his work and his beautiful shoes.

"Is anything wrong?" asked Lily.

"Is anything wrong?" echoed Gesset, tears beginning to leak from his eyes. "What am I to do?" he mumbled from behind his hands.

Lily moved closer to him.

"Today I got a fax from the Treuhand to fire 600 people. How can I do that? These people are my friends, my neighbors. How can I tell them the work we had pride in - the shoes - are so ugly there is no market anywhere for our shoes, our boots?" He looked at Lily as if she alone could supply an answer.

"Are they really unmarketable?" she asked.

"It is not a fair competition, Lily. The West Germans' real interest is getting rid of competition for their own production lines. They have to destroy us. It is not fair."

Lily sat down next to him, wanting in a way she could not find to comfort him. He took a handkerchief out of his pocket, blew his nose, wiped his eyes and looked at her.

"There's another problem, Lily."

"What is it?"

"They want to fire me. Make me leave my beloved factory."

"Why?"

"They say I have mismanaged the resources of the company."

"Have you?" Lily asked.

He poured a shot of aquavit into his glass before answering. He paused, a gesture inviting Lily to join him. She declined with a nod. He drank it slowly, looking at Lily. He got up suddenly, went to his desk and pulled out an elegant, thick, sales catalogue and placed it in front of Lily. Imprinted on the front page was the name, "New Age Shoes."

"Open it," he said.

Lily turned page after page of slick photographs of elegant shoes, totally unlike the shoe models he had held up with such pride the day before.

"What is this?" Her tone was almost querulous.

"I thought it was the way, Lily, the way to become a capitalist. I didn't mean to do anything wrong. Now the Treuhand is threatening to bring charges against me if they can find proof."

He finished the aquavit in one swallow. Lily felt sick to her stomach watching the man shrivel in front of her eyes.

She tapped the elegant sales brochure. "What is this?" she asked. "What are 'New Age Shoes'?"

"It's my company. It has nothing to do with you or your claim, which is for property."

"My claim is for the property and the business, Otto. What is 'New Age Shoes'?" Lily could feel the bile reaching her throat. Gesset looked at her, pleading with his eyes for some sympathy.

"The rumors about the Treuhand are all true, Lily. They are going to close the factory as soon as they rule on your claim. On one pretext or another, they'll rule against you. They'll break up the property and sell it to each other. I know the mayor's wife has put in a bid for the building we're sitting in. If you had money, well, maybe it would be different. But I had to do something for myself. Shoes — that's all I know."

Lily felt totally lost. The change from a charming host the day before to this creature who was abandoning support for her claim and leaping to save his own skin left her shaken.

"What is 'New Age Shoes'?" She found she could barely bring the words out. She got up, moved away from him and sat across the table.

"It's my idea, Lily. My own creation."

Seeing her blank look, he continued.

"There weren't many supplies left but I created a beautiful shoe line from them." Pointing to the sales catalogue, he said, "Look at the designs. The shoes will sell anywhere."

He saw the look of disgust on her face, but he elaborated anyway.

"When the workers were called back, there wasn't enough to do. But since the Treuhand was paying the salaries anyway, I put the designer to work creating a completely different line, and the salespeople. We've formed a new company. Everybody you met yesterday is part of it. We've opened seven retail stores already. It will go well for us, Lily. Even in the West, they'll buy my shoes."

Gesset's eyes glittered as he himself turned page after page of the sales catalogue.

"It takes nothing from your claim, Lily. Trust me."

Lily kept tight control over her words. "Is there anything else?"

"Yes." Gesset asked, relieved at how reasonable she was. "Please don't tell the Treuhand. I can make the books all right. I only told you because, given your family history, you already know how hard it is to survive."

"Then I need to ask you a favor in return," replied Lily. "Tell me exactly what you know about the taking of this factory by the Nazis in 1933."

He considered the bargain Lily seemed to be offering, and with an audible sigh of relief got up abruptly and came around the table. He reached his hand to her and pulled her with him toward the door.

"Come with me," said Gesset.

They walked down the almost dark corridor to a staircase leading to the basement, Gesset holding Lily's hand so she would not fall. Gesset turned on a flashlight as they descended the old iron steps. Their shoes clattered making a forlorn sound in the deathly-still building. They passed several closed doors before reaching one for which Gesset pulled out a key. Unlocking it with difficulty, he managed to open it, and they finally entered a large empty room. Open iron filing shelves, which might have once held documents, were instead bare. The dust of years covered the floor. Gesset threw a light switch. A single bare light bulb went on.

"When your claim arrived, I came down here to look for the history of the factory. Over on that shelf," he pointed to an empty area, "I found the minutes of the last board meeting of the directors of PrinzLine. The minutes from May 31, 1933."

Lily began to shake both with tension and cold. She asked, "Do you still have them?"

"No, someone from Berlin came and took them away."

"Who came?"

He looked at her in the half-light and said, "I don't know. They just came and demanded the records. I had to give them up."

"What did the minutes say?" Lily asked.

"They said that in April, 1933, there was a nationwide boycott ordered by the Nazis of all Jewish businesses. The boycott was not successful. A new law was written that, by June 1, 1933, all businesses had to be aryanized. That law included the PrinzLine. PrinzLine had to be aryanized by June 1 or all the directors of the company would have been driven out of Germany or killed."

He looked at Lily in the gloom and said, "You know we in the East were good Communists. We had nothing to do with the Nazis or their atrocities."

Finally sick of him, Lily said, "In 1933 there was only one Germany, not two, and your parents or grandparents were part of the Nazi taking of property, businesses and lives. You were no better here in the East than in the West."

She looked at him with contempt, and said in a commanding voice, "Tell me what the Board of Directors' minutes said."

"I will tell you all I know if you in return do not tell the Treuhand about 'New Age Shoes'."

They studied each other like two chary animals, each afraid of the power of the other.

"I agree," Lily finally said. "What happened here in 1933?"


FEHLEEN, 1933


Anticipation enveloped Fabrikstrasse, the principal street leading into Fehleen, on May 31, 1933. The crowd, which continued to gather, had lined the street for a parade. An official government announcement bearing the signature swastika seal had been posted earlier on a kiosk outside the factory's main building. It announced that May 31 would be an historic day for the town. It would be the day that all the Jews were finally driven out of business. May 31 was to be a day of celebration, of festivity. The announcement was drawing an ever-larger crowd toward the factory.

Fehleen was a town filled with history. The shoe factory, a five-story brick structure, was by far the largest structure in Fehleen, but it was hardly the oldest. Just down the street and around a curve in the next street was the building, which dominated the profile of the town as one approached it - the church, Marienkirche.

Construction on the church had begun soon after the founding of the town in 989 A.D. The prevailing architectural effect of the church remained Norman, even though additions over the centuries favored Gothic styles and, internally, even some Rococco effects.

It had originated as a Catholic place of worship, but had been transferred, along with most of the churches of northern

Germany, into Lutheran jurisdiction at the time of the Reformation.

The church itself was situated in the center of a substantial churchyard, well-landscaped and flowering on this last day of May.

The antiquity of Fehleen was represented even more clearly though, by the very ancient "donjon," or guard tower, two blocks from the church. Although its military purpose had long since become obsolete, it served as a symbol of the town's venerability.

The pride of Fehleen was displayed everywhere, including among the crowd, on this parade day. Nazi banners were hung from windows. Many in the crowd carried their own miniature flags bearing the symbol of Nazi Germany, which they waved vigorously from time to time.

The blue sky served as a design backdrop to the three factory flags, which had found a rhythm to keep in the spring breezes. The flags also framed the words on the tympanum above the main entrance to the factory, the words that told its name: PrinzLine.

Daniel Brodsky ran the corporation from offices in Berlin, overseeing not so much shoe production, which had been for years under the capable supervision of Misha Sagal, but more the corporation's continuously expanding retail branches.

Daniel Brodsky had traveled today the 90 kilometers from Berlin to Fehleen in dejection. He knew what to expect, and he was near despair.

He sat now in the PrinzLine boardroom, looking out the large boardroom window at the street, at the crowd.

The room, rich in the Jugendstil, was furnished with a massive conference table, scroll elements on the fireplace mantle, sideboards with etched, gold-rimmed glass in the cabinets and a slender accent band of light green on the ornate ceiling molding.

Four other men sat with him around the conference table, Daniel Brodsky at the head. The board positions at the table were occupied by Misha Sagal, the factory director whose task it was to keep minutes of meetings, and by directors Hans Erlich, Fritz Freden and Gerhard Steiner. All five could hear the crowd through the window glass; all five saw the brown-shirted man standing on the steps leading to the main entrance raise his arm in the now-familiar Hitler salute and shout, "Resign!"

Daniel Brodsky's sense of despair had required him to persuade his niece, Theresa, to accompany him from Berlin to Fehleen. She had agreed to come to help her Aunt Franziska, Uncle Misha's wife, pack the family's belongings. They planned to leave for somewhere farther into the countryside at the end of this Nazi-decreed festival day until the furor was over.

Franziska had always been Theresa's favorite aunt, but the bond between them had only increased after the death of Emma, Theresa's mother.

Theresa continued to grieve over her mother's death. Her mother had succumbed to the deadly influenza, which had also claimed the older Aunt Marie. Everyone in the family understood that Emma, "the sweetest mother of them all," had paid with her life for having tried to nurse Marie back to health. The effort had two failures: Marie died, and so did Emma.

Though Theresa was twenty-five, she now understood what being orphaned was like. Her father, Georg Brodsky, had died when she was eight. The death of her mother almost defeated her. She withdrew, suspending for a while her involvement in the cultural scene of Berlin. Her mother's death had left Theresa deeply saddened and reliant on Franz, the upstart film director. Aunt Franziska alone had supported Theresa's marriage to Franz, who was without old money, and an Aryan to boot.

It was the thought of Franz back in Berlin, struggling with the dilemma of principle which confronted a young genius, pleasantly yet not entirely willing to be the protege of Nazi leaders, which periodically took Theresa's mind away from young Ludwig. Franz had promised to come later in the day to help the Sagals with their hurried departure.

She was holding Ludwig on her lap, his crutches beside their chair on the floor. Ludwig was very clearly frightened by the clamor outside the house.

"Cousin Theresa, will they kill us?"

His mother, Franziska, spoke quickly. "Theresa, Ludwig, get away from that window."

How it could happen that the mindless chanting of the word "Resign, resign, resign" could orchestrate itself into rising and ebbing waves of terror is difficult to say. The effect was unintentional. In many ways, they who shouted "resign, resign" did not all know what they were saying. They were rather caught like human reeds in the wind, carried up and down on the fanaticism evoked by the brownshirts.

"Resign, resign!" crashed through the window of the house, deafening all it surrounded. The sound terrified Ludwig even more.

"Cousin Theresa, what will happen to Papa? Isn't he there with them in the factory?"

Theresa wanted to change the subject. "Your Papa will be fine. Come, let us help Mama finish the packing. As soon as this crowd has gone and Papa is home, we will drive to the country."

"But what about kindergarten?"

"You will be on vacation for a while."

The attention of the three inside was diverted from any attempt to resume the packing exercise by the frenzy of a powerful voice. The voice commanded they watch as three young men lowered the company flags from the front of the factory building, holding them up for wider view. They then tore the flags into shreds, and handed out the shreds one by one to members of the crowd.

"Take these souvenirs of a proud day in the history of the Fatherland! Now it is jobs only for Germans, not Jews! Businesses only for Germans, not Jews! Schools only for Germans, not Jews! Doctors only for Germans, not Jews! Heil Hitler!"

The crowd clapped thunder: "Heil Hitler!" Hundreds of posters were raised in the air. The slogans on the posters were all similar: "Don't Buy From Jews;" "Jews Are Our Misfortune;" "Defense Against Jewish Atrocities."

Inside the factory conference room the five company directors had been listening to the frightening mob outside. They had watched the three company flags come down, be torn to pieces, and be distributed, as if in some perverse sacramental way, to members of the crowd. When Klaus Langan entered the conference room, none of them took notice, so completely were they mesmerized by the chant, "Resign, resign." Langan lay his briefcase on the conference table. He was dressed as always in a suit so formal that it looked like armor. The man seemed encased rather than dressed. He cleared his throat. The men found their seats again when Langan started to speak standing beside Daniel Brodsky's chair.

"Gentlemen, as your corporate attorney, I must advise you that tomorrow will be your last day as either owners or directors of PrinzLine. As of tomorrow, June 1, 1933, the law prohibits people like you who are Jews from owning any business, which means you Daniel, and your absent brother Julius, and Misha. It also prohibits Jews from sitting on any board, which means everybody else in the room, forbid you from producing, selling, or buying goods, or working with any Aryan. You cannot be served by any teacher, doctor or lawyer, including me. As of tomorrow, you cannot enter any court in the Fatherland. You are no longer citizens of Germany."

The words heard by Daniel Brodsky, Misha Sagal, Hans Erlich, Fritz Freden and Gerhard Steiner were words they had expected to hear. Rumors were rife that every non-aryan business in Germany was at that moment hearing the same words. That these words seemed more shocking to them, more devastating, might have been because it was Klaus Langan, the long-time counsel for PrinzLine, who had spoken them.

Daniel Brodsky had often meditated on the long relationship between the company, its directors, and their attorney. On those occasions, he sometimes saw Klaus Langan, not himself Jewish, as a pleasant reminder of the assimilated nature of Jews in a sophisticated German culture. He knew that not many years earlier, in places to the east, pogroms had prevailed.

He knew, therefore, how his colleague directors felt as well. The sentence of death for their company had been pronounced by another colleague, a friend, and now one who betrayed them.

"Herr Brodsky," Langan continued," you have no choice other than to resign. I will manage the company and try to find a buyer. Even though the price will be heavily discounted, you will get something in exchange for your stock in PrinzLine. It is your last chance. It is all I can do for you, gentlemen." Daniel Brodsky slumped. Suddenly, the precision of attire that always characterized his presence wrinkled, like the man himself. At 42 years of age, he knew more about himself than many realized. He knew his strength had been inherited from his father's business, not from his father. The fight with Goebbels, Hitler's propaganda minister who controlled all newspapers, had disillusioned him about his role, his place in German society. He knew that personal strength was not a virtue he could tout. But, more important, he knew from the minute Goebbels left jail after losing the libel suit Daniel Brodsky had brought against him that the political events in Germany would lead to this day, these words Klaus Langan had just spoken, and the end of PrinzLine as part of the Brodsky dynasty.

He was going to pay dearly for not seeing clearly enough into the crystal ball of German politics to foresee the rise of the Nazis to power.

He shook off a portion of the slump.

"And if we refuse to resign?"

"Confiscation," replied Langan. "The government will quite simply seize the property, seize the assets and records, and dispose of them as it sees fit. I have done you this favor: I have provided you a choice. You may leave and eventually get something...or nothing. The choice is yours."

"You dare describe this as a choice?" Hans Erlich was a thin, ill-dressed, almost physically crooked figure. He knew nothing of shoemaking, but had served as financial advisor to Benjamin Brodsky in purchasing the land for the many retail stores. Daniel Brodsky had kept Hans Erlich on the board. He was known as the "silent director." He seldom furthered discussion, seldom disagreed. He voted when it was called for.

His sarcastic characterization of Klaus Langan's offer was out-of-keeping, but it captured well for the others the sardonic quality of Langan's "favor."

"Hitler will allow one of his loyal followers to 'buy' PrinzLine for a pittance of its value," said Misha Sagal.

Erlich continued unexpectedly.

134

"Herr Sagal, you will even lose most of that because of the 'flight tax' the Nazis have imposed. There are lists of other taxes as well. I shall miss my generous stipend as a director. I wish I thought this is the worst we shall see from this madman, Hitler. I for one am too old to think of emigration."

The board members began a conversation among themselves, ignoring Klaus Langan, setting aside for the while what Langan had presented as an immediate time for decision.

"I hear suicides are quite fashionable in Berlin this year," one said.

"The money, Daniel and Misha, even if you get a small sum, will be directed through the Nazi bank, in block funds, either to France or to Holland," said Fritz Freden. "There it will be discounted, perhaps by as much as 75 percent. You may end up with nothing for PrinzLine."

Gerhard Steiner's career was banking. He knew little except finance, but his knowledge of finance was considerable. He looked, quite deliberately, as he thought bankers did and should. He wore only waistcoats, morning or evening. They expressed openly the curved, bottle-like shape of his body. Often, when he spoke, the exactness of his diction caused the glasses which rested on his nose to rock, as if gestures to underscore his rhetoric.

As one in finance, he was suspicious at all times of men's motives. Money, he believed, and the quest for it, could explain most things.

"That is correct," Gerhard Steiner said. "You will never see proceeds from this forced sale, unless, of course, Daniel, you have already made an arrangement on the side without notifying the board."

"I have continued the honorable history of this company, even as my father began it," Daniel Brodsky replied angrily.

There was nothing more that he could say, nothing more to be said.

"Sturmmeister Streicher himself has prepared these papers, gentlemen," Langan said, pulling several long documents from his briefcase that he then lay on the table in front of Daniel. "You have much to fear from this ruthless man. You must resign. You must each sign the documents he prepared. If you do not, you will be imprisoned, or eliminated. Neither being owners or board members is worth your lives. Sign or not, you will never conduct Prinzline business again."

Daniel Brodsky stared at the swastika-embossed documents as one stares at a sign in a foreign country, offering directions to its beholder in a language he does not understand but which he who is looking at it, knowing that the sign is trying to tell him something he may need to know, continues to stare uncomprehendingly.

"And you, Mr. Langan," Daniel Brodsky asked, looking up from the pages, "what will you do?"

Langan stiffened, as if Daniel's question aroused the military in him.

"I am an Aryan and a good German," Langan answered. "I will, as I said, serve temporarily until a new owner can be found."

"And when," asked Misha Sagal, "did you join the party, old friend?"

"I must look out for my family," Langan said.

Daniel Brodsky reached into an inner pocket and brought out a pen.

"I am glad my father did not live to see this day. May he forgive me for what I have no choice but to do."

He signed, and passed the documents to Misha Sagal, handing him as well a fountain pen. Misha wept openly as he signed. Every other man in the room signed silently on the designated lines.

Outside, the crowd, whose patience at waiting had been restored regularly by the demonic incantations of their leader, shouted when they saw a man run out of the factory entrance waving sheets of paper.

"They have resigned!" he shouted, "they have all resigned!"

The chorus of the crowd's chant grew louder, but only, it seemed, after unanimously they knew to change the tense of the verb they had chanted, mouthed, and yelled several hundred, if not thousands of times, as they waited like an audience to a play they could not see.

"Resigned! Resigned! Resigned! The Jews are gone."

## FEHLEEN, 1991

Lily stood alone under the company flagpoles, then crossed the street to look at the factory built so long ago by her great grandfather. Her heart ached imagining that terrible day in 1933 when her mother with Franziska and Ludwig watched their lives, their hopes, their talents and dreams destroyed by townspeople who stood by or participated in the destruction.

"How is it possible that people stand silently by to such injustice? How can it happen?"

Lily knew that that simple question haunted the world.

She wondered if in her trade-off with Gesset she had found part of the answer. An embarrassing one. To get what she wanted from Gesset, she had promised silence. It was the first small step toward becoming someone she wouldn't admire. She was willing to lie to get a piece of property. How much would she lie if it were to protect her family, or for food if she were starving?

From Gesset's retelling of the history of the factory in 1933, she knew the house of the Sagals was close by. Her mother's description of it stood clearly in her memory. White, Victorian, on an acre of land, on Goethestrasse. She walked, following the map, and soon stood in front of the house. It had only taken minutes. It stood in its beauty undisturbed by war, Nazis or Communists, its architecture completely out of place in its context to the other grimy buildings on the street. She could hear children's voices as they played in the backyard. A sign over the entrance indicated it was a kindergarten. The City of Fehleen's kindergarten.

The gates were unlocked. Lily entered, and walked up the steps to knock on the double front entry door. A cheerful young woman opened the door and looked with surprise at Lily.

"Oh, we did not expect you so soon, but please come in."

She looked Lily up and down, noted Lily's confusion, and said, "The mayor's office called and said you were here to visit the factory, which you say belonged to your family."

There was nothing antagonistic in the woman's voice. Nevertheless, Lily felt chagrin as she said, "And this house."

"Well, be that as it may, it is now a city-owned building, bought from the county government after reunification."

"What did the city pay?" Past the woman's shoulder, Lily could see the huge stained-glass window, with a white unicorn in a field of green, that her mother had described in such detail.

The woman's look was less friendly as she replied, "One Deutschemark, because it was bought for the public good. The public good takes precedence over any other kind of claim."

Reaching out, she shook Lily's hand, saying, "My name, by the way, is Lisl Weber. I am head of the kindergarten. And your name? I'm sorry. I forgot it."

"Weitrek. Lily Weitrek. May I see the house?"

Weber cocked her head to one side. "The ground floor, yes. Some of the younger children — we have thirty here — are taking their naps on the other floors."

Lily was given a rapid tour of the large living room, equally large side rooms, an enclosed garden room, the kitchen, pantry, servant's room and a very antiquated bathroom and, next to it, the water closet — a typical German division of hygienic functions. A toilet was always in a different room from a washbasin and bathtub. Lily felt the woman breathing down her neck and finally asked if she could be alone for a minute.

As she stood on the staircase at the foot of the stained-glass window, Lily wanted to say something to her mother, to the unknown Aunt Franziska and the child Ludwig. She tried to imagine them together in this house, her mother visiting her favorite aunt in summer and later, after the child Ludwig was stricken with polio, lending her love to her family.

But nothing came out of Lily's thoughts except a sense of failure. "I have failed. I am failing in this quest. The Germans are too strong and I'm too weak."

Lily left the house without seeing Weber again, nor did she look for the woman. As Lily closed the gate behind her, she turned to look at the lovely house. In the background, the children were laughing.

On her way to the Victorian house Lily had passed the public park named, according to a monument sign in front of it, "Peoples' Park." Almost in the middle of the park stood Stadt

Fehleen's town hall. Remembering Mauer's story of the bonfire built to consume evidence of Nazi adherence as the Soviet troops stood poised on the outskirts of Fehleen, Lily concluded that she was standing on the exact spot of the bonfire. No evidence remained of that day in April, 1945, in this carefully-tended park, with flowers in orderly rows and pruned hedges .

Next to the townhall trailers had obviously been brought in fairly recently. A temporary sign read, Landesamt. "Land registry," Lily translated to herself. It was her last stop before leaving Fehleen. She knew that the acceptance or rejection of her claim to a great extent would hinge on finding the property deeds to the factory. She took a deep breath, and opened the trailer door into a single office, with stacks of documents covering every flat surface.

The young woman at the only desk looked up from the antiquated phone she'd been talking on, quickly said goodbye, and hung up. Moving papers around on her desk, she busied herself sorting them into various piles, ignoring Lily standing at the counter.

Lily felt a sudden lightheadedness as anger surged through her body. "May I have some assistance, please?"

The woman, tugging down her tight Western sweater over her shiny black skirt, staggered over to Lily on 6-inch heels. She stopped at the other side of the counter and pulled a pad of paper from beneath the counter and placed it in front of Lily. With each movement, the woman's long bright red fingernails clicked on the counter. Indifferently, she said, "Fill out the form. Name here." She indicated the top line. "Property address on the other lines." Having said that, she tottered back to her desk.

Tossing her hair, she suddenly looked at Lily and said, "Do you like my sweater? It's like your Hollywood look, yes?" Not waiting for Lily to answer, she ran her hands through her curly blond hair and said, "I want to look American, like in the movies." Suddenly unsure, she asked, "This is the look, isn't it?"

"Yes, very much so."

The woman laughed softly.

"Thank you." She looked at Lily more closely. "But you do not look like the pictures in magazines. You look —" She stopped. "Tired." Lily completed the sentence. "I look tired." Lily didn't add "depressed, sad and frightened," which was how she felt.

She had completed the form as best she could and held it out to the young woman, who teetered back to take it from Lily. She read it, and as Lily watched, the woman's face became concerned.

"I don't know if these very old files are even in the basement of city hall. Why should they be here after all this time?"

Seeing Lily's expression, she patted Lily's hand. "Let me do my best. I will call next door. Sit down. This may take some time."

Lily sat on the wooden bench watching the woman jiggle the phone hook several times before getting a connection.

"Helmut," Lily heard her say into the phone, "a woman is here looking for Brodsky files. 'B,' Helmut, not 'V.' Yes, it's an odd name, Polish probably."

She shook her head impatiently. Covering the mouthpiece, she asked Lily, "What years are we looking for?"

"Early 1930s."

"Helmut, look in the '30s, early '30s. Dumbkopf, then try 1930! Address — 1 to 48 Fabrikstrasse."

To Lily, she said, "1 to 48? That's a lot of property."

Lily just nodded, hoping against hope that at least one thing would go right on what had been a terrible day.

The woman drummed her nails on her desk.

"If I hang up, he'll take all day. I'm going to stay on the line so maybe that idiot will hurry," she explained to Lily while reaching into her desk and lighting a cigarette. She practiced blowing smoke rings.

"You did? You found them?"

She smiled at Lily conspiratorily. The smile disappeared as she said, "You found them under 'J.' What does 'J' have to do with anything?"

Her face lost all expression. "'J' for Jew. Stuff it, Helmut. Just bring the files to my office. Now!" Her eyes locked with Lily's. "I'm sorry. The Nazis were idiots."

After a short wait, a plump, balding man entered the office balancing a bound volume of unusual width and placed it on the counter. It looked 100 years old, which it was. He stared at Lily with curiosity.

"You can go, Helmut. Thank you."

Lily registered the woman's curt tone of dismissal. She sounded, Lily thought, more like a commanding general than a Hollywood starlet.

"Well, you are really lucky." Looking at the form Lily had filled out, she said, "Yes, Mrs. Weitrek, you are the lucky one. Imagine having these old records still here. Shall we look?"

She leafed gingerly through the brittle, wide pages until she reached the section with `F' written in old German. Lily felt her heart pounding and her knees buckling as the woman turned the first page. Even upside down she could make out the word `Fabrikstrasse,' and beneath it the numbers 1 to 48 running down the page. The woman turned the book around to Lily. A big 'J' was at the top. Next to each numbered entry heavy black lines obliterated the name of the property owners from 1933 to 1945. The black lines were so intense that nothing could be made out.

The young woman paled, understanding the significance of the obscene black lines. Lily felt her eyes fill.

"Please, Mrs. Weitrek, please do not be sad." She came around the counter to take Lily in her arms. "I don't know what to say. Why would we try to hide the history of these people? Were they family?"

Lily muttered "yes" into the new sweater.

"Well, we must find a way of reading through these lines. There must be a way to do that. The Stasi had equipment. Surely the Wessies do too. They'll want to help you, won't they?" The young woman led Lily back to the bench, afraid Lily was going to collapse.

Very much in command, she said, "Mrs. Weitrek, leave me your number in Fehleen and I will call you when I have made contact with the government."

She patted Lily reassuringly on the back. "There is no reason we would want to obliterate your family history."

Lily took a deep, shuddering breath and forced herself to regain some self control.

"I'm leaving for Berlin this afternoon. I'll give you the name and telephone number of my attorney. Please contact him if you have some information for me."

She stood up and began to search in her wallet for one of Wolfgang's business cards and handed it to the young woman. "Thank you," she said, "for your kindness."

They shook hands and Lily left. The young woman went back to study the old records. On a note pad she wrote out the years that framed the blacked out lines. When she finished she realized the first year was 1933, the last 1945.

"The Nazi years," she muttered to herself. She felt enormous sadness for the woman who had just left. "I wonder who she really is or whether she ever smiles."

As Lily walked back to the hotel to check out, the thought occurred to her that she was pursuing a claim in a country increasingly strange to her.

She checked out of the Hotel Stadt Fehleen and got into a taxi that was waiting outside.

On the way to the train station, she asked the taxi driver to pass by the factory. She wanted to imprint it on her mind. As the cab drove past the main building, she saw some activity at the farthest entrance, the entrance Gesset had identified as the workers' gate.

Four covered trucks were pulled up and parked. It became clear to Lily that the vans were being loaded with sewing machines, quickly hidden beneath the trucks' canvasses after being placed on the tailgates. The hasty placing of the factory's machines telegraphed fear of being caught. Lily asked the cab driver to stop across the street. She could hear the voices of the men, but did not recognize the language.

"What language is that?" she asked.

"Polish," the taxi driver answered laconically. "The license plates are Polish, too." He looked at Lily in the mirror. "It goes on all the time. Pretty soon, there will be nothing left. Shall we go on?"

"Yes." Lily felt numb.

"It's like the old days again," said the driver, starting the taxi. "When the Soviets pulled out in 1947, they took every piece of equipment, the lights, the nails, the switch plates, the wood from the floors and carried the factory, piece by piece, on their backs to Russia. Only the buildings remained. That's how it will be again. There will be nothing left by the time the Treuhand closes it." He turned to look at Lily.

"You want my opinion?" he asked.

She nodded.

"The Treuhand knows. Spying on each other was our way of life. In other places what was reported would just have been gossip, but here it was the way to report everything to the Stasi. Everything went into the Stasi files. Little things. Big things. A friend would report on a friend, a worker on a boss, sometimes a husband on a wife, a student on a professor or the other way around. So the Treuhand knows. Someone or many someones have told them that what you saw goes on. And you know what? They don't care. When the factory is empty of equipment, it will be easier to close, get rid of the workers. And easier without workers to sell the property."

"To whom?"

He looked at Lily through the mirror. "To each other, someone from the West or someone in power here."

"What will happen to the Stasi files?"

He thought for a minute. "The government will hem and haw and finally decide to open them."

"Why would they do that?" Lily asked.

"Because it is good to pretend to be an open democracy. But the real reason for the Wessies to do that is to weaken us in the East. We will look shiny and new on the outside, with new roads and phones that work, but on the inside we'll be destroyed. When the files are open, every person named in a file — and there are hundreds of thousands of files — will learn who reported them. Families will break up. Neighbors, friends, workers who worked side by side for years, will no longer speak. Our guts will spill on the ground."

"What will happen to the people who reported others?" Lily felt chilled at the driver's cynicism.

"They will try to find jobs and move to the West or drive taxi cabs."

Lily got out hastily at the little train station, waving away the driver's offer of help with her luggage.

Even the stares of the other passengers on the old Fehleen train didn't bother her. Nor did the thought of dragging her suitcase at the Magdeburg train station to catch the connecting train to Berlin. All she wanted was to get to the Metropol, sink into a hot tub and call Michael. She desperately wanted to hear his voice, the sound of the dogs barking in the background.

She planned to ask Michael to take the portable phone out to the front deck so she could hear the sound of the ocean in front of their house. Maybe then she'd feel stronger, more confident. "They can't scare me. I'm an American," she muttered under her breath as the train moved through the soot-filled, barren landscape toward Berlin.

# INTERLOG II

## IMPERIAL BEACH, CALIFORNIA
## 2002

I discovered in Lily's absence that my sense of "home" is altered when, unaccustomed to it, I am alone. The idea of home, it seems to me, with all its extensions - homeland, for example, is a philosophical center in itself. I have remembered these lines from T.S. Eliot (East Coker) which I first read in college; then, I looked at time from the beginning of the verse, now, somewhat otherwise:

Home is where one starts from. As we grow older/ The world becomes stranger, the pattern more complicated/ Of dead and living.

Lily went to Germany to try to get a factory and some property back. But both of us knew back then even as preparations for her departure were underway that she was going to look as well for "home."

Americans speak of "second homes," vacation spots often, "getaways," they are called, homes to get away to - from home.

Some Americans, on the other hand, even many who were born here, but especially those who immigrated, refer to the land from which they emigrated as "home."

A 12th century student at the University of Paris - I cannot remember his name - made an observation so striking that I have never forgotten it.

"An uneducated man is at home in his own land. An educated man is at home in many lands. A truly educated man is at home in no land."

I had been meditating on this when Lily called early that morning.

She had the entire conversation planned. I was to take the cordless phone out on the front deck of the beach house so that she could hear, she hoped, the sound of the waves. That effort was disappointing because, at low tide in the month of May, the water can be at considerable distance from our deck.

More successful, though, was the contribution the dogs made to the register of yearned-for noise, strong morning objections to dogs other than our dogs making their way to the beach.

Lily enjoyed that.

Lily's reported on what was happening, and again, that morning's account of yesterday's activities, seemed more and more to have placed her in not only another country but another world.

Together, we exchanged, due to the sporadic East German phone system. a summary of several days' information. She told me about her wide array of concerns and I supplied most of the amusement with anecdotes from the daily encounters of the small-town newspaper.

Lily did not seem to register much of this.

All trades, all professions, have their own and special vocabularies. Small talk originated, I think, in a desperate effort to be sociable in the face of the alienation of vocabularies between and among those whose work worlds are not the same.

The language of promotion and public relations of Lily's regular work world is different from the language of journalism, my work environment, as cases in point. But two people who marry have to shift from the common language of their courtship to learning the second language of their spouses.

In Germany, Lily had been learning a new language, I discovered, the vocabulary, less of shoe manufacturing, though we both expected there would be a lot to learn about that, than that of German civil service and legal documents.

I did not know, for example, what an *amt* was; I guess the English equivalent might be "office" or "bureau." And the vagaries of German corporate law, which Lily was now sprinkling about in her conversations with me, are not teachable by phone even if the speaker wanted to teach. Lily did not.

The result is that, in a time in history when international communication has become almost. instantaneous, words by phone, documents by fax, I was learning less and less about what

Lily was about with each phone call, and trying to come to understand that, when she returned home, a third language and a third vocabulary would, at least until I learned them, serve to thwart at least part of our conversational day.

There is no complaint here; it is only a challenge I had not expected to develop, nor do I think did Lily. Something is always to be gained from a new language. Its vocabulary, even only partially mastered, creates the bridges of human effort on which metaphors can be made.

One reason, among many for which I love Lily, is that she loves to learn, and never turns away from a dream or a hope because a learning effort will be required.

That was what was happening in Germany then. Lily was climbing the mountain of understanding about how that system works. She was in effect in class every day.

One day, from what she said, it was history, not only of the factory, which she said she had been scared about, but of real estate, blackened documents.

I knew that was what to some extent Lily was about those days in Germany, a country from which she knew she came, but did not know how, a country in which her forebears' business had been seized by the Nazis, then preempted by the Soviets, to which she had laid claim.

I have to say that the Lily who left, the Lily I knew, seemed not the woman I heard on the phone. She seemed no less affectionate, no less interdependent as we saw ourselves. Perhaps Germany had been changing her, had changed her.

Then it was time for me to go to work, to the newspaper office. Lily had gone to bed by then; she had called three hours earlier.

I had fed the dogs. They had lined up in the sequence of expected disappointment. I was to go, they were to stay, and when I returned, I would be alone.

They wondered, I thought, where Lily Weitrek had gone, and whether she would return the same person who left.

The truth is, so did I.

# ELEVEN

As Lily hurried down Unter den Linden she could see Wolfgang in the distance pacing impatiently in front of the East Berlin Statbibliothek, the mid-city library. She thought she had left the hotel in plenty of time to avoid making Wolfgang wait for her. If she had learned one thing, it was not to keep him waiting. Lily waved to get Wolfgang's attention but he seemed totally immersed in his own thoughts and did not see her.

Wolfgang was summarizing for himself exactly where they were in the search for documents. The briefcase that tugged at his arm contained Lily's family records. He would have to find a good moment to show them to her. Lily, he decided, was braver than he would be in the same circumstance. She had come alone to a foreign country and was learning things about her family and its history that kept tearing her sense of identity apart.

He spotted her and waved, noting a certain fatigue in her steps. It had been only five days, but she was changing. Fine lines, barely visible a few days ago, were etched deeper around her eyes. The confident step seemed more hesitant. He would have to ask her what had happened when she went back to the factory on the day after he left to go to Barby.

Barby. He shifted his weight, moving the briefcase to his other hand.

Barby. Miserable place. He had driven frantically to get to Barby. It was where all the businesses' property records were kept for the State of Saxony-Anhalt in which Fehleen and the factory were located. The records hall was actually in an old, historic castle.

"The old records," he thought ruefully, "have made a full circle." During the Nazi era and before, all business records for Saxony Anhalt were in Barby. Under communism they had been moved to East Berlin and now they were all being moved back.

"I wonder if I myself am like the old records, moving in a circle with Lily. This claim started with the Nazis, will it also end with them?"

The PrinzLine Shoe Company's property records were there, page after page of property, plot size, addresses, everything but the names of the owners of the company in 1933.

"How am I going to tell Lily that heavy black lines go across every page from 1933 to some time after the war's end?"

The shoe factory had been nationalized and the old PrinzLine Shoe Company re-named "The Peoples Shoes" by the East German government, created in 1951. From 1933 to 1951 there was nothing but black lines.

Wolfgang had exploded at the file clerk, who shrugged and said he had not even been born in 1933 so it was not his fault if some upstart West German lawyer did not like what he saw.

Somewhat more politely, Wolfgang had asked when the government planned to get equipment to x-ray the offending lines. Laconically the clerk had suggested a time frame of anywhere from two to five years. "The government has more immediate problems than documents almost 60 years old." Wolfgang had pounded the desk in frustration. The clerk had smirked at Wolfgang's display of temper.

The last word had been Wolfgang's.

He had ordered Xerox copies of the pages. "All of them," he had barked at the clerk, who complained that the brittleness of the pages made the task tedious.

"It will take days," said the clerk.

Wolfgang paid for the service in advance and, as he filled out the request forms, he permitted himself to say as a parting shot, "You have the money and the order forms - so my request is official. I expect the documents to be mailed to my office within the week."

On the drive back to Berlin Wolfgang began to question the government's lack of interest in acquiring a reader - some ultraviolet equipment that would reveal what was behind the black lines. "How can the government honor these Jewish claims if there is no way of reading the documents? On what will the claims be based?" The more he thought about it, the more clear it became to Wolfgang that not only Lily's claim but many Jewish claims could be denied for lack of evidence. The PrinzLine pages

were not the only ones in the thick portfolio in Barby that had
been blackened out. Wolfgang had to assume that the other
properties had also belonged to people the Nazis condemned as
"enemies of the state."

"Hi Wolfgang. I'm sorry I kept you waiting."

He had been so engrossed in his own thoughts he had not
noticed Lily's arrival.

She looked up at him with worry etched on her face and said,
"Wolfgang, all the personal records of my family in Fehleen were
blackened out. There was no way to read through them to see
which properties belonged to anybody in my family."

He put his briefcase down and put his arms around her. Lily
leaned her head against his shoulder, relieved to have friendly
human contact.

"The same thing is true for the business records in Barby." He
patted her shoulder as she pulled away and said, "We'll build the
case the other way. We will locate the addresses of the former
PrinzLine retail stores from old phone books. That will be the
start of a list of properties outside of both Barby and Fehleen.
There were PrinzLine retail stores in every major German city so
some of them must have been in Berlin. Shall we go in?"

The Stadtbibliothek was the oldest Berlin library. Because it
had been locked behind the Berlin Wall in the East sector, West
Berlin had built its own Stadtbibliotek, so now that the Berlin
Wall was down, and East and West Germany were one, Berlin
had two *Stadtbiblioteka*. For the same reason, it had two opera
houses, several symphony halls and quite possibly more museums
than any city in the world. The competition between the German
Democratic Republic and the Federal Republic of Germany had
been at its most fierce here in divided Berlin. Berlin was the
showcase. Berlin was the heart of both Germanys.

The building itself was large and imposing. It was also now
surrounded by decks of scaffolding which announced that this
venerable place of knowledge was to be refurbished for the new
Berlin.

Once they were through the entrance, they were informed by
a sign that visitors needed to go to a Visitors' Office to get a
required pass.

The Visitors' Office resembled a registration desk, the kind there used to be at schools long ago. There was a counter the length of the room, a room perhaps 75 feet long. Behind the counter were rows of racks for clothing where, Lily learned, their coats, their briefcases and her purse would have to be checked.

She was told this after she had signed a registration book of the kind also reminiscent of an old school procedure, handed over her passport to the clerk for examination, and was given a day pass.

Wolfgang knew all of this protocol, even though it was no longer the protocol at the new Stadtbibiliothek in what had been West Berlin, a library more of an "open stacks" affair than this old research library had been or was.

Wolfgang smiled at Lily's reaction when she understood she could not take her briefcase or purse with her into the library proper. He assured her that her possessions would be very safe. He also went to the back wall of the Visitors' Office, across from the long counter, and opened a door there to show her that there was a restaurant available. She smiled appreciatively.

The small, obsolete elevator carried a sign that it was out of order. From the tattered nature of the sign, it had been out of order for a long time.

The alternative to the unusable elevator was stairs.

They turned around to look at them. The staircase symbolized the grand design of the building from a grand era. The steps ascended up the center of the first floor and were very wide, probably 30 yards, and ascended gradually as if they had been designed, as indeed they had been, in a pre-elevator age with an aging readership in mind. When they reached the second level, the stairs split, ran flat along a corridor to the right and to left. Off this corridor were offices. It appeared that library officials worked in them; one, for instance, said "Director," another, "Assistant Director."

At the two ends of this corridor, the stairs, considerably more narrow now, went further up.

That was as far as Wolfgang and Lily could see when they were at the second floor corridor level. They saw a directory, which told them that the reference room they thought was the one they should go to, where records that had to do with matters before 1951 were stored, was on the fifth floor.

They exchanged a communicating look, as if they understood that the fifth floor is what they should have expected.

At the very top of the staircase, the building seemed suddenly smaller. There was a short hallway to the left at the top of the stairs, and in it was a window office, also on the left. Everything else was wall without openings. They learned later that, except for that short hall and its window office, all the other space on the fifth floor was devoted to archival rooms.

The woman behind the counter of the window office directed them to the end of the hallway and again up a narrow staircase to a door which, though closed, was the only exit at the top of the stairs. The sign on the door read what they hoped for: "Reference Room - Records Before 1951."

They entered.

The room had not apparently changed from the 1930s. Rows of tables lay out the length of the long room, chairs at the tables all facing the front where the entrance door also was. At the very front of the room - one might say the head of the room, there was an elevated dais behind which sat a single woman. She was going over papers, it appeared. But she looked very much like a head teacher overseeing students at work at their tables in an old high school gymnasium.

Bookcases lined the other three walls. Some people were at the bookcases, peering up and down with the kind of uncertain visual scrutiny afflicting only those whose bifocals or trifocals seem always to be betraying the acquisition of information by those who wear them.

There were stacks of books of different heights on the tables. The people sitting at the tables were examining books from their respective stacks one by one.

"Let us begin, Lily, with old phone books. If we find addresses for PrinzLine Shoes from before the property was seized, we can drive to the different locations to see if they still exist. Did you bring your camera?"

"Yes." Lily looked puzzled. "Why do we need a camera?"

"The Treuhand can only return or pay for property that still exists. Remember, Lily? That was even a condition of your government in accepting claims for property in East Germany."

Lily shrugged with a growing sense of fatigue. "You're right. I did forget. Lead on, McDuff."

Wolfgang looked surprised, prompting Lily to explain, "It's from *Macbeth*. 'Lay on McDuff and damned be him that first cries 'enough'.""

Wolfgang headed into a side room trailed by Lily.

Against one wall stood shelves filled in orderly rows with old telephone books. The years of issue were clearly marked on the front of the shelves.

Lily and Wolfgang eagerly pulled out the phone books of 1931 and 1932, seated themselves quickly at a nearby table and rather frantically began leafing through the alphabetical order of the books. Lily found herself holding her breath as her eyes ran down the `Bs' to get to Brodsky. She exhaled loudly as if someone had hit her in the stomach, prompting Wolfgang to look at her with concern. "Are you all right?" Lily's face had a greenish tinge, her chin quivered.

"They're here, Wolfgang. The Brodskys - their addresses, phone numbers." She looked up surprised. "Even their professions are listed. And where they work. Listen to this." Her finger slid across the old book.

"Brodsky, J., Jewish News, Berlin; Brodsky, D., Director PrinzLine Shoes, A.G. Oh look!" Her chin quivered uncontrollably. "I missed it at first. Here's my grandmother, Brodsky, Emma and F. What's `F'?"

"'F' stands for *familie* - family," Wolfgang replied.

"So my mother was probably still living at home in" - Lily flipped back to the front of the book - "in 1931. At Hohenzollendamm 179."

She looked wistful as she said, "I wonder if I were to call this phone number my grandmother would answer?" She caught Wolfgang's worried look.

"I know it's make-believe, Wolfgang. But just for a moment I wanted to call and hear the voice of what was once my family. Maybe to hear my grandmother's voice."

Tears were forming in the corners of Lily's eyes. "I don't even know what she sounded like."

Clearing his throat, which suddenly felt uncomfortably tight, Wolfgang spun the 1932 phone book around to Lily and said too loudly for a library, "And here are the listings of PrinzLine Shoe Stores." He was pleased that Lily shifted her attention to the shoe stores. "One each in Andreastrasse, Oranienburgerstrasse, Invalidenstrasse, Wrangelstrasse, Mollstrasse, and Berliner Allee. We will have to plot them out on a map to make the best use of our time. I have a map in the car. I will go get it while you write down the addresses." Lily nodded. Instead of leaving, though, Wolfgang walked to the shelf and began pulling out other phone books. Lily watched curiously as he unceremoniously dumped 1929, 1930, 1933, 1934, 1936, 1937 and 1939 telephone books on the table in front of her.

"What are you doing?" she finally asked.

"We may as well be thorough," he said. "What we are doing is comparing the list of stores before the factory and its assets were seized to the years afterward. Under the new owners."

"Why?"

He was surprised Lily hadn't made the connection, but he tried to soften his normal pedantic style. "It's a matter of value, Lily. If the new owners not only got the factory but all the stores too, your claim has one value. If the stores were closed, it diminishes the value. If the stores stayed open, it means they - whoever they were - got everything, in an American phrase - lock, stock and barrel. So we need to compare the addresses from when your family still owned PrinzLine to the list of stores after the properties were taken."

Wolfgang pushed half the pile toward her and was quickly engrossed in jotting down shoe store addresses against the different years in which the phone books were published. Lily followed his example. They were done in thirty minutes.

"The store in Wrangelstrasse is listed in 1929, 1930, 1932 and 1933. It disappeared in 1934. How's your list?"

Wolfgang replied, "You are correct. Everything is the same except for that one store in 1936, 1937 and 1939. So it is safe to assume that the value passed without significant loss directly from your family to the Nazi owners. In addition to which two new stores were opened in 1939. It appears the company thrived."

Wolfgang reached for the phone books in front of Lily, beginning to stack them to be returned to the shelves. Lily put a restraining hand on his. "Please - one more minute. The Sagals. We didn't look for them."

"Lily, we know they lived in Fehleen."

"I know that, but I'd like to think that for a while at least they were here in Berlin, nearer people who loved them."

He nodded. They quickly went to "S" in each book. None of the phone books held the name of Misha or Franziska Sagal. Wolfgang noted Lily's sadness.

"He was the factory director in Fehleen, Lily; it was unrealistic to think we would find them in the Berlin phone book. I promise we will find them."

Lily smiled at the casual way he said "we." It was a change.

Wolfgang gestured to Lily to pile the books in his outstretched arms.

She stopped when they reached Wolfgang's chin. "I'll do the rest," she said.

After they had retrieved their belongings from the cloakroom, Wolfgang hustled Lily to his car. He pulled out a city map of Berlin from the glove compartment and unfolded it on the hood of the car. Lily saw the year of issue in the top right hand corner.

Lily stared with fascination at the map, which had been printed in 1989 before the Wall fell. It contained the locations of the border crossings and checkpoint transit roads from East to West Germany that had divided one Germany from the other. The map also contained different symbols indicating which of the crossings were for West Germans, West Berliners or for foreigners. Wolfgang watched her with amusement.

"History, Lily. It moves very fast. Too fast for me to have bought an up-to-date map that no longer has the Wall on it."

155

He smiled, reached out and in an uncommon motion touched her hair. "You are too serious, Lily. There are thousands of these old maps."

"Maybe. But they are no longer sold anywhere. I'd like to have it."

Turning back to the map, Wolfgang said, "And so you will. But right now it is very useful for our search for old shoe stores here in the East." He put his finger on the map. "We will start here," pointing to Mollstrasse, "and make a circle and end up by having lunch. I have heard of a very good restaurant near here. I shall 'lead on, McDuff.'"

Two hours later, standing in front of the only existing shoe store they had been able to find from 1932, even Wolfgang's earlier enthusiasm had been stilled.

At the old Mollstrasse location a park had replaced the former store. Large apartment complexes covered the former store in Andreastrasse. An empty street made it impossible to find the location of the Berliner Allee site. And now they stood in front of the Oranienburgerstrasse address. Lily had dutifully taken pictures of each 1932 shoe store location and its 1991 replacement. Every time Wolfgang stopped his car to study the map with increased frustration, Lily's hopes sank lower.

Standing now in front of their last stop and finding that one former shoe store site still existed did little to raise her spirits. She stepped out of the car to focus her camera on the storefront. As she did, the iron security window guard went down quickly. Passers-by gave her barely concealed looks of hostility as they made a wide circle around her. Lily stood baffled at the overt gesture of the window guard being lowered. It was almost, she thought, *as if someone knew I was coming.*

Wolfgang leaned across the open window on the passenger side of the car to ask, "What is the matter?"

Lily did not answer.

Wolfgang climbed out of the car, took the camera from Lily and snapped a picture, the address of the former PrinzLine shoe store his primary focus. He handed the camera back to Lily and said, "I will go in. Even though it is a music store now," a fact the outer sign proclaimed, "maybe the owner knows some of the history of the store." He looked at Lily. "Are you coming with me?"

"No."

He gave her a gentle push. "I suggest that you walk around the building while I go in?" He cupped Lily's elbow in his hand, leading her across the street. He entered the now shuttered small music store. Three narrow streets converged to the small plaza. The store stood on the far side of the plaza next to a butcher shop. The butcher shop displayed the only visible sign on the street that times were changing. A clearly new, blue awning draped the entry door. Lily walked to the space between the music store and the butcher shop and found herself in a small alley between the two stores.

Old cobblestones caught her heels as she walked farther down the alley to find herself in a "hof" so dingy and dirty she could not imagine that it had once been elegant. Laundry hanging up to five stories above the two stores bespoke another century. At ground level she saw what once were stables for working horses. In her mind's eye she could hear their hooves making clip-clopping sounds as they arrived 100 years ago laden with the shoes from the Fehleen factory. She stood in the dark connector between an old family shoe store and a meat market moving into the new world order.

Wolfgang's voice echoed in the "hof." "Lily? Lily, are you in there?"

He stood in what little light reached the plaza and could not see her.

Lily called out, "Yes."

"It will be all right, Lily. The owner will let us take pictures, so come out of there."

When they were back in the car, several pictures having been taken by Wolfgang, he said, "The owner doesn't know anything of the history of the store. But he did say that with the press so full of claims stories everyone is afraid that they will lose what little they have gained since reunification. He apologized, Lily, for making you feel unwelcome."

He touched Lily's shoulder reassuringly. "We found one store still standing, even if its use has changed. That is not so bad, is it?"

Lily had to agree.

"We have to go back to the library this afternoon, but I think a bit of lunch is called for first. Are you hungry?"

He looked so concerned Lily felt a wave of gratitude. "Actually, I'm starved."

"Good."

"Wasn't it just a few days ago you told me nothing in the East is good?"

"Maybe I have to learn a few things myself about this new reunited country," he answered.

Lily looked absently out of the window as they followed the path they had taken earlier in the day in the search for old shoe stores. Shoe stores were less on her mind than documents. Wolfgang was surprised when she suddenly asked, "Did you get the documents of my family?"

Even though Wolfgang was paying total attention to the road, his mind was searching for how he was going to present the documents in order to do Lily the least harm. He had hoped that Lily would ask to see the documents later. He began to worry that the meeting he had set up at the Stammbaum with a film historian who knew Lily's father and the showing of her family documents at the same time might overwhelm her.

He glanced at Lily and wondered to himself at what point in time she had become so central to his being. When he was not with her, Wolfgang found himself thinking about her. The phone messages from his office were piling up at home, ignored. Greta had scrawled a note across the growing pile sarcastically suggesting Wolfgang tear himself away from his "fascinating" client long enough to check in with his boss - her father. Wolfgang had to assume that someone in the office had told Greta who the client was.

"Why is she so important to me?" he asked himself when he was alone at night in his room. "Because." Because why?"

He forced himself to answer his own question, to try to understand his growing emotional involvement with Lily.

"Because I could tell Lily about growing up in the rubble of postwar Germany, about being afraid, of being ashamed of who I am and she would understand." He concluded that through Lily he was taking a personal journey in which he was the student, Lily the teacher.

"It is a journey I could not have taken alone. I need someone to lead me and it is this woman with a Jewish claim who will tell me who I can be." Wolfgang felt both exhilaration and fear as he analyzed his innermost thoughts.

He would, he promised himself, protect Lily as best he could from the revelations in the documents and whatever the film historian would reveal about her father.

"What are you thinking? You haven't said a word for miles." Lily's voice logged in his mind.

"Nothing much. We are almost at the restaurant." He smiled at her reassuringly.

Lily turned in her seat so she could study him more carefully. "Wolfgang, you're acting very strange. Is there something wrong? Did I do something to upset you?"

It wasn't the opening he'd hoped for to tell her that lunch at the Stammbaum wasn't as casual a suggestion as he had pretended earlier in the day. Nervously he cleared his throat. "I arranged for someone to meet us for lunch."

"Who?"

"Someone - a man named Arla Schermer, a film historian." Out of the corner of his eye Wolfgang saw Lily straighten in her seat, a jaw muscle clenching. Lily was grinding her teeth.

In the coldest voice he had heard, and up to that moment Wolfgang thought he knew Lily's emotional range, she snapped, "Would this - person, have anything to do with my father?"

Wolfgang sighed. They were directly in front of the restaurant. Already late, there was no time to get into a fight.

"Lily, Arla Schemer knew both your parents. I thought you would want to hear what he has to say."

He switched off the ignition and turned to Lily, who glared directly ahead.

"Why couldn't you leave it alone, Wolfgang? I precisely asked you not to bring my father into it."

She turned to look at Wolfgang and, in a voice dripping with sarcasm, she said, "Our Wolfgang is such a busy, meddling person."

"I will overlook the insult, Ms. Weitrek."

Wolfgang was so angry he had to fight off the impulse to shake her. "He is an old man and, as I said, knew both your parents. Show some strength, Lily."

He was immediately contrite. "I am sorry. You have more courage than most people. I will make a deal with you, Lily. Let us go meet the man. If you do not want to hear what he has to say, just say that and we will leave."

Lily stared ahead, refusing to look at him. Almost pleading, Wolfgang said, "It may help us in the long run to know what happened to your father." It was the use of the word "us" that prompted Lily to finally look at Wolfgang.

"Be fair," she said to herself. "Be fair to this man who for reasons I can't even guess took my case and has driven all over the place to help me. He deserves more than a tantrum on my part."

He looked at her with worry in his eyes. Lily realized only Michael looked at her with the same intensity of feeling. There are never many people who care very much, so why am I being so childish instead of grateful that he cares at all?

"You're right. Maybe it's time to confront the old demon, my father," she said, unbuckling the seat belt and opening the car door.

Wolfgang let out a sigh of relief. He gave a small prayer that whatever Arla Schermer had to say it would help Lily, not hurt her.

The film historian was waiting for them standing uneasily inside the restaurant entrance. Isolated strands of white hair straggled down to meet the collar of his suit jacket, shiny from many applications of too hot, old-fashioned irons. Schermer was old and frail. He gazed at Lily with unabashed adoration, bowing over her extended hand after Wolfgang had introduced them, muttering repeatedly "such an honor, such an honor to meet the daughter of Franz Weitrek."

Lily was nonplussed. She moved toward the corner table Wolfgang indicated was theirs, one Wolfgang had obviously chosen since the waiter whisked the "Reserved" sign off the table as soon as the small group was seated.

Schermer's repetitive, "Imagine meeting his daughter. What an honor it is, revered lady, to meet you," grated on her nerves.

Lily looked helplessly at Wolfgang who, she thought, resembled a cat closing in on a bowl of cream. She kicked him under the table. Rolling his eyes at Lily, Wolfgang handed Schermer one of the menus and said, "Perhaps we should order first. Before any discussion."

He smirked at Lily as Schermer said, "I am much too excited to eat. I just want to gaze at this beautiful woman who looks so much like her father...the same deep-set eyes, the same way of tilting her head. It is just like seeing Franz again."

Wolfgang proclaimed loudly, "I am starving." He snapped his fingers to bring the waiter to the table, and when the waiter came, Wolfgang said, "I'll take the liberty of ordering for us." He rattled off a list of dishes Lily could not catch except for the first course, which would be "oxensuppe."

For herself Lily conjured up a Big Mac and french fries at Imperial Beach's McDonald's. The waiter faded from view and so did her imagined "Big Mac."

Schermer looked at Lily, his bright blue eyes sunken behind the wrinkles of old age and said, "I remember the last time I saw your beautiful mother and your father together. Later I learned - because after that evening I was sent as journalist to cover the eastern war - that they were never seen again in public as a couple. I was at the time a film journalist and was in the car interviewing your father on the ride to the 1939 premiere of one of his films. It was to be a grand event. Goebbels, as Hitler's Chief of Propaganda, had invited every high ranking Nazi he could find in Berlin."

Schermer's eyes twinkled. "Of course, `invited' is the wrong word. They were ordered to attend."

Tania Wisbar and John Mahoney

For Lily, the world she was sitting in disappeared. In its place was only the soft voice of the ancient film historian as he led her through his memories of 1939.

BERLIN 1939

Friederichstrasse, one of Berlin's theatre streets, sparkled with light in August 1939 in much the same way as Times Square did. And it was an opening night besides. The Auerbach Theater, as it was still referred to by those who momentarily forgot it had been re-named the Volkes Theatre, was particularly well-lighted for the occasion and the drapes of Nazi banners reflected the light. A swastika was centered above each of the three theatre doors, and a stern, uniformed policeman stood directly under each swastika.

A crowd was forming from each direction on the street, kept back from the doors by a ring of mounted police who formed a half-circle, itself almost like a stage, in front of the doors.

The crowd's attention went to an elegant polished black Mercedes limousine that its chauffeur brought to a stop outside the police ring at the curb. The occupants of the passenger bench in the back of the limousine, Theresa and Franz Weitrek, waited for the chauffeur to come around the back of the limousine to open the curbside passenger door.

Next to the chauffeur, Arla Schermer hastily continued to scribble notes from his interview with Franz Weitrek, notes given to him as the car traveled to the theatre.

Schermer could not get comfortable in his Nazi uniform. It showed in his dirty cuffs and the cigarette ashes falling unnoticed down the front of his shirt. He was a journalist through and through; his passion was film, not politics.

Theresa appeared first. She loved red. And even though her appearance here tonight for the private premiere of her husband's film was an unwanted occasion and one she both hated and dreaded, she was too stylish to affect a drabness of dress which otherwise would have matched her mood.

162

The red evening dress was exquisitely simple, so simple that those whose eyes it caught imagined it to be complex and even daring.

Franz followed her out of the limousine. His lean, ascetic look was enhanced by evening clothes, he being one of those men whose confident appearance in formal dress belied the uniform discomfort such attire seems to visit on most men.

In spite of their style, the couple looked exhausted. Those who were being kept waiting by the mounted police stepped back as if under orders, creating a path for the couple to enter the center theatre door.

Franz put his hand under Theresa's left elbow; she stopped flat just inside the door.

"I am not going in there."

"But you must. The only way we can get through this is together."

She stiffened. "I am not going in."

Franz looked around, a slight desperation in his manner, to see who was watching, what they were now thinking.

"We have a daughter to protect, Theresa."

"And your career."

"What do you think is going to happen to us if I refuse outright to make their films?"

"Others have."

"And they are either in prison or in other countries. Or dead."

This exchange at the door of the recently re-named Auerbach Theatre was a well-remembered dialogue for both of them. Franz' brilliance in this new art had attracted the attention of Goebbels very early in his new-found career as propagator of official art. And Franz, even as Arthur Auerbach had once somewhat discourteously observed, was ambitious. He had made two films, then another - this one that was about to be screened.

"I'm begging you," Theresa said without moving her lips or changing her emotionless expression. "Please let us leave! We have to get out of Germany. France has fallen. Pretty soon there will be no way out. You promised me that we would leave after your last film, and here we are again, dragged before monsters one more time. You promised…"

Tears interrupted her sentence, but she recovered quickly. "I have to get out of Germany."

"Alone?"

"No. With you. I am pregnant."

Franz drew her close. Her head rested for only a second on his chest.

"Remember," he said, "I love you. We will name our new baby Lily - surely the baby will be a girl - after your favorite flower. Now come. We need to protect…our children."

The theater's banquet hall was completely full, full of elegantly dressed women and uniformed men. There were a few exceptions to be seen - men in evening dress just as Franz was, but otherwise all the women's escorts for the evening wore either the black of the S.S. or the brown of the S.A.

The result was an image drawn by inadequate rotogravure. Because of the brightness of the attire of many of the women, the brown and black of the uniforms connected themselves into swaths and lines across the face of the image. The result was color crisscrossed with black and brown stripes; the people wearing the clothes faded behind this abstraction.

Theresa and Franz picked and worked their way through this image, Franz nodding occasionally to some but speaking to no one, and Theresa, head rigid and eyes straightforward, stayed beside her husband.

The stage to which they were headed appeared at the end of the crowd. It held a long head table set with china and crystal. Several centerpieces punctuated the table's length. These were groups of flowers arranged around small Nazi flags.

The head table had been waiting for Theresa and Franz. German officials in Nazi Germany did not expect to be kept waiting, but the man who occupied the center seat, Joseph Goebbels, had directed them to patience. Like many Nazi officials, especially the high-ranked ones, Goebbels had found prominence and success in the party of the National Socialists in the wake of continuous early failure. He had been an aspiring writer whose work interested no one. His journalistic efforts, which included slander of Daniel Brodsky, had earned him a prison sentence. But his release nearly coincided with Hitler's success in the election of January, 1933, and allowed Goebbels to go from jail to the position of the second most powerful figure in the Nazi hierarchy.

Nor did Goebbels forget while in jail that Daniel Brodsky's suit against him had led to his stint in jail. He had managed to bring quick focus on Brodsky's shoe factory, force him into sale and allow the new Aryan owners to delay paying even the thieves' price that Brodsky had no choice but to accept.

Goebbels often thought, as he reviewed the episode, that he could almost claim responsibility for pulling the trigger of the suicide gun in Daniel Brodsky's hand.

And he was not unaware that his prize director, Franz Weitrek, had married the Jewess niece of Daniel Brodsky.

By then the crowd had sorted itself out from the confluence of color, brown and black, and was seated at tables throughout the hall. They were waiting for the event to start, engaging in small talk as they waited.

Goebbels arose, and with a symbolic clink of a spoon against crystal, brought the great crowd to silence.

"I, Joseph Goebbels, as Propaganda Minister for all Germany, declare our pride in the film which you are about to see. It reflects the true German, Aryan spirit of our Fatherland. And now we will hear a few words from our talented young director. Heil Hitler!"

To a man, to a woman, the crowd stood, saluted and shouted, "Heil Hitler!"

All, that is, except Theresa, who neither stood nor saluted. Goebbels' eye went to her.

Franz did not salute either. Instead, standing with the others at the head table, he used the moment to move to the podium.

Everyone sat down, quiet, waiting, so they thought, for Franz Weitrek's words.

But their eyes turned, along with those of the officials at the head table to its far end, where Theresa Weitrek, lip curled, shouted:

"Why do you not tell them that your wife hates the colors black and brown...that they are the colors worn by murderers?" Those who direct Greek tragedy and comedy labor, rehearsal through rehearsal, to coordinate blocking, particularly to ensure that the figures in chorus react as one to the exchanges. But, off-stage, no director could have ever achieved the unanimity of the crowd's reaction to Theresa Weitrek's words. They were a tableau, frozen, waiting for what would come next.

Theresa got up, and looking at no one, eyes fixed on the door out of the hall, left the room.

The frozen tableau cracked; bedlam followed. Franz turned away from the podium and headed after his wife.

He got only as far as the center of the table. His arm was seized there by a furious Goebbels. He kept the vise-like grip on the director's arm as he turned to his orderly.

"Start the film!" he ordered and, to Franz, "You will stay!"

The stage curtain lifted to reveal a screen. As the film began, the audience fell silent. Goebbels, still gripping Franz' arm, shoved him off stage, exiting stage right. After walking about 20 feet of backstage area, Goebbels reached around Franz and opened a door inward. Schermer planted his foot in the doorway to wedge it open enough to overhear the conversation that ensued. Inside there was a small reception room. Goebbels went to the bar at the far end to pour himself a cognac. He made no offer of a drink to Franz. Goebbels drank his cognac as if it were whiskey in a shot glass. His fury transformed his speech almost into a hiss.

"You married this Jewess because you were young and ambitious and her family owned many film houses. But this embarrassment has to end and end now!"

"They owned only a few," Franz replied, trying not to further antagonize Goebbels.

"Of course, they now own none. Jews no longer control films, film houses, anything else. The control now is ours - for the German people. Give me your papers!"

Franz reached into the inside pocket of his evening jacket and took out his identity cards. No German could ever allow these papers to be out of his possession.

"Reichminister Goebbels, you know my papers are in order; you yourself signed them!"

"But I am now taking them back. Tomorrow I will issue an exit order for your wife. She will receive a permanent visa out of Germany. You and your daughter will be placed under house arrest until your wife is out of Germany."

"My wife is pregnant, Herr Goebbels. She has nowhere to go. She would be alone. Please, I will do anything."

Goebbels looked up at Franz over his glasses. It was a deliberate move, a deliberate posture.

"There is a very good script - a good propaganda film. The one you refused to make before."

"But I was working, at your request, on the film we came to see tonight."

Goebbels seemed to be calculating, not numbers, perhaps, but ideas, terms, or conditions. He took the time it appeared he needed to find the result or come to the conclusion before he resumed the conversation.

"If you agree to this film, exactly as I tell you, I will permit your wife to stay until the child is born. We will then have two children for the Fatherland. But when the child is six months old, your wife must leave Germany forever. You and your children will stay, like good Germans. The children will be 'Aryanized.' I myself will conduct the ceremony. Hitler may even attend. He would like that. He loves children. Do you agree?"

Franz knew that the conditions Goebbels would set for Theresa's stay, even for a while, would be hard. So while he thought he was prepared for the worst, he was nevertheless shocked.

"Yes," he said.


BERLIN 1991

Even in the retelling of that long-ago night in 1939, Arla Schermer seemed to age in front of Lily's eyes.

167

"Who knows today what any of us would do under the same circumstance?" he asked into the air above Lily's chair. He hesitated for a minute as if unsure if he should add further to the story he had told.

Lily encouraged him to continue with a small nod of her head.

He hesitated again before speaking. "There was another factor complicating your parents' situation. At that premiere your father saw an old sweetheart, an actress, from before your parents' marriage. Her name was Gisella Von Melling. She was a beautiful young woman from an excellent background."

The words "racially pure" hung in the space between Lily and Schermer. Lily's glance left his face to focus on her own tightly clenched hands, hidden in her lap.

Wolfgang reached under the table to put his hand over hers. "It is my fault. I should never have put Lily at risk like this," Wolfgang thought to himself.

He shoved back his chair to stand up and said, "Thank you for coming Mr. Schermer. I think we've heard enough."

Eager to get away, Schermer also stood. Looking at Lily he said, "I'm sorry, Madame, to have distressed you." He pulled out a picture from an envelope he had laid earlier on the table and said, "I found in my personal files a picture of your father from then. I thought you might like to have it." He placed it on the table, bowed in her direction, gave Wolfgang a nod, and left. Lily looked briefly at the picture, then turned it face down. The waiter appeared and cleared off the luncheon dishes. He shook his head, amazed that people were so rich they could waste food.

Wolfgang sat down again, wondering how he could apologize for his lack of judgment. The silence lengthened.

As if reading Wolfgang's mind, she finally said, "Don't blame yourself, Wolfgang. You couldn't know what he was going to say." Her voice was flat, lifeless as she continued. "I've heard all I want to about my father. This is to be the end of any further inquiry." Her voice rose, "Do you understand, Wolfgang? No more!" Gently he said, "I wish we could just leave it like that. But among the documents I found there is one relating to your parents."

Lily looked at him with growing impatience.

He rushed on, "I think you should see it. Then, as you asked, we will drop any further discussion about your father. Please, Lily."

She gave a defeated shrug.

Wolfgang pulled his briefcase onto the chair Schermer had vacated. As he opened it, Lily could see three manila folders with Wolfgang's meticulous handwriting on the tabs. Her stomach turned over. Wolfgang pulled out the folders, re-arranging them so he could present their contents one by one.

The look of dread on Lily's face made sweat break out on his body. He shuffled the folders back together. "Lily, this is not the right time. You've heard enough for one day. Please forgive me. We'll do this some other time."

She stopped him.

"No," Lily said. "Show me the documents. All of them."

"Where does she get the strength?" he wondered.

Reluctantly, Wolfgang placed the first folder in front of her. Lily did not reach to open it. Neither did Wolfgang. He was at a loss as to how to proceed.

"What's in it?" Lily asked like a person seeking a verbal buffer against the reality of bad news, sudden shock.

As matter of factly as he could manage, Wolfgang said, "Your parents' divorce decree."

"Open it, please."

The document lay between them in all its ugliness. Time had not softened the swastika seals at both the top and bottom of the decree. Lily refused to touch it. She barely glanced at it. She looked instead at Wolfgang.

"What does it say?"

He cleared his throat several times, pulled reading glasses out of his suit pocket, put them on, and lifted the paper so it shielded most of his face.

"It says, 'In the Name of the German people, the plaintiff, Franz Weitrek, an Aryan and Lutheran, files for divorce from his wife, Theresa Weitrek, born Brodsky, a Jew, the defendant. The marriage entered into on the 12th day of May, 1932 is hereby dissolved.

169

The divorce petition is immediately granted on this 24th day of November, 1939, in Berlin, at the plaintiff's request.' I can't read the signatures but underneath is each person's title. One is the civil records notary, the other the Justice Inspector."

Wolfgang slid the document back into its folder and reached out his hand. "Give me your hand, Lily."

She placed her hand in his and gave Wolfgang a small smile, which did nothing to erase the pain in her eyes. "He left my mother while she was pregnant — with me."

She took a deep breath and slowly let it out. "That's my father. A Nazi and a coward. Some pedigree, eh McDuff?"

"So it's not the British Royal Family, but what can we do?"

His fake upper class English accent took the curse off the moment.

Almost defiantly, she reached across to tap the other two folders. "Let's have the rest of - whatever it is you found in the civil records of this uncivilized —"

"Go ahead, Lily, say it."

"Country."

"It is something we all have to work on, Lily, to make up for what happened. It is very important to me to not let the past be forgotten. You are also very important to me."

As Lily looked up at him, she saw something in Wolfgang's eyes she had not seen before, a gentleness, a longing. She shifted her gaze to his hands still holding the folder. "They are nice hands," she thought. "What would it be like to be held by those hands?"

Abruptly, he put the folder back into his briefcase and placed the remaining ones in front of Lily. Businesslike, he said, "I told you I found the marriage certificate of your grandparents with the brothers and father of your grandfather serving as witness. That is in this folder."

He lifted the remaining one and said, "And this is your mother's birth certificate. Obviously your grandparents are listed on it, as the married couple having this child."

She noticed a certain reluctance in Wolfgang's willingness to pull either out of its folder.

"May I see it?"

"Of course." He handed her the document from 1908.

She glanced at it briefly. "I can't read it. It's in old German script. Can you read it to me?"

Wolfgang moved his chair closer until their shoulders touched so she could follow as his fingers marked out each line on the certificate.

"It is Birth Certificate Number 800 issued in Wilmersdorf on May 15, 1908."

"My mother's birthday." She looked up at Wolfgang with a look of surprise at something important, unexpectedly remembered. "This coming Wednesday is her birthday. The day I fly home."

Wolfgang, embarrassed that his hands had started to shake, quickly continued reading. "Here on this line," he pointed to it, "it says 'before me, the civil records keeper residing at Wilmersdorf, PfalzerStrasse 34, came George Moishe Brodsky of Mosaische religion and notified this office that Emma Brodsky, born Auerbach, his wife, Mosaische religion…'"

"What's Mosaische?"

"As in Moses," Wolfgang replied, sliding past the word.

A look of total bewilderment covered Lily's face. "Moses?"

"Jewish, Lily. It was the designation for Jews. Mosaische from Moses."

"You mean to tell me that every person born in Germany had to list a religion?"

"Yes." Wolfgang closed his eyes. He could feel the heat emanating from Lily. He knew without looking at her that it was caused by anger.

"That's disgusting," she snapped.

Not only disgusting, dear Lily, he thought to himself but the requirement that led ultimately to murder. When he was young his mother had once, accidentally it seemed to him at the time, remarked how difficult the process had been in 1938 for a German family to prove it was not tainted by Jewish blood, by the Jewish race. Every family in 1938 had to register its family tree at the Aryan Office. The family tree, to be declared racially pure, could not contain even one Jewish member for three generations back from those living in 1938. Even one of four grandparents could lead to being marked as a Jew and made to wear the yellow star, and be marked for dismissal from all walks of life.

All over Germany families scurried to find old Lutheran or Catholic bibles in which birth and death records were noted, scurried to find baptismal records, scurried to find archival records, scurried to prove they were not and no one in their family had ever been Jewish. It was the scurrying to distance themselves from their Jewish neighbors, colleagues and friends that isolated the Jews so they could be registered city by city, town by town, village by village and finally house by house as an unwelcome presence in Germany. When the roundup of the Jews began, those Jews who had not left Germany or committed suicide, which whole families did together, were easy to pick up and mark for deportation to the camps.

Wolfgang remembered once seeing a rare book he accidentally stumbled on, perhaps one of the few remaining in the world, on a trip to the Vatican. At first he thought he was looking at cartoon characters from the 1930s with grotesque figures with large noses on skinny faces. When he looked more closely, he realized he was looking at Jews as they were interpreted by racially pure Nazi doctrine. A full Jew was colored in black, a half-Jew was striped, a quarter-Jew was polka-dotted.

There was also some coding for eighth-Jews, but Wolfgang could not remember what it was. Sitting with Lily as the ugly images crossed his memory, he felt ill.

"Go on, read the rest," Lily demanded.

It took him a minute to shake the cartoon figures out of his mind. "Here it says, 'His wife, living with him at Wilmersdorf, a daughter was born at home on the 15th of May in the year 1908 at 8 o'clock in the morning named Theresa Eva.' Your grandfather signed here."

Lily studied the scholarly handwriting. "What is that? There at the bottom," she asked, her attention caught by the additional lines below her grandfather's signature.

Wolfgang looked puzzled. "I don't know. The date is 28 September, 1939. It looks like a copy was sent to another agency." He shrugged, "I'm sorry. I don't know what it means."

He put the last folder in front of Lily. Just as Wolfgang had told her in Fehleen, it contained the marriage certificate of her grandparents, witnessed by brothers Daniel and Julius and the father of the bridegroom, Benjamin Brodsky.

Lily's face, Wolfgang observed, seemed to have lost muscle strength, her eyes were half closed, her jaw slack, and her cheeks caved in.

"I find I am very tired. Would you mind, Wolfgang, if I go back to the hotel? I'd like to lie down for a while."

"Of course. You should rest for a while." What else was there to say? Nothing. There was nothing to say to comfort her. Wolfgang knew that. He quickly gathered up the folders, swept the picture of Lily's father up with the rest, and placed them in his briefcase.

The short ride back to the hotel was made in silence. When the car pulled up to the hotel's revolving door, Lily jumped out before Wolfgang had a chance to turn off the motor. She was desperate to get to her room, to think. To sort out the overwhelming confusion she felt about her father. And her mother. Had Theresa deliberately lied to her about her father? If so, why? What could explain the monstrous lie that he chose to be a Nazi filmmaker? Wolfgang called after Lily's disappearing back, "I will call later to arrange a time for us to have dinner."

Lily gave no indication that she heard him.

Lily entered the lobby absentmindedly, stopped at the desk and asked for her room key.

The young people in immaculate hotel uniforms behind the desk looked up and each let their best professional-friendly smile of recognition appear as they saw her. Their predecessors had smiled the same way at Nazis, communists, spies, Stasis. It was the way they were, had been and needed to be.

Berthold, the young man behind the desk, watched her approach, wondering how anyone could change so much in a few days. The confident energetic American woman of a week ago walked unsteadily toward him and said almost in a whisper, "My key, please." As she turned away after he placed the key in her hand he noticed the absence of a smile or "thank you." She had always given him that wide smile before and he missed it. And then he remembered. Calling after her he said, "Mrs. Weitrek. There is a fax for you." She returned to the desk as Berthold reached behind him to retrieve the fax. It unrolled in his hand. He glanced at it, struck by its heading. Unable to stop himself, Berthold broke every professional rule of the Metropol and any other good hotel. He read the fax aloud.

"It's from the International Red Cross. Search Division. 'Franziska and Misha Sagal - wife and husband, dead in Auschwitz. Ludwig Sagal - son, also dead in Auschwitz.'" Berthold voice quavered. He looked at Lily with shock, then stared with horror at the fax. "My God," he said, "Did we do that? Really kill them? I never believed all those old stories were true."

A couple registering at the next desk space, looked up, the husband dropping the hotel pen on the half-filled out form, picked up the two suitcases from the floor and said loudly to his wife, "We leave. Now." They hurried out the revolving door. The hotel manager moved in front of Berthold, nudging him to one side. He picked up Lily's room key, which she had dropped on the counter, took the fax out of Berthold's hand and gave both to Lily. Smoothly he said, "I believe both of these are yours; the key and this fax. We are pleased to have you as a guest but would prefer if you settle your bill every day rather than wait until your departure. Which is, I believe this Wednesday." He checked the calendar. "Three days from now."

Heartily he said, "Well, Mrs. Weitrek, I expect then to see you at the cashier in the morning. Now have a good day and enjoy our fine hotel."

Instinctively, rather than consciously, Lily found the elevator and got to her room. All she wanted to do was hide. She lay down on the bed and wept.

# TWELVE

Although the Hotel Metropol lobby was elegantly refurbished with its grand sweeping staircase leading to a mezzanine bar, the elegance did not extend to the hallways leading to the guest rooms. The corridors were only dimly lit. Dated light fixtures threw circular patterns of light and darkness on the frayed hall-length carpet.

Wolfgang reacted to the change in light between the bright interior of the elevator and the darkened hallway as a man who had suddenly lost the ability to see. He stood momentarily unsure of where he was and even less sure of his right to be there.

Wolfgang's frantic hours of trying to reach Lily by telephone – always busy - had prompted raised eyebrows from his office partner, Hartmund Gerber, and was followed by Gerber's sardonic lecture on keeping a lawyer's professional distance from someone who was after all just a 'client.' Gerber also suggested Wolfgang might want to return some of the business calls piling up on his desk. With one sweep of his hand Wolfgang dispatched the memos into a drawer and slammed it shut. Gerber threw him an amused look and left the room.

When the office closed Wolfgang went home to a far less amused wife. Greta had watched Wolfgang's distracted interaction with their two sons at the dinner table, interrupted every few minutes by Wolfgang jumping up and closeting himself in his study to call Lily. Greta could hear his angry voice through the study door as he shouted commands at the hotel switchboard operator to find out if Lily was in her room.

Greta sent the boys to their rooms to do their homework so she could have a private discussion with her husband about his increasingly aberrant behavior. She had practiced her speech listing Wolfgang's faults standing in front of the mirror that morning. Chief among them was his obvious obsession with this 'Jewish' case. Her speech died on her lips as Wolfgang emerged from his study struggling into his suit jacket and, without another glance at her, left the apartment.

Now, standing in the dark hotel hallway, Wolfgang hoped he remembered Lily's room number correctly. The hotel desk had declined, by policy, to either confirm or deny that Lily was in room 221. If he was wrong, Wolfgang told himself, he would look like a fool. Maybe she had gone out, he thought. But where would she go for all these hours? He should never have dropped her off at the entrance. He should have stayed with Lily rather than agree to her request to have some time alone.

Wolfgang found room 221 and knocked. That there was no answer only made him more unsure about what he remembered. After another and somewhat louder patter of knocks on the door, he stepped back as if to regroup. Wolfgang was uncertain whether the lack of answer to his knocking meant that the occupant, if indeed there was one, was asleep, was ill, or was deliberately ignoring him.

Wolfgang could feel his heart hammering. The 100,000 laws that regulate how German citizens behave also include laws against the noise created by hammering on hotel doors and lurking in hotel corridors as an uninvited visitor. Rather than back away to deal again with the hotel clerk in the lobby, Wolfgang's legal mind told him the worst outcome to continued hammering on Lily's door would be a charge of disorderly conduct.

That embarrassment he thought would suit Greta just fine. "Don Quixote and his Jewish client." The sudden image of his father-in-law's face turning to stone as the police report reached his desk stating that one of Gast & Gast's attorney's had been booked for loitering at the Hotel Metropol caused Wolfgang to chuckle.

He decided it was more important to find out if Lily was in the room than worry about the reaction of the hotel's security force if other guests reported his incessant knocking.

He banged on the door forcibly, calling out loudly, "Lily open the door." And held his breath.

She must have heard him and already decided to admit him because the door opened inward immediately.

His shock at how she looked must have registered with her. She moved her right hand quickly up and over her hair, reducing the unkempt look somewhat. But there was little she could do to cover the information her eyes conveyed about crying.

"Have you been here all this time?" It was one of those useless questions, a bridge of rhetoric that served to carry in an innocuous fashion the resentment of realizing that hours worth of phone calls went deliberately unanswered.

There was no time for the self-indulgence of resentment, he realized. She must have had a reason.

"What happened?" he asked. She took the message the hotel clerk had given her on her return out of her pocket. She handed it to him. But, obviating his need to read it, she said,"It's Franziska, Misha, and Ludwig. The Red Cross fax states they died in Auschwitz in 1944."

He moved to close the few feet between them. It put him completely inside the room. Behind his back, his hand closed the door.

He extended his arms, open, offering her, quite literally, a shoulder to lean on. His arms stayed empty.

She turned and walked away from him toward the bed. She slumped down, sitting on the side of the bed in clear discomfort with his presence, an intruder on her sorrow.

"You are, as you say, 'stuck' with me, Lily," he said. "You paid for a lawyer's time and skill. And that sometimes includes comfort." He could not tell whether Lily had even heard him.

Lily moved farther back in the bed, head down, hands clasped so tightly together the blood drained out of them as Wolfgang watched.

So softly that Wolfgang had to strain to hear the words, she said, "Can you even imagine their agony? To be so demeaned? To become a bundle of skin and bones, considered nothing human, to be shipped with thousands of others like refuse to be murdered?"

She looked up at him and said, "I want to remember them differently." She paused before continuing. "I have no way of reaching out now in my mind to them except as they must have been at the end." Hesitatingly she continued, "I'd like to talk to them. To hold them just once, to hold them once as my family."

Her voice broke and tears began to trickle down her face. She wiped them away briskly, impatiently.

Wolfgang took his handkerchief out of his pocket and knelt in front of her. He dabbed silently at her tears. He was not a man who gave easily into emotion, but he felt unwelcome tears on his eyes' brims.

Lily looked at the man kneeling on the floor. She was shaken at the change in Wolfgang from the prim and uptight person she had first met in the cemetery.

Wolfgang suddenly moved toward her closet. He talked to Lily over his shoulder, "We will remember them differently."

As he spoke he went through the clothes hanging in the closet and pulled out a silver blouse and a white suit jacket with a matching long skirt.

Wolfgang paid absolutely no attention to women's fashions so he could only hope Lily would approve of his choice.

Placing the outfit on the bed next to a bewildered Lily, he said, "We will remember them differently. You will have to trust me."

He pointed to the clothes that he had placed on the bed. In spite of his normal indifference to fashion, he was confident that his choice would be proper for the celebration he had planned. "Please put these on. I will wait outside."

"I don't want to go anywhere, Wolfgang. I want to stay here. Alone."

He chose his words very carefully, making sure by both pace and cadence that Lily was very aware of how carefully he was phrasing what he was about to ask. Kneeling down in front of her he said, "Allow me to take you out, Lily. To celebrate their lives. They were once a happy, glamorous couple, much beloved by their family here in Berlin. Allow me to take you out to remember them, not at the end, but at the beginning."

He arose, took Lily's hand, bowed over it, his lips just shy of actually touching her flesh and said, "I, Misha Sagal, ask you, Franziska Auerbach, to honor me by going out for the evening."

"You?" Lily replied. "Misha Sagal? A Jew?"

"I am free to be anyone, and I choose to be Misha. Come, Franziska, I will be waiting for you."

Lily dressed quickly after she had applied enough makeup to cover as best as possible the traces of her tears. She brushed her hair forward to soften her appearance.

The sudden brightness of the lobby as she left the elevator caused her to wince at the glare reflected from the ceiling-high chandelier. Wolfgang was tapping his foot by the open passenger door of a taxi when he saw her coming through the revolving door and waved to get her attention.

They exchanged silent looks as he helped her into the taxi. In response to Lily's surprised look, Wolfgang tersely said, "It's better to take a cab." The only break in the silence occurred when Wolfgang said to the taxi driver, "To Wedding." For a moment it looked as if the cab driver might refuse.

He explained to Lily, "Wedding is a suburb of Berlin, not an event."

The cab sped quickly through the almost empty streets of the East Zone before turning toward West Berlin. The cab first traveled through the center of West Berlin, with its glittering shops and restaurants, then left it and headed into what to Lily's eyes was clearly a working class district. Store signs were no longer written in German but in Turkish, in increasingly narrower and rutted streets.

As the cab stopped for a red light, Lily saw small groups of dark-skinned men smoking on the street corners and some sitting on benches at the perimeter of a large park. Three blocks beyond the park Wolfgang abruptly told the cab driver to stop. To Lily he said, "We'll walk from here," and gestured for her to get out of the cab.

She stood uneasily in the empty street next to Wolfgang as he waited for the cab to disappear from view before turning to her with a smile. "It's all right." His expression softened as he looked at her, all traces of tension gone from his face. "It's all right, Franziska. There is nothing to worry about now. You must trust me."

Lily vaguely remembered hearing about neo-Nazis hunting for victims in Turkish neighborhoods and quickly scanned the dark street. Wolfgang reached up, putting one hand on each side of her face, forcing Lily to look at him.

"Do you trust me?"

"Yes."

Taking Lily's hand, Wolfgang turned right on the next street. Halfway down the block he stopped in front of a secluded entrance. Wolfgang opened the door and they found themselves facing a short flight of stairs. Wolfgang led Lily down the stairs into a courtyard.

Across the courtyard under an arched entry lit by coachman lamps stood a single figure who simultaneously gave the impression of guard and host. He waited for Lily and Wolfgang to cross to him. Only as they got closer could Lily see the small, gold plate on which was engraved "The Berlin Foundation Club" next to the entrance.

The man's clothing was so strange Lily felt her mouth drop open. He wore a derby which he tipped as he said, as if they were expected, "So you have come!" Out of the corner of her eyes Lily could see that Wolfgang found nothing out of the ordinary at this unusual greeting. Or the rest of the man's clothing, which Lily quickly cataloged: a stiff-winged collar with open cravat, the suit tight-fitting by contemporary standards, pin-striped and vested. But Lily was most struck by the fact that the man wore spats over his shoes. The entire ensemble came from the 1920s.

The man, whose name was Helmut Holder, was used to the look of bewilderment on the faces of first-time visitors to his establishment. So he stood quietly as Lily studied him from head to foot. "And you, pretty lady with the sad face, eyes red with weeping, what sorrow brings you here?" he wondered to himself.

Holder gave no indication that he recognized Wolfgang. That would be to betray a confidence and violate the very principles of the establishment that Holder had founded very quietly, very privately in 1951 — the year a few thousand German soldiers out of the 91,000 captured by the Soviets at the battle of Stalingrad were released from Russian prisoner of war camps and allowed to return to their "Fatherland."

Holder often thought of the irony of opening his club in 1951 as if he had deliberately intended to honor the memory of those who did not return from Russia. Nothing could be further from the truth. It was for Bernard and no one else. The one frayed snapshot of Bernard he had was always in his shirt pocket above Holder's heart. At night the small photo stood on the nightstand by his bed. But there was another image of Bernard carried in Holder's head. It tore at him in restless sleep and bad dreams that even after almost five decades caused Holder to weep. It was the image of their last meeting in a rubble-strewn street in Berlin. As the allied bombers pounded the city, the few Jews being held at the collection point at the Jewish Hospital waiting for transport to the death camps from the Grunewald Station were brought at gunpoint to clear away the rubble, dig out the Aryans who might be trapped below the bombed buildings. Holder, himself trapped, heard bricks and boulders being removed from around him as he, a fourteen-year-old boy, cowered, afraid that the digging would cause whatever was left of the building to fall on him. Intermittently he would lose consciousness then awaken again to hear curses and kicks aimed at those sent to rescue him. Holder could not tell if anyone else had survived the direct hit on the building. Outside of his ragged breath and the sounds of the debris being removed, he could hear nothing. It was too dark to see, but with his hands he could make out the small box-like prison he was in.

"Is anyone in there?"

How many hours Holder had been there he could not tell but along with the voice a sliver of light also reached him.

"Is anyone in there?" The voice was followed by a thin arm poking its way through the slender opening.

Weakly Holder answered, "Yes. I am in here."

He could hear the voice call to someone else, "There is someone alive."

A much deeper voice screamed out, "You pigs, you lazy pigs, hurry up, there is a German to save!" Holder thought he heard the sound of a stick against flesh and a soft scream of pain. Dozens of hands scratched at the rubble, removing it piece by piece until Holder could begin to see heads bobbing with effort as bodies strained to free Holder of his prison. It was the yellow stars on the tattered clothes that Holder saw first. Then the shaved heads and the eyes sunk deep into the skulls of his saviors. While they kneeled looking at Holder through the space they had created to pull him out, a tall, uniformed figure poked his rifle down toward him and yelled at Holder, "You're not a Jew are you, boy? We don't save Jews."

"No - he's not one of us," said a young voice. Holder's throat constricted at the sound of the voice.

The uniformed man swung his free hand at the impertinent speaker, striking him across the shoulder and tumbling him down into the hole next to Holder. The body of a boy his own age landed next to Holder. He turned, his gaze in the half-light registered first shock, then recognition. A low moan came out of Holder as he reached out - "Bernard? Is it really you?"

Holder threw his arms around Bernard, who gently pushed him away.

"It is I. Do not let on you know me, or they will punish you."

"You are my brother. I will tell them you are my brother. They will have to let you go."

"It is too late for me, Helmut. They know I am Jewish."

Running his hands over Bernard's shaved blond head, over his face and down his skinny body, Holder cried out. "How could they do this to you? I have looked for you everywhere, but no one would tell me where you had gone." He began to cry, hiding his face in Bernard's neck.

The rubble that had become dislodged with Bernard as he fell was systematically being removed again. Both boys knew it would be only a matter of minutes before they were pulled out under the watchful eyes of the commander of the Jewish work battalion. Something like Bernard's old grin lit up his face for a second, the grin that Helmut had always counted on to persuade his mother that neither Helmut nor Bernard should be punished for some childhood prank.

Bernard said, giving Helmut a quick hug, "Remember me. When this is all over, remember me living with your family during the good years. Being your brother was the gift of my life."

Hands reached out and the boys were pulled to the surface, both blinking in the sudden light. The sun was visible even through the clouds of dust that hung over the street, slowly descending back to earth over the destroyed building. Bernard went as ordered to stand in line with the rest of the work battalion. Helmut looked around uneasily and realized that Bernard was the youngest in the line. The others, he thought, must be some of the last of Berlin's Jews who had been in hiding, only to be discovered so close to the end of the war.

The commander yelled, "March, pigs!" In a disorderly row the weary two-dozen men and Bernard began to move away, leaving Helmut alone. His father was gone, his mother a recluse, and now the adopted brother he loved above anyone else was also going to be taken from him. The big brother who had excelled at so much and made Helmut train long and hard at every lesson so he, too, could, if not excel, at least be better than life itself intended him to be, always with gentle encouragement from Bernard.

Half in shock and half in a frenzy of fear and loss, Helmut ran after Bernard screaming, "Do not leave me, Bernie, do not leave me." Tears streamed down his face as he grabbed Bernard's sleeve and pulled him out of line.

"Run, Bernie. Run." As Helmut half dragged Bernard down the street, he did not see the work battalion commander pull out his pistol, but Bernard did.

"Save yourself, little brother." With his last bit of strength, Bernard pushed Helmut out of the way and took the bullet intended for either. It threw Bernard backwards. He was dead before his body hit the ground.

Helmut stood, unable to comprehend. The gun came up again, aimed directly at Helmut. A skeletal member of the work battalion closest to the commander placed himself in front of the gun and said, "Sir, he is only a boy. A German boy." For a frozen second the boy, the Jew and the Nazi stood in the destroyed street. Abruptly the commander holstered his pistol and yelled, "March, pigs, march." The group, lessened by one, moved as ordered. Helmut, alone in the street with Bernard's body, wept over his dead, adopted brother.

Bernard's and Helmut's parents had been close friends in the late 1920s, both fathers lawyers during that brief period that Germans tucked away their anti-Semitism. The families lived in the same apartment building in Berlin, and visited each other often. When each of the families had a son born just three months apart, Bernard being the oldest, the women often laughed at the fact that each had two sons since the boys, even as toddlers, refused to be separated. Bernard was a blond, blue-eyed Jewish Dane, as was his mother, Rachel, who had moved from Copenhagen to Berlin to marry a prominent Jewish attorney, Fredrick Feldstein. Helmut was dark-haired and brown-eyed, both of his parents, Bettina and Juergen Holder having their origins in Catholic Bavaria.

The day before his third birthday Bernard's parents were killed in a boating accident. Helmut's parents knew that the Nazi laws of 1934 against inter-racial households would make it impossible to formally adopt Bernard, a child no one else wanted in the rush of many Jews seeking visas to leave Germany. But the laws could not prevent Bettina and Juergen Holder from using their considerable intelligence to circumvent the racial laws.

Bettina went to a parish priest who did not know her and under the pretense that her husband, as a Lutheran, objected to having his son baptized in the Catholic Church, begged the priest to perform the ceremony and give the child the baptismal name of the saint, "Bernard." Helmut's birth certificate was thrust into the priest's hand confirming for him that the child to be renamed "Bernard" on church documents was actually Bettina's child. The priest did not even blink as he studied Helmut's birth certificate, on which both his parents were clearly listed as Catholic. It was, after all, 1934.

"Where will it all end?" the priest often asked himself. The Catholic Church was funded directly by the German government. What was the Church to do now that a madman was at the head of the government, holding the purse strings to the Church's survival.

As the boys grew, Bettina and Juergen Holder gave a prayer of thanks that Helmut and Bernard did not mature at the same rate. By the age of five Bernard was very tall for his age, athletically skilled, while Helmut retained his baby fat, looking a full year younger than Bernard.

Using the Church document to register Bernard in school, Bettina delayed a year to register Helmut, using her son's birth certificate. The problem of obtaining a forged birth certificate for Bernard kept Bettina awake at night as the full impact of the racial laws became clearer to the family. Bettina and Juergen burned Bernard's real birth certificate, fearful it might be discovered and his Jewish parentage exposed.

Perhaps the fiction might have held if Helmut's father had not died suddenly of a heart attack. The death of her son-in-law prompted the sudden announcement from Bettina's mother, Dorothea, that she would be moving from Stuttgart to live with her widowed daughter so they could suffer the war together as a family.

The antipathy between Dorothea, a rabid Nazi, and her daughter and the now-dead Juergen had been so bitter that Dorothea had not set foot in her former son-in-law's home since Helmut's second birthday.

Overcome by panic as the sweep for hidden Jews intensified, and deprived of Juergen's guidance and help, Bettina moved herself and her two sons to Grunheide, a rural suburb of Berlin where Juergen had owned a small farm, a fact never disclosed to Dorothea. The Holder family often spent summers there and the villagers were used to seeing the two brothers.

When Dorothea arrived in Berlin, "The apartment is yours to use," said Bettina's note to her mother. "But we have gone to the country for a while."

The family always attended the village church services on Sunday when in Grunheide, and this visit was to be no different Bettina determined. To not attend would be to attract attention.

Bettina did not recognize the fat woman who, one Sunday after they had been in Grunheide several months, squeezed herself into the last pew, forcing Bettina, Bernard and Helmut to move over. The woman's voice filled the church as she leaned across the boys to peer at Bettina. "Frau Holder, how nice to see you again after all these years." She raised her hand to pat

Bernard's blond hair, "And I suppose this is the wonderful little baby boy I delivered thirteen years ago." She looked closely at Helmut and said, "And who is this Jewish-looking boy with you?"

Stiffly Bettina replied, "That 'Jewish-looking boy' happens to be 'the wonderful little boy' you delivered. My son, Helmut."

Fortunately, the priest came down the aisle, preventing any further questions from the meddlesome woman.

As the last "Amen" was said, Bettina Holder, boys in tow, rushed home. They were packed within an hour. The knock on the door came as they were leaving. The local S.S. officer demanded to see "papers." When he had finished scrutinizing Bernard's baptismal and confirmation documents, he seemed momentarily satisfied. "You know, Frau Holder, it is against the law to hide a Jew."

Pretending outrage, she replied, "Of course I know that."

"Very well." He turned to leave. "But your son Bernard's birth certificate, where is that? Is it here?"

"I must have left it in Berlin. At our apartment." Her voice was so calm Helmut thought his mother should have been an actress. His knees on the other hand were shaking so badly he felt sure the S.S. man would hear them knocking together.

Bernard was fortunately in the boys' bedroom hiding the packed suitcases under their beds. So many years later, waking in the middle of the night, Helmut knew his cheeks were wet reliving those last hours with Bernard so long ago in Grunheide.

The S.S. officer returned later that night. He was still waiting, he said, for a return call from the Aryan Amt in Berlin. But it really was not necessary to wait. He himself had had a very interesting conversation with the woman staying in Bettina's Berlin apartment, her mother, Dorothea. Bettina's mother would be happy, she said, to serve her Fuehrer by swearing that she had only one grandson, not two. Furthermore, she remembered that her daughter and former son-in-law were once very close to a neighboring Jewish family named Feldstein, who had a son very close in age to her own grandson. She added bitterly that on her last visit to her daughter's apartment the little Jewish boy was constantly under foot, spoiling her grandson's birthday party.

Bettina and her two boys had sat holding hands, praying during the long wait for the S.S. officer's return. "Turn over to me the boy who is not your son," he ordered Bettina.

Bettina fingered her rosary beads and said, "Take me. I will not give you either of my sons." Her voice was calm. She seemed unaware that she was looking death in the face. Bettina knew she could not choose between the child of her flesh and the child of her heart.

"For the last time, Frau Holder, give me the Jew." His tone was menacing, but he seemed totally perplexed by the obstinate woman. Changing tactics, he shouted, "Remember you are a good German!"

Bettina laughed softly. "My memories are of a 'good' Germany. Yours will curse us for a hundred years and beyond."

Fury crossed the S.S. officer's face. He turned to Helmut and screamed, "Jew, get up."

It was Bernard who stood up. Carefully, he placed his rosary on the table, and he said, "It is I you want." The S.S. officer looked taken aback, so sure had he been that the dark-haired Helmut was his target. The officer's gaze fell on the blond, blue-eyed child in front of him and, almost with regret, said, "I have to take you in."

The wild grin that lived in Helmut's dreams crossed Bernard's face as he said, "You will leave my mother and brother alone!" It was a challenge, not a question.

"As best I can," the officer replied.

Bernard knelt beside Bettina, burying his head in her lap. Her hands stroked the blond-haired child she loved so much as she listened to her heart break.

"You could not know," she murmured into his hair. "You were so young; we thought you would forget."

"I always knew. I love you, Mama. Goodbye."

Bernard stood, lifted Helmut out of his chair, held him close for a minute and said, "Little brother, live for me." Bernard kissed Helmut on both cheeks, put him gently back in the chair, replacing the dropped rosary beads in Helmut's hands.

Bernard was gone. Only the sound of Bettina's weeping filled the room. Within weeks, on his fourteenth birthday, Helmut was commanded to join other young boys and very old men in the Volks Army in Berlin, a rag-tag group thrown together to fight the fires caused by the allied bombing of the city.

It was on the way to fight one of those fires that the air-raid sirens sounded and Helmut ran into a building seconds before it was leveled by a bomb.

In the last days of World War II Helmut deserted and made his way back to Grunheide, knowing that once the Soviet Army entered Berlin Bettina would be caught behind Russian lines. He found Bettina sitting in the farmhouse exactly as she had the night Bernard was taken away, at the table praying over her rosary beads.

Helmut packed a small bag of his mother's belongings and forced her to join him with all the others fleeing the approaching Russian troops. Their apartment miraculously still stood and, even more miraculously, Bettina's mother was gone, having fled farther south seeking safety behind the American lines.

In the chaos of the next few years Bettina and Helmut barely existed, but were grateful that their apartment was located in what had become the French sector of occupied Berlin. Bettina said little except when she and Helmut planned the memorial they would build for Bernard. Bettina died before it could be created. But both she and Helmut knew exactly how it would look, whom it would serve, and its purpose.

In Helmut's careful screening of those hundreds of people who sought reservations, he turned the tables on the Nazi process of requiring documentation proving that a family had no Jews hiding in branches of the family tree. Before allowing a person or group into the 'Berlin Foundation,' he demanded the war time record of his older guests and the war time record of those they came to mourn. Helmut's scrutiny could take weeks or months. He had to be satisfied that no one entering had any connection to the camps, neither the death, labor, nor holding camps, the S.S. or any of its divisions.

There was not a single swastika, flag or officer's uniform of the Nazi era in the club. Without any publicity, word spread from the guests who came that there was a place to mourn for those for whom there had been no funeral, no service, no flower, no song. Bernard's memorial was a private place to mourn, remember and to say a final goodbye. It was the only place of its kind in the confused nation whose very soul cried out for forgiveness, while the words spoken on the nation's behalf refused an apology, acknowledgment or even a single day of commemoration for the innocent dead. At the intersection between personal memory and public posture, a band-aid replaced the heart of the country. For some of his countrymen, the band-aid was not enough.

Helmut knew why so many of his countrymen came to the 'Berlin Foundation.' They came looking for the missing pieces of themselves, the dreams and innocence forever lost with the dead and questions about how and why they had died.

The true origin for his establishment was his private secret, the missing piece to his life. The discreetly monogrammed glasses, napkins and small pins on the waiter's lapels reflected what was missing. The `B.F.' monogram did not stand for `Berlin Foundation' at all, but rather for Bernard Feldstein, lost son and beloved brother.

"For whom have you come?" Holder asked.

"For family," Wolfgang replied.

Lily was mystified by the strange dialogue.

"Whose family?" Holder asked.

"Hers," Wolfgang replied.

"You may enter. Wait at the end of the corridor. Someone will seat you."

Inside the entrance, where Lily might have expected to see a large dining room, or a clubroom, there was instead a long corridor to the right which they began to walk down.

The corridor down which Wolfgang and Lily walked after entering the Berlin Foundation was a passage back in time. The decor of the hallway modulated from the modern of 1991 back in stages, looking soon like the 1930s, then like the 1920s.

Lily asked, "You have been before, isn't that so? The doorman recognized you, I thought. Why were you here?"

"To say goodbye. To my older brother. We think he died at the very end of the war, killed by the Soviets. His body was never found. We could not bury him. I came here."

"And?" Lily wanted to encourage him.

He stopped. So, then, did she. They could see now that at the corridor's end it opened into a large room. At that distance, the room seemed to exist in a haze.

"I came to let him go. I grew up missing the brother I never knew. There are still many of us who could not bury their dead. When our soldiers came home from war, there were no parades. There were no flowers. There were no funerals for those who did not return.

"We are still a divided Germany. One Germany looks back over its shoulder to ask why and how we allowed so many to die, and to ask forgiveness. The other is afraid, or angry, will not look back. Looks straight ahead...build a new Germany...make sure the trains run on time."

They began to walk again as he finished, and entered the hazy room.

The haze made perception less than ready. It was not smoke; no one there was smoking. The haze was praeternatural.

Lily could see from where they stood at the entrance to the room that perhaps as many as twenty private cubicles were placed around a large dance floor. The cubicles were on a raised platform. Each cubicle contained a table around which a family-like group sat, the men in evening clothes, the women in long dresses and wearing many jewels. No one spoke.

The cubicles were framed by heavy curtains, pulled open and pinned by large, gold knobs embossed with the initials "B.F." Lily realized that the curtains could be pulled shut to create total privacy.

Vases of fresh flowers had been placed on the floor around the room, catching the shimmers of light from chandeliers that flickered also on the jewels the women wore.

In the center of the room, an old woman caught Wolfgang's and Lily's eyes as soft waltz music issued into the room from some source outside the room. Her arms were around a young man dressed in a German soldier's uniform from World War I.

190

They turned slowly to the music. The young man, a mannequin, followed her lead readily, but seemed oblivious to her happy tears.

Lily was dumbfounded. Her eyes were fixed on the woman, the mannequin, the dance. It was as if this room had been transformed into a theatre, a theatre in which she was the only member of the audience. She was oblivious in her fixation to Wolfgang's presence. The other families seated at other tables, miming their apparent responses to one another, seemed part of some dramaturgy, choral in their role, themselves an on-stage audience to the dancing woman and mannequin.

Wolfgang watched her. From his own, single experience before in the "Berlin Foundation," he knew how she was reacting. He thought it best to allow her, without interruption, to have understanding evolve, even as it had when he, alone, had brought his purposes to the Foundation for the first time.

"How can I be of service?"

Neither he nor she had noticed the formally attired maitre d's approach. The words he spoke came as a shock to the environment of silence to which Lily had been growing accustomed.

"I am Misha Sagal, waiter," Wolfgang said. "We are looking for....Franziska, this is our celebration. Whom shall we have join us?"

A kind of giggle almost found voice out of the chill she felt about what was said. She felt as if her spirit had flown out of her body. With no ability to stop the flight, she felt her conscious self slip away to be replaced by the persona of a long-dead great-aunt, Franziska.

"I suppose Isador, my oldest brother. He is the one to whom you will have to speak about us. He of course will not approve of you, so then we must invite my sister Emma. She will help us."

"And Marie," he said. "She likes me."

"But we must invite also Daniel and Julius. They are business partners whom you must not offend."

The maitre d' nodded. "Very good. Please give me both years and descriptions of those whom you wish to invite."

"About 1925, I think," she said. "The family is quite prosperous. Isador is somewhat pompous, I think, my sister Marie is jolly, and fat, and my sister Emma is very beautiful and quite reserved."

"A tall, blond family, then?" said the maitre d', "like you, Mademoiselle?"

He turned to Wolfgang, "As it was back then, Monsieur?"

"Yes. As it was back then."

The maitre d' knew what to do now. He beckoned to Lily and Wolfgang to follow him.

The maitre d' directed them with a gesture of his right hand, palm up, to one of the cubicles, at which were already seated lifelike mannequins whose images conformed to the descriptions which had been given to the maitre d' of Franziska's family members.

The maitre d' pulled out a chair for Lily. Wolfgang seated himself next to her.

After being seated, Wolfgang and Lily studied silently the "family" which had been given to Lily. She stared at each one in turn before reaching out shyly to touch the face of the patrician-looking woman with the upswept brown hair. Wonderment replaced shyness as she said, "Look, Misha, my family. This is my sister Emma." She turned to Misha and said, "Isn't she beautiful? Imagine having such a beautiful family."

Her excitement grew as she leaned toward the plump female figure with tousled blond curls peeking out from under a small hat.

"And you are my sister Marie."

Wolfgang knew as he watched Lily become Franziska that she was unaware of the tears that ran down her face. She made no sound of weeping, but there were tears behind her words. In a split-second, she was giggling.

"And this gentleman," she whispered in an aside to Wolfgang as Misha, "is of course my eldest brother, Isador.

"Really, Isador," she said more loudly, "you must give your permission for us to marry."

She shook her head, looking away from Isador to concentrate on the last figure. "Why, Daniel Brodsky. You honor us with your presence."

The mannequin nodded, as if in reply. The mannequins lifted their empty teacups with fluid, realistic motions. As Franziska spoke, they turned their heads to the sound of her voice. And, it seemed to her, they nodded in recognition and acceptance.

The maitre d' arrived unobtrusively with a bottle of wine, and, just as unobtrusively, left after filling just two goblets.

Franziska lifted her goblet and whispered, "What did Isador say, Misha? Does he approve?"

"He is disappointed in you, my dear. He expected you to marry a lawyer, as he is - at the very least a banker, not someone who supervises shoemaking."

"What nonsense." She addressed Isador with disdain. "You are so old-fashioned, Isador."

Franziska turned to Emma, "Emma, sweet sister, please talk to Isador."

The dumbshow continued, human beings exchanging pretend words with pretend people. One by one, the mannequins, including the one of Isador, began to nod in apparent assent. So it seemed as if Emma did talk to the older brother because when she turned back to Franziska, Emma was smiling and nodding her head.

The Isador mannequin finally raised an arm, as if in some gesture of prayer, a rabbinical acknowledgement, and a blessing for the couple.

Misha spoke very seriously, and said very formally, "Thank you, Isador. Yes, I do love Franziska with all my heart, and I promise no harm will ever come to her while I am alive."

Franziska flashed Misha a smile and then spoke to her sister, Marie, as if in answer to a question.

"Well, of course we will bless the family with many healthy children." She turned to Misha. "We will, will we not, Misha?"

"Of course. But now, my dear, it is time to dance, to celebrate our engagement."

Misha got up, extended his hand to Franziska. She took it, and they both smiled at her family as they left the table.

Other couples were already on the dance floor, circling gracefully to the music of another time. Under the shimmering half-light, the real and the imaginary blended.

Misha took Franziska in his arms to celebrate their betrothal, her face nestled against his neck, breathing in his scent as they circled the floor.

His fingers played over her spine and she leaned her body into his.

Stopping in the middle of the dance floor, he cupped Franziska's face in his hands as she stood completely still. Misha gazed at his fiancee with wonder in his eyes, and ever so gently learned her face with his fingertips. His fingers followed the line of her eyebrows, eyelids, the line of her cheeks, and finally, her lips.

He bent to kiss her, but stopped himself, his mouth so close to hers that their breaths mingled, but their lips did not touch.

Franziska broke away first, and, with a shaky laugh, took Misha's hand and led him back to the table. They sat again, surrounded by family, only briefly, only long enough to say goodbye to Emma, Marie, Isador and Daniel.

And finally to each other as Misha and Franziska, a glamorous, newly-engaged couple from long ago.

As Lily and Wolfgang moved down the long corridor to leave, they passed a room that had not been open when they first entered the club.

Wolfgang's gasp, almost of pain, made Lily follow him as he entered the room.

They stared, shocked into continuing silence by what the room contained.

The room was twelve feet high and circular. Huge, enlarged photographs of Berlin in the last days of the war covered the walls. The pictures ran from ceiling to floor, seamlessly connected, so that Lily and Wolfgang were dwarfed by the images of total destruction that surrounded them. For Wolfgang, the pictures brought remembered nightmares into the present.

The floor space was taken up by four statues so lifelike that Lily wanted to cry out for help.

In the very center, a boy in his early teens knelt weeping over the body of a dead friend or brother, who wore the infamous yellow star on a ragged jacket.

Caught by the sculptor, frozen in time, was the figure of a uniformed man in mid-stride, holstering his gun as he looked back at the two boys. On the other side of the central figures, a solitary woman sat in a chair praying, fingering rosary beads which Lily thought she saw move.

Lily looked at Wolfgang. He seemed almost catatonic, and she was frightened for him.

She reached over to him, took his hand, and pulled him to the door.

"We have to leave here, Wolfgang."

Once outside in the corridor, he shook his head several times, as if to trying to rid his mind of the images. He took a deep breath.

"I am fine, Lily, I am fine. Do not worry about me. I am fine."

He smiled, almost apologetically, and shrugged.

"It was so unexpected- to see my childhood again. My playground as a child."

They paused outside the street entrance, leaving behind the secluded premises that housed the Berlin Foundation.

As they were leaving through the door of the Club, Holder had said that a taxi would be waiting.

"I shall await your bill," Wolfgang said. Holder nodded.

On the street, before entering the waiting taxi, Wolfgang turned to Lily and said, "I am a very lucky man, Lily, very lucky to have met you."

Once in the taxi, Wolfgang said, "I think that should conclude our adventures for the night."

In answer to the driver's questioning look, Wolfgang said, "To the Hotel Metropol on Friedrichstrasse."

Lily put a restraining hand on Wolfgang's arm. "No. I have a favor to ask," Lily said.

"What is that?"

"I would like to see the Friederichstrasse Bahnhof," she said. "I am staying at the Metropol because of it, but I have not yet been there. I would like to see it."

The driver had turned his head around and was listening. Wolfgang nodded to him to do as Lily had asked.

They rode in silence, Lily in anticipation of seeing the station, Wolfgang unhappy at the prospect.

The taxi stopped to let its passengers out. Wolfgang paid the driver and, exiting himself, turned to offer his hand to Lily as she left the taxi.

They were standing under an arched walkway at second-floor level over the street that connects the Friederichstrasse Bahnhof to the S-Bahn station. They crossed to the main entrance of the train station.

The station was closed, just as Wolfgang had told Lily. A sign declared that fact, as did the yellow tape stretched across the entrance.

Lily saw the sign, saw that the place was closed.

"I would like to go in anyway," she said.

"We cannot. The sign says we may not."

"But I will go in; I need to go…"

"Why is this so important, Lily? This is only an empty, closed train station."

"I do not know why it is important, but it is."

"Lily. It is against the law."

"Well," she said defiantly, "I will go alone." She took three quick steps ahead of him, stopped, and turned around to face him.

"You are Misha Sagal. There is something here that has to do with living, and dying. I do not know more, but I am going to enter. Come, Misha, if you can."

The barricades of simple yellow tape proved to be no problem. She simply stepped over them. She saw, as she climbed the steps, that while the station might indeed be closed, it was not locked up. In fact the main entrance at the head of the short staircase was wide open.

There once had been shops and concessions on both sides of the entry way. She could see that as she reached the main level. If the station had been functioning, the signs would have directed passengers to the proper gates for their departures or arrivals. But, as further evidence the station was closed, these signs were hooded.

Two qualities characterized this place, Lily thought. It was ghostly, and dusty.

Emptied places all seem ghostly, and the more or less so according to the number of occupants, users or patrons a place was designed to hold. An emptied house is still filled, but only with the memories of the family which once lived in it - four, five, six, even ten people. But the Friederichstrasse Bahnhof had been designed for hundreds, even thousands a day. Lily only knew the statistic that the Hauptbahnhof in Frankfurt, assuredly the busiest train station in Germany, saw 2,400 trains pass through it each day. The Friederichstrasse Bahnhof traffic had been much, much less, perhaps four or five hundred trains daily. Nevertheless, its emptied status still registered ghostliness many multiples of that of a home. These were the unearthly recollections of thousands of travelers over many years whose thoughts about something that happened to them, good or bad, in the Friederichstrasse Bahnhof were now the only occupants of the closed train station.

Lily proceeded up the longer and much wider stairs to the train platform, and stopped when she reached the top at the platform for Tracks 3 and 4. There were more hooded signs. There was also a closed kiosk in the center of the platform, halfway down its entire length from where Lily stood.

The door of the kiosk opened quite suddenly and a group of five young men burst out from inside it. One of them unfurled a long banner while another held its rigid, short pole. Opened, Lily could see that it was a Nazi banner, with a huge swastika.

She froze in fear.

Three young men began to goose-step around the banner held open and at full extension by the other two.

They were building themselves into a furor as their goose-stepping pace increased, as they shouted, certain no one could hear them in the cavernous, closed Friederichstrasse Bahnhof.

"Heil Hitler! Heil Hitler! Kurt! It is perfect!" one of them said.

Lily made a ghostly apparition in the white outfit Wolfgang had chosen for her to wear, and she knew that if any one of them looked her way, she would be seen.

But fear did not make her move; it made her freeze. She stared at the five young men and their danse macabre, unable to blink, unable to think clearly.

Wolfgang had decided after all that he could enter, not that his ethical standards had been set aside, but only that, upon reflection, he decided that his obligations to his client might well include an imperative greater than respecting the quasi-lawfulness of the train station's "closed" sign.

He had followed closely enough behind Lily and was on the stairs leading to the platform when the five neo-Nazis had burst from the kiosk and started their short-radius, goose-stepping circle. His attention was attracted to them first, then to Lily. He saw that she was terrified.

He whispered as loudly, he thought, as he dared.

"Lily? Lily, listen to me. I want you to move very slowly, very slowly, back toward the stairs."

Her answer was silence; her answer was terror. She could not move.

"Just one step. Slowly. No quick movement. Lily."

Wolfgang's eyes kept shifting from Lily, back to the neo-Nazi group, back to Lily. The goose-steppers had not heard him, yet. But he had to get Lily to move.

She was still without words, without ability to act. "Franziska. My love. What am I to do with you? It is time to leave. This is hard, I know, but we must not let these bullies see us, find us. One step; take one step."

Lily backed toward the staircase, toward Wolfgang's voice, still staring at the neo-Nazis, still shaking from head to toe. But her movements, however, cautious and careful, caught the eyes of one of the group, who stopped his march and shouted,

"Over there! Get her!"

Wolfgang was only two steps below her. He grabbed her hand, turned, and almost dragged her out through the tunnel, out of the station, past the shuttered shops and dusty past, back into Friederichstrasse.

Outside, Wolfgang, after several reconstructive deep breaths, conceded.

"I was wrong about your train station. It is not closed. Someone could still die inside."

The shock that they both had experienced in the Friederichstrasse Bahnhof had lessened somewhat. Wolfgang had continued his grip on Lily's arm as he hustled them both back toward the Metropol, just a block away. As they entered the hotel, he turned them both to the left and up the sweeping, curved staircase to the mezzanine which circumvented the hotel lobby. Once on the mezzanine, they both knew to head to the other end where there was a bar and several comfortable sofas.

After one cognac, the inarticulate nature of their shock began to find some words. After a second cognac, they were able to recount mutually just what had happened.

Wolfgang's role of providing reassurance, the role he took on earlier in the hotel when he invited Lily to the "Berlin Foundation," was a role he felt slipping because of a greater and known reality about the many racial attacks as unemployment increased. There was a question he had begun to ask himself: "Could we Germans do it all again? Make the same mistakes?" His words for Lily were the proper ones - that the encounter with the neo-Nazis was not to be generalized, that such incidents were few and far between, that the government would not tolerate any even small return to Fascism. But in his mind, he tried to sort out alternatives they might have chosen. He wondered if he was comforting Lily - or himself.

Lily had asked to go to the train station as a favor. He might well not have agreed. He could have told her that he knew the building was closed.

Even so, after he had agreed to direct the taxi driver to go to the station and it was clear the place was not open, he still could have resisted the idea of allowing Lily to enter.

He had, of course, resisted. He stayed behind when Lily asserted her determination to go in with or without him. Thank

God, he thought now, that I decided over my own better judgment to follow. Invisibly, he shuddered. What might have happened to her if he had not followed?

Just as a man who is driving toward some precise destination can lose his way, probably by mistaking a road where he was supposed to make a turn for a road still short of the proper place to turn, Wolfgang began to go over and over the events. The logical sequences of conditions contrary to fact kept circling.

When the driver who discovers he is lost turns his car around to retrace his steps back to a required turn, he is almost compelled to speculate about time lost. His mind masticates the alternative conclusions - how much time was lost, where he would be if he had not missed the turn, so that by the time he arrives back and negotiates the needed turn on a different road, the compulsion is inevitable to try to recapture both the time and distance lost.

So Wolfgang indulged his mind in such conditional suppositions. But they were safe here, now, on the mezzanine of the Hotel Metropol. He became suddenly aware of the fact that Lily was speaking, trying to elicit his attention.

"Are we still going back tomorrow morning to the Stadtbibliotek?"

"Yes."

He rose and she followed. He checked the amount he had left on the table for appropriateness, nodded to the bartender and once again cupped Lily's left elbow as he led them back around the ring of the mezzanine.

They stopped before reaching the escalator at the deck of elevators. Wolfgang, resuming his normal formality, bowed over her hand. He then saw her into one of the elevators, and before the doors closed, said, "On Unter den Linden, then, outside the library tomorrow morning. Shall we say 11 o'clock?"

The closing elevator doors clipped her confirmation.

After the doors had closed, he said, almost as an afterthought, "Sleep well, Lily."

# THIRTEEN

Lily straightened her back trying to ease the pain between her shoulders. Her head ached from staring at old documents. She looked across the library table at Wolfgang, totally absorbed in business records from the early 1930s. Lily took off her glasses and closed her eyes. "Headache number 2,000," she thought trying to find some humor in her frustration. "Every German word - particularly legal words - has at least five syllables." Even when Lily sounded them out softly to herself it was impossible for her to make sense of them.

Wolfgang looked up as she groaned out loud. He smiled and said, "Keep working," his nose back in the documents. She dutifully resumed the tedious task of sounding out incomprehensible words.

The head research librarian whose nameplate identified her as Dr. Elisabeth Gross, had been more than helpful. She had listened attentively to Wolfgang's detailed explanation of the documents needed for Lily to justify her claim to the Treuhand for property in what had been East Germany. She stared at Lily with growing interest, only interrupting Wolfgang to say, "I see" or "How very remarkable" several times. Dr. Gross jotted down a list of topics for herself as Wolfgang spoke, studied it and finally said, "Much of what you need is I think here. Some will be in the basement and take time to bring up."

She pulled a stack of old fashioned off-white newsprint quality order forms and placed them in front of Wolfgang. "Old newspapers are in the basement archives. Fill out a separate form for each newspaper you want with the year indicated. We will most likely have the Halle newspapers but I doubt we will have anything from Fehleen." She indicated a series of open shelves that ran along the back wall of the reference room. "Under the heading of 'Law' you will find bound volumes from before 1951." Lily and Wolfgang followed her gesture with their eyes until they found the 'Law' section. "You should find what you need." She looked puzzled momentarily. "I know we have the 1935 Jewish

Racial Laws, the `Nuremberg Laws'. I really don't know about those stemming from 1933." Wolfgang moved to turn away, impatient to get started. "One more thing," Dr. Gross stopped him. "Also on the open shelves under the section 'Business Corporations' you may find 'PrinzLine' listed from its first year of incorporation to its last year." She turned to Lily saying, "I do not know how well you read German."

Lily gave a small shrug of defeat. "Not that well," she replied.

Dr. Gross smiled and said, "It is difficult, I know. In our card catalogue, which is very complete, you might find some of what you look for in English." Seeing Lily's look of surprise the librarian continued, "We pride ourselves and always did in collecting information about what others write or wrote about Germany. That was also true during the time of Fascism. In the West sector many of these publications were destroyed or disappeared. But here in the East we were also the victims of the Nazis since we were Communists. So we safeguarded records to document the evil committed by the West in the 1930s and 1940s."

Lily kept her expression neutral. It was the same strange pretension she had first heard from Otto Gesset at the Fehleen factory. Four decades of brain washing by the East German government had eradicated responsibility for Nazi war crimes in one German country by blaming all of them on the other German country. Pretending they weren't just one country under Hitler until the Allied victory in 1945.

Lily could read enough German to follow the headlines in the newspapers lying around the Metropol Hotel lobby. There was, Lily understood, a nationwide debate beginning to emerge. The debate seemed to focus on the 'victim mentality' presented by the East Germans. If the East Germans saw themselves as victims of Hitler, why shouldn't the West Germans join them, asked one journalist. It would once and for all get rid of feelings of guilt. Germans, said another headline, should begin to develop national pride. A psychological ploy in its infancy which already had outspoken adherents who scrawled "All foreigners out of Germany," "Germany for Germans" on walls of buildings.

Lily realized Dr. Gross was speaking to her. "I will look myself to see what other material we may have here," she said.

"Thank you," Lily replied and turned away with Wolfgang who had impatiently been drumming his fingers on the several filled-out order forms he had placed in front of the librarian.

Three hours later surrounded by old, bound, heavy newspaper portfolios, law books and equally large corporate record volumes, Lily finally straightened, stretched and groaned for the second time in a matter of minutes. She deliberately said, too loudly, "Have you found anything yet?"

Wolfgang jumped at the sound of her voice, threw Lily a look of reprimand and said, "I'll answer if you give up this childish behavior. Groaning every minute like a school kid."

Lily realized he was teasing her. "Tell me what you have found."

He turned the heavy volume around so Lily could see what he had been studying. The long brittle page was headed by the words "PrinzLine & Cie, A.G. - in Berlin and Fehleen."

"What is it?"

"Everything, Lily. It's everything." He was so excited he jumped up, came around the table, grabbed the empty chair next to Lily and shoulder to shoulder Wolfgang's finger tracing each line said, "It's PrinzLine's annual stock report from 1932." His voice had dropped low so only Lily could hear him.

The print was so small Lily had to put on her glasses to follow the text as Wolfgang read it. "See here? PrinzLine was founded in 1883 but was restructured as a corporation - in Germany that's `A.G.' - stands for Aktien Gesellschaft - means it issued stock shares in 1911. It had two primary locations. Berlin and Fehleen. Here it explains the purpose of the company: to make and sell shoes." His voice rose slightly as his finger dropped several sections. "Here, Lily, it states the property owned - Look - it says that 1 - 48 Fabrikstrasse belongs in 1932 to the company. Also owned in 1932 were 10 houses, 300 acres of undeveloped land, 8 rental properties and 20 vacation villas." He stopped and searched the paper before continuing and somewhat taken aback said, "The value seems to be set at just about 140 million Reichmarks."

"What does that mean?" Lily asked,

Wolfgang looked at Lily and said, "It's good you're sitting down. Using today's terms that's about 14 million Deutschemark." Seeing her bemused look he said, "Of course, since 1932 there has been a war, and all of this fell under Soviet and then East German control. So what its value is today is hard to say."

Wolfgang searched the paper again. "Here, the directors are listed. The names, Lily. The 'proof.' The General Director was Daniel Brodsky, situated in Berlin; the Director in Fehleen was Misha Sagal. The lawyer for the company was a man named 'Langen'. And here," his finger trailed towards the bottom of the page, "is the list of everyone who served on the Board of Directors."

Lily and Wolfgang, heads touching, studied the names. None was familiar.

"There's one more thing of interest, Lily; the company had 48 retail stores as part of the company and another 91 separately incorporated in-" he counted to himself as he finger ran down the list, "in 23 major cities and in the 'provinces'."

Wolfgang put the heavy book down and leaned back in his chair. "1932 was a good year for your family - the listed profit for that year was 720,000 Reichmark." He studied the library's ceiling, frowning.

"What's the matter?"

Whispering, Wolfgang replied, "We have to find out who seized the factory. Find out what was paid, how much the value was discounted because it was a 'Forced Sale' because of Nazi law. Until we know who those people were, the puzzle isn't complete. This book ends in 1932."

He straightened in his chair and said, "So we keep looking, 'McDuff.' Back to work." Noticing Lily's reluctance to pick up the portfolio she'd been studying before Wolfgang's find of the 1932 PrinzLine stock report, Wolfgang tapped Lily lightly on the shoulder and said, "I release you from German legal documents, Fair Lady. Why don't you go through the card catalogue and see if there's anything useful in English."

"Everything in English is useful," Lily shot back, making a face at Wolfgang as she got up. She stopped and turned back to Wolfgang. "The stock report is very important, isn't it?"

"Yes, very," Wolfgang replied. "We'll have copies made and spend some time tonight putting a folder together to present to the Treuhand." He suddenly smiled. "I can hardly wait to see Dr. Lautermit's expression. Now, Lily, go to work."

"Yes, sir."

It was the librarian who found the 1907 promotional sales catalogue of PrinzLine shoes, published on the occasion of the company opening its 100th retail store. Dr. Gross was pleased, she said to Wolfgang, to have found the little booklet under "The History of Shoe Manufacturing in Germany."

From where she was standing at the card catalogue Lily could survey the large room and had followed the librarian's movement towards Wolfgang. Lily could see that the librarian said something to Wolfgang who immediately beckoned Lily back to the table.

The booklet was an odd size, about eight inches long and twelve inches wide. Lily sat down, amazed at the black and white pages filled with high top shoes from 1907. Even for someone disinclined to wear shoes, they looked elegant, if not too comfortable, she thought to herself. Interrupting Wolfgang repeatedly, who finally gave up his own reading, Lily read various passages aloud. The German was simple enough for Lily to make sense of what she was skimming through. "This contains the whole history of the factory. The first building was built in 1885. In 1883 a shoemaker named Hans Prinz sold his little store to Benjamin Brodsky. Brodsky introduced a steam engine and an automatic nailing machine he had bought from the Americans and English to shoe making in Germany. She flipped through several passages "as conscientious employers we provide all workers health coverage, a recreation hall and villas for their use during their month's vacation and holidays." She looked up. "Pretty progressive stuff for 1907." She thought for a minute. "Actually better than we have in the U.S. in 1991."

Paying attention to the booklet again she said, "Here's a picture of Benjamin Brodsky. What a big, bushy beard you have, Great-grandfather."

"Is there a picture of me in there?" asked Wolfgang.

"You?"

"Misha Sagal - my other self."

"Let me look, dear Misha, to see if your portrait is included." Quickly leafing the pages Lily finally said, "Sorry, Misha. The younger generation is not here. Neither you, Daniel nor Julius. But look - here's the house in Fehleen in which Misha and Franziska lived." She turned the booklet around so he could study the charming Victorian house that was now a kindergarten.

"Were we happy living there?" he asked.

"Of course, Misha. We were always happy until - well, until..." Lily's voice dropped off.

Abruptly, she got up leaving the booklet on the table and said, "Back to my hunt for something in English."

It was Wolfgang who found the 1933 newspaper article. He went searching for Lily and found her sitting in the middle of the floor between two book stacks. "German women do not sit on the floor," he dryly commented.

"Americans in jeans do. That's why we wear jeans. So we can sit on the floor of libraries in other countries." Lily replied nonchalantly. "What's in your hand?"

He handed the xeroxed page down to her and said, "Read it."

The 1933 article was only two paragraphs. It was dated June 2, 1933. "What is this strange word 'gleichschaltung'?"

"It means 'to bring or force into line'." Wolfgang paused. "In the sense of bring into compliance with the Nazi law that a Jewish owned business must be aryanized. Replacing the Jews with 'pure Germans,' 'aryans'."

"I see. Please read it for me," she handed the page back to Wolfgang. He took it and began to read and translate at the same time.

"The headline says 'Shoe Company Complies with Gleichschaltung'. Daniel Brodsky, representing the majority interest of his family-owned shoe business with headquarters in Berlin and principal place of manufacturing in Fehleen, led the resignation of the entire Board of Directors of PrinzLine on May 31st. A new Board it is anticipated will be named shortly after the new owners are identified. Until then company attorney Klaus Langen, a loyal member of the Nazi party, will manage the company. The 'gleishschaltung' order is the reason for the change in ownership and Board members.' That's the entire article."

Lily made only one comment. "That's a very short article for such a monstrous event."

Wolfgang left Lily sitting on the floor, books piled around her. She picked one up and studied the index. Lily had been through every book written in English in either the 1930s or 40s, looking for the Nazi era and its laws. She carefully replaced each book she had pulled until she had only one left in her hand.

"Damn it," she said out loud. Lily was tired, hungry and ready to jam the last book into its slot on the shelf, rather than reach towards the back to find out what prevented the book from easily sliding into place. And there it was. The book she had been looking for most of the afternoon. *The Jews in Nazi Germany*, published by the American Jewish Committee in 1935 and *The Economic Destruction of German Jewry by the Nazi Regime*, published in 1937 by the World Jewish Congress. The books were bound into one volume. Lily sat back down on the floor and soon was unaware of how long she was there. Both books warned the world of what was to come.

When Wolfgang came to find her he saw her head buried in the book, her face chalk white. "Lily?"

She didn't hear him. Louder, he said, "Lily, what is it?"

Lily looked up at Wolfgang. "Did you know that when the Nazi party was started in 1919 it only had seven members? One of whom was Hitler."

Stonily, Wolfgang replied, "No."

Lily continued. "In February 1920 the Nazis, the National Socialists, announced their program. Anti-Semitism was the foundation of the Nazi platform. That became the driving power in attracting millions of followers during the 1920s and early 1930s when Hitler became Chancellor."

Lily stopped to take a breath. "Do you know what the 'Aryan Paragraph' is, Wolfgang?" Wolfgang looked uncomfortable.

Lily continued; "It was the very first Nazi decree - the first law put on the books in 1933. 'None but members of the Nation may be citizens of the State. None but those of German blood, whatever their creed may be members of the Nation. No Jew therefore may be a member of the Nation or a citizen.' That led to the removal of all Jews from every walk of life, every profession and removed from them every right to find a way of staying alive in Germany. Eventually Jews weren't even allowed to buy milk or own a cat. They were completely isolated from their neighbors because they weren't any longer citizens. Because they did not have German blood'? What color is German blood?"

Finally angry, Wolfgang's reply was curt. "Your bad mood is yours to manage. Why would you make me resposnible for bad laws?"

"Spoken like a true German attorney," Lily snapped back. "Did it ever occur to you that it was your colleagues back in the 1930s who wrote every Nazi law against the Jews? And it was the court judges who carried out the laws. If the attorneys and judges had taken a stand against Hitler's racial laws maybe 50 million people would not have died in World War II."

"I was not there, Lily. I cannot answer for them." Wolfgang's voice went up a notch. He tried very hard to control his temper. "Do you wish to tell me if you were able to find laws more pertinent to your claim, or not?" He stressed "your" claim.

Wolfgang moved down the aisle away from Lily as if to leave. Over his shoulder, not unhappy to have the last word, he said, "I suggest you get off the floor - bring that book over to the table. It is possible your mood will improve sitting in a chair like an adult."

He left the narrow aisle. Lily could see Wolfgang stiffly sit down at their table. He angrily pulled the xeroxed copies of their combined research and pretended to study the pages.

Lily seated herself across from Wolfgang, scraping the chair noisily as she sat down. Without preamble or apology she rattled off Nazi laws of 1933. She whispered these at Wolfgang but made certain he heard every syllable. Wolfgang fixed Lily with his eyes, jaw clamped shut as she ran down her mental list.

"A non-Aryan is one who is descended from a non-Aryan, particularly Jewish parents or grandparents. All Jews are removed from the legal profession and all courts; all Jews are removed from the teaching profession, the arts; press and radio; publishing field, both scientific and literary; banks, insurance, real estate - a Jew may not own or acquire land, or owe a debt. No Aryan needs to pay a debt to a Jew; no Jew may hold a license to practice a profession or trade; no credit may be extended to a Jew, no Jew may represent any company in sales; all businesses must have Aryan owners; no business may keep other than Aryan employees. No Jew may be a citizen of Germany."

Rather sharply Wolfgang interrupted. "That's enough, Lily. I'm sorry you are upset but you are reading a history book. Bad, I know, but it must not deter you from our research purpose. Please calm down."

"The laws also allowed an Aryan spouse to get an annulment from a Jewish spouse just like that," she snapped her fingers. "Do you want to hear what it says about children born of this mixed marriage?"

"I do not think so," Wolfgang closed his eyes.

"Well, I'll tell you anyway. It says that these children are 'harmful to the German people'."

"Is that what upset you?"

Grudgingly Lily had to admit that it was a small part of her anger.

Wolfgang finally gave a small smile. "I don't think you are `harmful' - except of course when you are angry with me. Then you are quite - how do you say - intimidating. But not as intimidating as Dr. Lautermit will be if your file is incomplete. What have you found about the aryanization of businesses, such as PrinzLine?"

Lily picked up the book in which she had stuck a pen to mark the page. "It's under that strange work – 'gleich' something -"

"Gleichschaltung," Wolfgang said helpfully.

Lily read from the book, "Here it is defined as 'co-ordination between the Nazi government's anti-Jewish laws and private businesses. The decree was from 1933 and is listed under "Commerce" points 7, 17 and 23 in the Nazi program.' There was a nationwide boycott of all Jewish businesses - from large to small - on April 1, 1933. I'll read what it says. 'Every branch of the National Socialist Party, led by Stormtroopers, will systematically carry out a national boycott of all Jewish businesses. The boycott must hit at one stroke on Saturday, April 1st, at 10 am'."

Lily looked across the table at Wolfgang. "It goes on for pages describing exactly what the posters to be placed in front of each Jewish business have to say. For instance, 'Don't buy from Jews'; 'The Jews are our misfortune;' 'Defense Against the Jewish Atrocity'.

It says here that `the Nazis have utterly driven the Jews out of the leather products industry. The great shoe factories founded on the American model, such as Benjamin Brodsky's PrinzLine, have, because of `gleichschaltung', passed into aryan ownership.'"

Lily took off her glasses and rubbed her eyes before saying, "That's the story."

Wolfgang got up, glad to get away from Lily. He took the book out of her hand and said, "I'll get these pages about the PrinzLine xeroxed and then we'll go back to your hotel and complete the files for submission to the Treuhand."

Once the xerox copies had been made, Lily and Wolfgang stopped at the librarian's desk to thank Dr. Gross for her help. The librarian said she would continue to search on her own for more material and get in touch with them if she found anything else. Wolfgang gave Dr. Gross both Lily's hotel number and his office number, saying they'd be working in Lily's room into the evening.

Exhausted, Lily and Wolfgang made the short trip in silence to the hotel. The first thing Lily did as they entered her hotel room was to kick off her shoes. The second was to order food. "Food," she thought, "might put us both in a better mood."

They sat surrounded by all the documents they'd found during the week, discussed each one, as they ate. Their choice of food told something about them. Lily had ordered a hamburger, French fries and coke; Wolfgang a knockwurst, sauerkraut and hard roll.

It was late when the phone rang. Lily, thinking it was Michael calling from Imperial Beach, said a casual "Hi." Her voice changed, becoming more formal as she listened to the caller occasionally saying, "I see."

Wolfgang watched with curiosity as Lily gave a 'thumbs up' sign. Before replacing the phone on its cradle she said, "Thank you. We'll be right there."

Lily's eyes sparkled with excitement. "Guess what Dr. Gross found!"

"I can't," Wolfgang replied. "Tell me."

Lily with a skip and hop covered the short distance from the phone by her bed to the small table at which Wolfgang sat surrounded by copies of documents. "Our search, dear Wolfgang, is over. Dr. Gross has found the name of the Nazi family who seized the factory in 1933."

A strange foreboding caused Wolfgang to shudder. In a tight voice he asked, "What is the name?"

Lily pursed her lips and said, "I think it's something like 'Von Jaegerlied.' Translates to the song of the hunter, doesn't it? Or burden. 'Song' or 'burden' it doesn't matter. Dr. Gross said they are `The Family'." She gave the words emphasis.

Wolfgang stood up shakily. His legs had no strength in them. He grabbed the table edge to keep upright as the room did a full spin. "It cannot be. Must not be. They are one of Germany's most prominent families." Wolfgang rattled on helpless to stop himself. "After the war they founded the first German-Jewish Cooperation Association. They funded it themselves. They give money to it each year. The Von Jaegerlied family could not have been Nazis. Could not have taken your family's factory. It's impossible." Wolfgang sat down heavily as if utterly exhausted.

Lily had watched and listened with first astonishment and then dismay. The excitement in her eyes had been replaced by doubt. "There's only one way to find out. We'll have to see what it is Dr. Gross has found."

Wolfgang chose to drive the short distance to the library. He knew his legs would not carry him the few blocks. The sauerkraut and knockwurst churned in his stomach. Wolfgang realized he was very frightened. What was going to happen to him if Dr. Gross was correct? Who could he turn to for help if the Von Jaegerlieds were really the people who seized the factory? Old Jaegerlied must be in his 80s. The huge conglomerate was run by his sons. "No one will help me," he thought to himself. Greta will say, "I told you not to look into the past. Only harm comes from it." His employer would be even more direct. Much more direct. "I could lose everything. My job, my children, my standing in the powerful legal community," went through Wolfgang's mind.

The library was dark. Dr. Gross met them, as she had told Lily on the phone she would, at the side door.

Dr. Gross quickly led them to her office hurrying up the many flights of stairs. Their steps made echoing, hollow sounds in the deserted building. Lily was reminded of the ghostly feeling she'd had at the deserted Fehleen factory on her second visit to it.

As they entered Dr. Gross' office Lily and Wolfgang immediately saw the magazines laid out on a long table. The covers were imprinted with bold black swastikas at the top of each issue and the title "The German Worker & Warrior at PrinzLine Shoes" jumped out at them. Lily and Wolfgang were drawn to the display like magnets. Breathlessly Dr. Gross said, "I found these in the basement a few hours ago. They are Nazi propaganda magazines published in Fehleen after the factory was taken from your people. I read several of them to make sure of what I told you on the phone, Frau Weitrek."

They crossed to the display and Dr. Gross opened the first magazine saying, "We may have the only copies of these still in existence. I am sure the family thought they were all destroyed. This was apparently the first issue published in October 1933." She opened to the first page. "Here you will see at the bottom of the page the signature of the publisher 'Gottfried Von Jaegerlied' with his picture." She carefully turned to the first article. "On this page and subsequent pages, the article is quite long - Von Jaegerlied writes the history of how he, as a good German, had to, of course, support the aryanization of the factory, following the

212

boycott of all Jewish businesses on April 1, 1933. I could only find 10 issues in all. This one from 1933, two from 1934, and one each from 1935 to 1941. The pages are brittle, so please be careful.

I also looked at the index we keep here in the East of those charged with industrial war crimes by the Soviets in 1947. Until the Wall fell and reunification of the two Germanys took place that list remained. We in the East would not do business with those on the war crimes list. Now of course it is all different. We have no say."

Wolfgang stared with horror at the signature of Gottfried Von Jaegerlied. The room seemed to be getting smaller, pushing out the air. Wolfgang could not breathe in the confined space.

He backed away from the display of "The German Worker & Warrior at PrinzLine Shoes" bumping into the door as he backed away. "I have to leave," he blurted out. He took the steps down three at a time, found the small side entrance and ran into the dark street. Fumbling in his pocket for his car keys it took several attempts to unlock the door. He sat behind the steering wheel gulping air, willing his heart to stop beating so wildly. He spent the night driving aimlessly around Berlin ending up in front of his own apartment. Wolfgang sat looking at it, empty of any hope at all. By the time dawn broke Wolfgang had made up his mind. He had to reclaim the order and stability of his life.

Lily and Dr. Gross had watched Wolfgang's flight from the small library office with stunned surprise. It was the librarian, perhaps trying to explain Wolfgang's reaction to the magazines to herself rather than to Lily, who broke the silence that had fallen between them. "For some it is very difficult. They come here looking for one thing and find something quite different. Very often some information they do not want. Then they go away to try to put the new knowledge together with all the lies they were told."

She looked at Lily as if suddenly remembering something. "I do not know if this will be of interest to you but I found two old films about the shoe factory in the basement. I doubt anybody has looked at them for many, many years." She smiled suddenly. "It

213

is just amazing how thorough we were - or better put, my predecessors were in collecting information."

Lily continued to turn pages of the old magazines, finding a picture of the Victorian house in Fehleen. The caption underneath explained that the Victorian house was now the residence of the recently appointed Fehleen factory director. Appointed by the new owner, Gottfried Von Jaegerlied. It crossed Lily's mind to ask herself where Misha, Franziska and Ludwig had fled to after losing their home. No longer citizens of Germany, who had sheltered them? What happened to them between losing their home and dying in the concentration camp? Would no country take them in with a handicapped child?

The librarian asked again, "Would you like to see these old films?"

"Yes, thank you. Very much." Lily followed the librarian down flights of old iron rung staircases until they reached the basement. They walked down barely lit long hallways. Stacks of old newspapers, pages curling with age filled iron stands against walls of cavernous rooms. Lily's overwhelming sense was of dust and things forgotten by most. The open stacks were on one side, small offices on the other. Wooden doors scarred with age held single handwritten tags revealing a room's contents.

Dr. Gross finally stopped at a door marked "Industrial Films 1933 – 1940." The room was surprisingly large, containing film canisters stacked against the walls. The old canisters came from the celluloid age of a film industry in its infancy. The only light in the room came from a naked bulb suspended on a grimy electrical cord. An old 16 millimeter projector stood on the table in the center. There was a large empty take-up reel on the projector. Two folding chairs had been placed by the table. The librarian had, it was clear to Lily, anticipated her response - that she'd like to see the films, for two canisters were next to the projector.

Dr. Gross spoke to herself as she studied the label on the first canister. "Well, let's see if I remember how this works." She read the label on the canister before pulling out the film reel. Lily could see that whatever was on it made a very short film. Lily pulled the canister to where she sat to read the label herself. It

read "PrinzLine, Fehleen - April 1, 1933 boycott - Factory Director leaves."
Lily watched nervously as the librarian struggled with winding the beginning of the film onto the take-up reel. After several attempts Dr. Gross, satisfied it was firmly in place, reached up, turned off the naked, overhead bulb and turned on the projector. The film began to roll with the grainy leader showing first. The librarian struggled, but finally succeeded in getting the film into focus. It was the first title shot that caused Lily to suddenly sit upright. It read:

`Boycott - April 1, 1933
Sagal family leaves Fehleen.
Director Franz Weitrek


Lily felt time stop; felt her body leap towards the 1933 scene. Scratchy, grainy, in some places blank, the silent film showed the 1933 parade of aryanization, the three proud PrinzLine company flags torn up and tossed to the rejoicing crowd as small pieces of confetti.
And then it changed focus. The day had grown dark, the parades were over, the crowd dispersed. The focus was now on the Victorian house and the people living in it, hurriedly leaving with a few suitcases. The director panned the large stained glass window over the staircase and then down to a young woman carrying a suitcase out the front door to a waiting car.
"It's my mother," Lily gasped out loud.
The film went blank momentarily, as the director changed perspective. The next image had a tall lanky man coming down the staircase carrying a young boy holding crutches. The film wobbled a bit as if someone unsteadily held the camera. Suddenly the man was placing the child in the car, hovered over by the woman Lily had identified as her mother. When the child was safely in the car, the woman turned to the man. They embraced.
Tears ran down Lily's face.
She was seeing her mother and father together. For the first and only time in her life; for one flickering moment, Lily saw

them together. A film made almost 60 years ago had given Lily her parents. The film reached its end. The librarian rewound it, her back to Lily, leaving Lily to her private grief. The next film was made in 1940. Lily's father was listed as the director. But the subject quite different. The title shot stated:

PrinzLine Boots -
The Von Jaegerlied Heroes
Work for the Fatherland

Lily clenched her teeth as the propaganda film rolled. Scratchy and silent, the camera traveled through the busy factory employing thousands around the clock apparently producing boots for Hitler's conquering armies. The camera traveled quickly past women who looked emaciated to focus finally on a woman who resembled none of the others. This woman was not part of what looked like a slave labor group of women brought from countries conquered by Hitler. The woman, clearly a professional actress, had patrician features and a perfect smile. She lifted a black military boot and ran her hands over the boot, lovingly, almost sensually. With her fingers and hands the actress displayed the thick soles, the pliable but strong leather of the boot. The camera left the actress to come to rest in the packing room. Each box top firmly placed over a packed box of boots had a large swastika and the name "PrinzLine - a pure German business - a Von Jaegerlied company."

The credits repeated at the end. The actress lovingly demonstrating the strength of the boots was Gisella von Mingen. Franz Weitrek, the director.

Then it was over.

The librarian led Lily back up one flight of stairs and down a long dark corridor to the side entrance. Dr. Gross promised to make xeroxed copies of the "Warrior" magazines for Lily. Given their age, she said, it might take some time but she would send the copies to Lily at home, in California. The bill for the service could be paid later. As they stood at the side entrance Dr. Gross said shyly, "Some day I hope to see your country."

"When you come to the United States, please come to San Diego. I would be honored to have you stay with my husband Michael and me. The invitation is open." Lily smiled through her tears, knowing her mascara had run down her face and she probably looked as bad as she felt. "The invitation is open - forever. Thank you, Dr. Gross."

Once in her hotel room Lily finished the task of putting together the folders to be submitted to the Treuhand, to Dr. Lautermit. As she picked up each file folder she studied Wolfgang's carefully written tabs. "PrinzLine stock report - 1932;" "Brodsky marriage certificate;" "1933 Boycott of PrinzLine;" "1933 Gleichschaltung newspaper article;" "Nazi Aryan Paragraph - 1933."

When she was finished Lily stacked the painstakingly gathered information before carefully placing the folders in a large envelope. On the cover she wrote "My Family." When finished she said to herself, "We did it. We did the impossible."

She walked to the hotel window overlooking Unter den Linden and the Friedrichstrasse train station and said out loud, "Thank you, Wolfgang. I could not have done this without you."

As she thanked him in her mind Lily began to worry about Wolfgang. She scanned the street below looking for Wolfgang's car, glanced from time to time at the phone hoping it would ring and she would hear his voice. As the night passed Lily stood, waiting at the window.

# FOURTEEN

Lily's hand shook as she lifted the small portion of Asbach-Uralt to her mouth. The German brandy stung her lips and the back of her throat.

"I hate him!"

She quickly put the snifter back on the table as she continued to shiver as a cold wind blew down the side street and through the outside café that she had stumbled upon right after she fled the Gast and Gast office.

"Wolfgang Schmidt, you are a coward!" she thought to herself.

Her encounter with Wolfgang at the end of the meeting in the Gast and Gast office had been brief and surprisingly violent. Until that moment Lily had never thought of herself as a violent person, had never wanted to see herself as anything other than someone always carefully controlled. But that episode with Wolfgang and the outbursts that took place offered her a glimpse, a shadow of another person, a person of quick and flashing anger. She felt a small knot form in the pit of her stomach as she recognized how much in the heated exchange with Wolfgang she had sounded like her mother.

The day had started pleasantly enough with a cordial-sounding voice on the hotel telephone calling to invite her to a meeting with Wolfgang at the offices of Gast and Gast. Lily was looking forward to hearing Wolfgang's explanation about why he left the library so abruptly the night before.

But she was also eager to see the inside of the law firm that she had hired by mail to pursue her claim for the factory property.

The cordial voice had requested that Lily arrive for the meeting by 11 a.m. When she arrived on time, the receptionist in the outer office had indicated that it would be "a while" before Dr. Gast would see her. Her first sense of uneasiness followed upon this statement of delay.

Lily looked around the reception area. The interior of the Gast & Gast office was in contrast to its exterior. The office was in an elegant old house that had been converted for professional use. It was located on a block of similarly converted homes, offices, restaurants, and an occasional expensive retail shop just off the Ku'damm in the most elegant section of what had been the center of West Berlin.

Entry to the building required ringing a bell and being admitted, after identification, by an inside control button. A half-staircase up, a gold sign on the door greeted the visitor: "Gast & Gast: Dr. Heinrich Gast, Dr. Johann Gast & Partner."

Lily had taken a few steps around the reception room before choosing an expensive and uncomfortable-looking straight-backed chair.

The room abounded in art; all German expressionism, it appeared to Lily.

Sometimes when one has to wait, or, rather is coerced into waiting, counting objects is the same sedative for the mind as folk wisdom says counting sheep is for the sleepless.

Lily counted 17 paintings, mostly oils, a few watercolors, and all very large. They were hung two and three tiers high, reaching almost to the very top of a very high-ceilinged room, perhaps 18 feet high.

Layers of paintings, two and three deep, also stood directly on the floor.

This exhibition of swirling chaotic color bled from one picture into the next, lending a sense of disorder rather than the sternness of most attorneys' waiting rooms.

The room was more a gallery than a law office, disorienting Lily as to the purpose of this appointment she had been told was "urgent." She could see through the door into the main part of the law offices that the art continued on out of the waiting room and down a hall until the view escaped.

A voice came from among the artifacts. Lily realized the receptionist was evidently repeating her message.

"Dr. Gast will see you now, Ms. Weitrek. In the conference room. Please go down the corridor to the last room on the right."

Lily rose and headed down the hall. The paintings, she noted, did in fact continue the length of the corridor, in two tiers on both sides, with periodic floor placements of those the wall could not contain. Lily rekindled her apprehensions about the unknown purpose of this meeting as she made her way to the conference room. Nevertheless her apprehensiveness did not keep her from the sardonic thought that legal fees apparently could buy a lot of art.

The door to the conference room was open. She went in. There were three people in the room: one stood at the far end of a very long table, a man she assumed to be Dr. Gast, Wolfgang, and, unexpectedly, she thought, Haftig, the red-headed man she had found so unpleasant at the meeting with the Treuhand.

Wolfgang was looking out the window of the conference room when she entered. He did not turn around until Gast began to speak.

"Ms. Weitrek. How courteous of you to come on very short notice. I am Heinrich Gast, senior partner in this firm. I must say I have heard much about you from Herr Schmidt."

Lily's experience with German meetings was brief, but each meeting prepared her better for the next one. She assumed immediately that the gentility of this man, who was somewhere in his early seventies, expensively dressed, and very suave, was a preamble to some harsher message.

The very large conference room was dominated by a long, polished walnut table, some fourteen or more chairs around it. A dozen or more other chairs were placed next to the room's inner walls. In addition to the door through which Lily entered there was an exit door that was open and that led, Lily could see, into a smaller office space.

"You asked to see me?"

She had been right. Gast went immediately to his message. He did not even invite her to sit.

"A most unfortunate matter has come to my attention. This claim of yours, the one in which Herr Schmidt has been aiding you, has developed, shall I say, unwanted reverberations.

Herr Haftig, whom I understand that you met at a meeting with the Treuhandanstalt, has had to excuse himself from further involvement in the factory associated with your claim because he is one of the attorneys who represent the Von Jaegerlied interests.

He joined me here earlier to help persuade Herr Schmidt that he cannot continue to represent you in this matter."

He bowed slightly to each man as he spoke.

"This claim, your claim," he continued, "challenges, let me say, the unblemished reputation of the Von Jaegerlied family."

He turned around completely, looking away from Lily, fixing his stare instead on Wolfgang.

"That family is among our oldest clients. I, personally, am related to them by marriage. This puts my firm in an impossible position. Herr Schmidt will be released from whatever responsibility to you and your claim that you may think he has or that he intended to accept."

He then picked up an envelope that was lying on the conference table closer to where Lily was, still standing. His arm extended the envelope toward her.

"We are returning your money, the down payment you sent, in its entirety."

Gast affected an artificial smile, as if money reimbursed is exonerative.

Lily ignored the envelope. She was beginning to comprehend what was going on more clearly than the succinct speed of Gast's speech had at first allowed. She was, she realized - in a remembered American phrase - being fired as a client. She sat down suddenly in the nearest chair.

Gast moved away.

"One more item, Ms. Weitrek. Dr. Lautermit of the Treuhandanstalt has asked us to notify you of a meeting at 2 p.m. today to discuss your claim. You may acquire the room number from our receptionist as you leave. Goodbye, Ms. Weitrek."

He left the room, followed by Haftig, who bowed to Lily as he left.

Lily stood speechless as she stared at Wolfgang, still in the room, praying that he would quickly assure her that he was still "her Wolfgang," "her attorney."

Instead he said, "I have no choice. I cannot give up my profession, my future, my wife, my family... I have no choice. You must understand!"

His words played a melody that combined the strength of despair and the weakness of whining.

Lily lashed out. "Well, Herr Wolfgang Schmidt, what will you tell your children now? That you did your best to undo the past? To try in some small way to redress the injustices of your history? But you sold out. You would no doubt have been comfortable helping to write the `Aryan Paragraph' as a good German attorney in 1933." Wolfgang suddenly rushed toward Lily and roughly grabbed her shoulders, lifting her out of the chair. He put his face near her face, his nose almost touching hers. A decision one way could have led him to embrace her, but he chose another. A hatred older than either clutched at both of them.

Wolfgang let go of Lily's shoulders and pulled back. He began shouting at her.

"You sniffed around, poked around and stirred the ashes until you found someone you could say was guilty. Are you satisfied? You would ruin the reputation of a fine family, leading German industrialists. A family noted for its philanthropy. Are you satisfied?" he yelled at Lily.

Lily's anger matched his.

"Are you accusing me of being guilty instead of them?" Her voice dropped to a hiss. "In this scenario, is it the victims who are guilty? Tell that to your children. Tell them the same lies your father told you."

Lily turned abruptly away from him. She took the envelope, removed the check contained inside and said, "Keep the money, Mr. Schmidt. I don't take favors from cowardly German attorneys." Lily put the check back on the table. She stalked out the door, and, for good measure, slammed it behind her.

Out on the street, Lily walked down a house or two and stopped. Physically, she had to catch her breath in the wake of the stormy exchange and her furious exit. Emotionally, the task was greater. She saw a little café, entered, and sat down. A waiter immediately brought her a coffee. She nodded.

The contrast between yesterday and now was hard to believe. Wolfgang had wanted to be, was, Misha Sagal. He had taken up her cause, had turned to comfort her as her history under discovery altered her view of herself, her understanding of herself.

Little else that she had found, and almost no one in authority she had met, seemed really on her side. Taxi drivers, office clerks, a waiter here and there all could project politeness. Some, like the clerk in the records office in Fehleen, and certainly the librarian, could even muster sympathy. But they had no authority to right wrongs.

Only Wolfgang. He had ventured out of his skepticism, overcome his reluctance to move tombstones, set aside his shibboleth about not crossing barrier tapes at the Friedrichstrasse train station. He had become... her friend, perhaps something greater than a friend.

It had all ended when this Gast, his father-in-law, had dictated. Wolfgang had saluted and renounced Lily.

Three days of her stay in Germany still remained, with two tasks yet to undertake. The first was to return to the Treuhand as she had been notified to do by Gast. In her mind it was to present the documentation she and Wolfgang had found, a visit that until a half-hour ago she had expected would be with Wolfgang. Now she had to go there alone. And she planned to see Hanine Hoffman, if she could. In what turned out to be Wolfgang's last favor, he had identified for her where Hanine lived.

Lily picked up the check that the waiter had placed on her table. The 10 Deutschemark note she had placed beside the check was sufficient, and she raised her hand to get the waiter's attention. He came and took the bill and the money away.

She looked at the clock on the back wall of the café. There was time to take a taxi back to East Berlin - perhaps get out of the cab while still a few blocks from the massive Treuhand building and walk the rest of the way. Walk and think, she thought.

Three blocks from the intersection at which the Treuhand building sprawled, Lily told the driver that it was where she wanted to be dropped.

She paid him, left the taxi, and stood still. She could see the site of what she expected to be a decisive session at the end of the street.

She double-checked her belongings to make sure she had her purse and the large manila envelope firmly clutched in her hand. The large manila envelope contained the documents both Wolfgang and she had obtained in their searches. All that she had not known but now knew about her family and its business was in that envelope. It was the information Lautermit had told them they needed to provide to authenticate her status as a bona fide claimant in the eyes of the Treuhand.

She held the envelope even tighter, and started walking.

The street crowds increased as she neared the Treuhand, and she felt somewhat intimidated by the thought of the importance of her meeting today. How many of those going to, now coming from the Treuhand had learned decisions today?

Would she?

Lily was not aware that an elderly gentleman was following her. He seemed to make no attempt to quicken his steps as if to overtake her; he simply kept pace with her progress from about three yards behind her.

It was as if he had timed it so that when Lily reached a crossing, and stopped at the curb to check traffic, that he would catch up to her.

The sound of a man addressing her made Lily jump. "Mrs. Weitrek." He spoke from behind her. She turned around. The man was staring at her with such intensity Lily fought off the impulse to run.

Hostilely, she asked, "Who are you?"

He offered her a card. She took it, looked at it, and then looked back at him.

He almost intoned his reply.

"I am Dr. Johannes Kroner, a business attorney for the Von Jaegerlied family."

"What do you want?" She saw the light had changed to green. Lily began to cross.

Kroner dropped his avuncular look, realizing he would have to hurry to catch up with Lily.

He reached Lily as she stepped up the street curb. "I offer you some advice. If you cause any more whispers about my clients, or succeed in causing anything to be written in any newspaper, we will file action against you." Kroner reached out to grab her arm. Lily stiffened and roughly pulled her arm out of his grasp.

"Are you trying to scare me? Is that a threat?" Lily deliberately raised her voice. Passers-by made a wide circle around Lily and Kroner.

"I am telling you, not threatening you. You may threaten yourself, however, if you ignore what I say."

"Don't you think I know that Von Jaegerlied was charged after the war as a criminal?"

"Ah, but thanks to his attorney, Heinrich Gast, the worst charges were dropped and Von Jaegerlied was released. His company only made boots for Hitler's army. They killed no one."

"You mean he made boots for the army at what had been my family's company."

Lily's fright was hidden, she hoped. What did this man mean to do to her? How did he know where to find her today, where she would be? Had Gast told him? Or Wolfgang?

"Go home, Ms. Weitrek. We have put in a claim with the Treuhand for the factory ourselves. In fact, we have claimed all the property. It all belongs to my clients. And you, you have neither the time nor the funds to contest them."

Lily snapped.

"PrinzLine belongs to my family. I have the proof right here!"

She shouldn't have said that, she thought. I've in effect told him I have new evidence, and that it's probably with me now. He knows I'm going to a Treuhand meeting, knows I've papers with me.

She looked around to see whether this exchange was attracting special attention. It was. But nobody wanted to get involved. Whatever this woman and man were arguing about was their business. Just off the street corner where Kroner had approached her was an old East German apartment building. People were walking back and forth on the street, but the crowd seemed to have diminished from what it was when she first set foot out of the taxi.

The rest of the block had more apartments, all of them almost derelict in appearance.

"Quite probably in that large envelope you guard so carefully. We learned about that from our colleague, Dr. Gast," Kroner replied.

Wolfgang told them, she thought.

"You have no claim, Ms. Weitrek. We can prove that after the war Von Jaegerlied was cleared of all charges and released. You are on a fool's errand here. It is most regrettable that Dr. Gast, unaware that your claim would besmirch a fine German family, permitted that importunate Schmidt to represent you. Go home, Ms. Weitrek. I repeat, you are on a fool's errand."

Just then from around the next corner a large gang of skinheads raced into the street, perhaps as many as forty. Their goal was clear. They ran to the entrance of an apartment building just off the corner where Lily and Kroner were still standing. Almost all of the gang waved shiny banners that bore the Nazi symbol, the swastika, and several of them also had lighted torches.

There seemed to be three leaders in the gang; the others seemed only to be running back and forth aimlessly, energized by their own shouts.

"All foreign workers out of Germany!" they shouted, soon getting into unison.

The three in front threw their torches at the apartment building; one of them also threw a rock and broke a window. Chains were being dragged by other gang members, their scraping sound on the pavement adding to the cacophony.

"Death to Turkish pigs! Heil Hitler!"

A small Turkish family made the mistake of coming to their apartment window to investigate the commotion. Several gang members saw the terrified mother, father and two small children at the windows.

"There they are! There are the Turks!"

Another rock, another broken window. The leaders waved their followers into the building.

Another group had assembled, however, also brought forward by the noise. They were only ten in number, perhaps, but they succeeded in getting in between the apartment building and some of the gang trying to enter. A woman shouted at them, "What are you doing? Leave these poor people alone!"

A man's voice: "Filthy Nazis, have you learned nothing? You are destroying our country again!"

The fight was about to be engaged when the sound of sirens first, and the sight of two police cars coming down the street toward the groups, compounded the confusion. The crowd effectively blocked the police cars. Most people there wanted to open the way for the police, but the physical scuffling between the two groups slowed the cars' progress.

Lily had been staring at all this, forgetting about Kroner altogether. Suddenly, Kroner grabbed the envelope from under Lily's arm, her fast grip loosened a bit because of the fray. He bolted into the street, where he collided with the three neo-Nazi leaders who, in spite of the fact that they were leaving because of the police' arrival, were goose-stepping in derision as they left.

One of the skinheads said to Kroner, "Well, old father, you can remember this march, is that right?"

He kicked Kroner's knee and yanked his arm up and down, forcing him into the goose-step march. Kroner lost the envelope he had taken from Lily at that point, and, as it fell, it opened, scattering Lily's family documents.

The march of skinheads turned the corner, left-face, and began to sing the Horst Wessel song of the 1930s.

Lily then moved quickly then to try to retrieve the envelope and its contents, but she bumped into the last of the skinheads in the group. She shrugged that off, and got down on her knees to shovel the papers together. The skinhead crouched down.

"Pretty lady, let me help you."

He joined Lily on his knees. He picked up a single piece of paper and looked at it.

"Please," said Lily. "May I have it?"

"What is it?"

"Please," Lily repeated, as courteously and carefully as she could. "It's my family. It's..." she said very carefully, "my history."

227

"Yah," said the skinhead. "Family is important. You should not be so careless about your family's history." He gave the single document back to Lily.

He ran to catch up with the rest of the gang. But he turned to look at Lily once more.

"Heil Hitler! Pretty lady" he shouted as he ran away.

Lily stood open-mouthed. The crowd was being directed away by the police. The threat of further civil disorder had passed. The Turkish family had retreated into the cover of its apartment lodging and, shortly afterwards, Lily was standing on a nearly deserted street.

"What else can happen today?" she said aloud.

Not only had Gast and Wolfgang dropped her just before the crucial point in her pursuit of her claim, but it was obvious that they had seen fit to inform this Dr. Kroner where she would be going next, to the Treuhand, and when that meeting was to take place. Thus Kroner could intercept her, try to scare her off the claim and actually try to steal the evidence of family history that she was bringing to the meeting with the Treuhand.

She walked very quickly the remaining one and a half blocks to the Treuhandanstalt. She entered the main door at ten minutes to two.

Once inside, she started the sign-in process she had learned with Wolfgang's help on her second day in Germany. Then, she reflected, she had no idea what to expect at the meeting. Nor, she realized, did she know what to expect now.

Recollections of eight days churned in her mind as she negotiated the paternoster to the fourth floor again.

She paused after she jumped off the machine. She had, metaphorically, to shake her head to clear it.

She was Lily Weitrek of San Diego, California, the United States. She was married to Michael, from whom she was very far away. She had been caught, suspended, during these days in Germany, in a decision process over which she had no control.

Yes, the protocol was there. Documentation, evidence, certificates of vital statistics - births, deaths, marriages, paths of inheritance.

But there was no jury, she realized, only judges. She had counted on Wolfgang to assure her fairness. Otherwise, she now suddenly understood, she would have quit. Gone home.

These were thoughts of many recent days, suddenly clear and articulate in the three minutes she allowed herself, to herself, before going to one more conference room.

She had come alone to Germany. She had found, unexpectedly, a friend, a colleague in her effort. Now she was alone again.

She headed for Room 4635. She was as puzzled this time in the same way she was when she and Wolfgang had come to this building the first time because she could not invent an understanding for the curious and inexplicable room numbering system. She moved slowly down the long corridor, her senses registering with discomfort the chemicals of the new carpeting mixed with the freshly painted walls.

She was studying the doorways as she passed them at the same time thinking how much she would give to smell instead the fresh ocean breezes of Imperial Beach.

"Between the soot, the paint and the carpeting," she mumbled almost aloud, "one's life could really be cut short."

Lily tried to avoid focusing on the importance of what undoubtedly was to be her last meeting with the Treuhand officials, among them a man she had come to dread seeing again, Dr. Lautermit. To reassure herself as she walked, she touched the thick envelope that contained her family history to make sure that it was still there and intact. She stopped. The number on the door beside her was 4635.

Lily took a deep breath, opened the door into a small conference room.

"I think I am in the wrong room," she said to the solitary man in the room. He stood looking out of the window that faced the remaining sections of the Berlin Wall with its graffiti-sprayed messages of joy merged with political statements including a few that issued the imperative "Foreigners out!"

The man turned toward Lily. "Not at all, Ms. Weitrek; you are in the right room."

Lily judged the tall, white-haired man to be in his early 60s. He had wide-set blue eyes, a very straight nose and a propensity to smile that gave Lily a sense of some reassurance.

"I am Dr. Johannes Petermann, Deputy Director of the Private Property Executive Sector, Treuhand." He gestured toward a chair at a small conference table. "Please sit down."

He seated himself. Lily chose a chair one chair over from the one Petermann had taken. She found herself admiring his broad-collared blue and white shirt that was a twin to one she had bought for Michael at Nordstrom's in San Diego. But while Michael chose casual jackets whenever possible, this man was dressed quite precisely in a charcoal-gray suit.

"Where is Dr. Lautermit?" Lily asked. "I was told he had arranged this meeting."

Petermann began to roll a pen between the thumb and first finger of his left hand as if deciding how he would answer Lily's question. He shrugged slightly, hunched his left shoulder. "Dr. Lautermit has left this agency."

"May I ask why?"

He studied Lily before replying.

"This is a very difficult time for us, Ms. Weitrek. We are – the Treuhandanstalt is – right now, today, the world's largest industrial enterprise, a second government in Germany."

"That doesn't answer my question. Where is Dr. Lautermit?"

Petermann sidestepped the repeated question.

"It is necessary for us to locate investors for 40,000 businesses in the former East Germany or close those for which no investors can be found."

He rose from the chair abruptly and went to a sideboard disguised as part of a newly-painted wall, opened it and took up a tray already set with cruets of water and a thermos apparently filled with coffee.

"Coffee, Ms. Weitrek?"

"Yes, please." Lily was fiddling with the edge of the large manila envelope that she had placed on the table.

Petermann was silent as he poured two cups of coffee, busying himself with that task before eventually placing a small, delicate, fine china cup on the table for Lily. He then prepared his own cup before returning to his seat.

He smiled suddenly. "I had rather dreaded meeting you, you know. You must be aware that your claim has caused quite a stir in the agency." He chuckled. "I can imagine old Gast furious at his son-in-law for accepting your case once he learned what it was about."

Lily asked, just a bit more loudly, "Where is Dr. Lautermit?"

"Dr. Lautermit has become an entrepreneur."

Lily was unable to judge whether Petermann was conveying any reaction to what, so far as Lily could determine, was a classic case of insider trading. "Is this what it seems to be?" she asked, "Dr. Lautermit took over a claim?"

By way of answer, Petermann continued, "My government has recently replaced its former priority of returning East German business property to former owners. Instead, it now allows investors to take over such properties."

In a kind of afterthought, he went on. "Of course, these new investors such as Dr. Lautermit must assure us in their business plans that they will employ some of our displaced, and now unemployed workers. Their bank loans will depend on their keeping this commitment."

Lily saw quickly that Petermann's statement had something to do with her claim for the shoe factory.

"What about my claim?"

"Your claim, Ms. Weitrek? Well, I am afraid it is most complex."

"My government had no problem with it. Nor, apparently, did the former East German government."

Petermann took a sip of coffee before replying, hesitating again as if trying to choose from among several possible answers.

"Your government, Ms. Weitrek, has turned over to us, the Treuhand, the claims of those people who, like you, want property returned. Your government is preoccupied with a recession, the Middle East, a war with Iraq."

Lily's look was blank as her mind interpreted and then applied this man's message to her claim.

"I am very sorry, Ms. Weitrek, but I have more bad news for you."

"What is that?" she said almost inaudibly.

"As you have already learned, the Von Jaegerlieds have filed a claim for the same property.

When Lily found her voice, she shot back. "Your government set last October as a final deadline for claims for property in East Germany."

"Ms. Weitrek. I said the Von Jaegerlieds 'filed;' I did not say their claim had been accepted."

"Oh," was Lily's one word response.

"Now within your own claim there are a number of omissions that we or someone would be required to correct before the claim could be recognized by us in any case. But even if that were accomplished, it is quite doubtful the property would be returned to you."

"What omissions?" Lily picked up the manila envelope and began to pull out the family history that she and Wolfgang had compiled.

"Please hear me out."

She had no choice but to listen. She nodded in agreement.

"In the past month my government has determined that it must now reject all such claims as yours and instead accept offers from those who propose investing in now bankrupt East German businesses. Can you, Ms. Weitrek, invest the millions it would take to re-build the shoe factory and modernize its business practices?"

Petermann was warming to the task of challenging Lily.

"Could you design shoes and market them to sell internationally? Do you have experience in negotiating with labor unions? German labor unions? Can you accept a 14 million Deutschmark debt that exists for us, the Treuhand, for the necessity of keeping the factory open when your claim delayed closing it?"

"This is a travesty of justice." Lily's face flushed. She bit off each word as she went on. "If Dr. Lautermit can become an 'entrepreneur,' if he, with his close ties to this 'second government' can so abuse his role that he personally profits from it, then this agency, this country will eventually be charged with unlawful destruction of property, abuse of claims, fraud and corruption." Lily drew breath and exhaled.

Petermann had anticipated Lily's anger and deflected it with a soft response.

"Ms. Weitrek. Try to see it from our perspective. We have four million people who are unemployed. We must weigh the future of the many against the interests of a few."

Lily's reply was immediate. "Strange, I just read that very same statement in a book written in 1935."

Petermann stood up and said, "We will succeed in building a unified German democratic country." He bowed to Lily, indicating that the meeting was over. But Lily continued to sit. He turned to her and said, "Well, why did you really come to Germany, Ms. Weitrek? Did you not know that claims are handled far better through attorneys? The history in a nutshell, Ms. Weitrek? The crimes were too great, the losses too large. Will the return of an art work, or a shoe factory, money paid out for a lost life...? His rhetorical question went unfinished. "I know, and you must know, these will be only gestures in history and for history. That is all they can ever be."

His speech was over. He became almost solicitous. "So why did you really come to Germany?

Lily stood now and faced him directly.

"I think," she hesitated, "I think I know now, - to hear one person offer an apology, maybe one person say 'I am sorry.'"

# FIFTEEN

There was very little time left for Lily in her stay in Germany, but there was one thing she had to do before returning home, notwithstanding the outcome of her claim and struggle with the Treuhand.

And that was to visit Hanine.

When Wolfgang had asked over their first dinner if Lily could name anyone who knew both her parents, Lily had answered Hanine. The only thing Lily knew was that her mother occasionally referred to this woman who lived in East Germany and had been Lily's nanny when she was a baby.

Wolfgang had found Hanine.

He had been able to get the information that she was still alive and about where she was living more easily than might have been expected because one of the partners at the law firm specialized in laws regulating geriatric facilities, and was able through his contacts to locate her in the East Zone now that the Wall was down.

Wolfgang had been quite precise in his written directions about how to get to the Elderheim, a senior residential center in Fuerstenwalde, formerly in East Germany, not far from Berlin.

Lily set out to see Hanine with a complex of emotions.

First, of course, was the effort to absorb in her mind that Wolfgang's unexpected decision to drop her case left her on her own. The impact had been lethal.

In the space of fewer than ten days, her dependence on Wolfgang, the regularity of his companionship and, quite soon after they met, his leadership of her claim effort had installed him in her view of each beginning day.

Now, not only was Wolfgang gone, but so was any real hope for her claim - her mother's claim. The opinion expressed by Petermann to her yesterday at her meeting at the Treuhand, she knew, was less an opinion than a closet decision. It was unlikely that she could successfully fight the Von Yaegerlied competing claim.

Nor was it too likely there would be any compensation for the losses. The Von Yaegerlied claim had smothered that possibility with the cozy relationship from the past now drifted into the present.

But also, all of this bad news came without the armor of Wolfgang's resolve, and friendship, between her and the blows.

So she faced as well the emotional unknown of visiting Hanine alone. Not, of course, that Wolfgang would have gone with her; but Wolfgang would have cheered her intent to go, and would have listened to whatever she would have to say about the experience when she returned, the experience of visiting one who was very old, no doubt, and who had been important to Lily in ways to which her mother alluded but never stated.

The train to Fuerstenwalde was on the S-Bahn. It was a quick trip, one speeded more by the distractions of regret that billowed in Lily's mind. She got off at the Fuerstenwalde station, found a taxi waiting outside and asked the driver to take her to the Elderheim.

The ride from the train station to where the Elderheim was located passed with no conversation.

Lily was headed toward a visit which she knew would require her energy; she had almost no energy left. Lily was tired to the marrow of her bones.

There were several buildings spread over a considerable amount of land. The taxi left Lily standing at the gate. The Elderheim had a central information desk in Building I, according to a sign posted on the main gate. The sign also said that the buildings were apparently designated according to care needs.

She began to worry more now suddenly about not only seeing Hanine for the first time in her memory, but about in what condition she would find her.

Lily's momentum stalled at this new intimation, wondering whether the person she had come to see might be living independently in a building named, according to the sign, Goethehaus, or where the residents needed, as the sign described it, "full care," in a building named Mozarthaus.

She fell into a brown study, just standing there, collecting the references together, both regular and stray, to Hanine. She wished her mother had said more than "she helped us when we left Germany after your father died."

She stared at the buildings of the Elderheim. They were not old. They bore some resemblance to the monoliths of Soviet architecture that greeted the eyes of the visitor venturing for the first time across where once there was a Wall. What would inside be like? She wondered what was next.

Lily's thoughts coalesced back to reality. She decided to start her search for Hanine in the building closest to the path she was on. She had been apprehensive as she walked the length of the well-tended grounds to reach the building. She did not know what she would do or which way she would go once inside. She said a "small prayer" that this building, "Mozarthaus," a full-care building, would not be where she would find Hanine. Once inside Mozarthaus, she saw a reception desk much like one finds in an American hospital. Lily gave Hanine's name to the woman behind the desk, a woman named Frau Gertrud Walther according to her badge.

"Frau Hoffman is in room 433," Frau Walther said. "Does she expect you?"

This was not what Lily had wanted to learn. Hanine was indeed in the full-care unit.

"It is the time for the noon meal," Frau Walther said. "We do not normally allow visitors at this time because those in Mozarthaus require assistance at their meals. When did you last see Frau Hoffman" - she looked down at Lily's signature in the guest book put there before any conversation began - "Frau Weitrek?"

"I can't remember," Lily replied, "Could you make an exception? Please, this is my last day in Germany. I leave for the United States tomorrow."

"You are from the United States? Here? To see one who lives with us? In Mozarthaus? Fraulein, you are the first American to visit Mozarthaus. Of course we will make an exception. In fact, perhaps you can be of some assistance in helping Frau Hoffman with her meal."

When Lily emerged from the elevator on the fourth floor, the wall signs told her room 433 was to the right. The room numbers were quite large above the doors. Outside room 433 there was a cart with food dishes on it.

A woman in a gray uniform came out of room 431, stopped, and looked at Lily with a question evident in her eyes.

"I have come to see Frau Hoffman," Lily answered before the question could be asked. "Frau Walther said I might be able to provide some assistance to Frau Hoffman, if she needs it. I leave tomorrow for California. For home."

"Very well. I was just about to wheel in her tray. I will set it up for you to help."

Lily was puzzled. She followed the attendant into Hanine's room.

The old woman, dressed in a loose-fitting housecoat, sat in a chair that was positioned so that the food tray might be moved directly in front of her. She turned at the sound of their footsteps, her head cocked, her eyes empty.

Lily suddenly understood. Hanine, this old woman, was blind. Hanine, familiar with the sound, knew that the tray was being moved in. She did not know anyone unusual accompanied it.

Lily felt a void.

The attendant placed the food on the tray. Cheerfully and loudly as if the patient was deaf rather than blind she said, "Frau Hoffman, here is your lunch." Hanine reached out her hands to assure herself of the tray's position in front of her. "And in addition to this lunch, you have a surprise visitor." She beamed at the sightless old woman. "A woman from California." The attendant marched out of the room.

The frail body seemed to grow still as the attendant's words registered, causing a hunt for understanding in the deeper recesses of memories buried in the brain. With a sudden sharp intake of breath Hanine said, "I only know of one person in California." Color suffused the parchment yellow skin and the woman turned her head, not knowing where her visitor stood. In a quavering voice she said, "Can it be? Can it be after all these years it is you Theresa? Frau Weitrek, are you here?"

Lily made sure the sound of her shoes would allow the blind woman to track her movement towards the chair.

She said softly, "No, Hanine. It's Lily Weitrek. Her daughter." Lily was afraid that the shock would cause the woman to collapse as Hanine placed her hand over her heart as if protecting it from its irregular beating. Lily could feel her own heart beating a rapid tattoo.

Hanine took rasping gasps of air into her lungs. She moved her head from side to side as if searching for someone from the past. "Lily? My little baby, Lily? Is it possible?" She gestured Lily closer, moved the tray stand out of the way and indicated Lily should kneel down directly in front of her.

When Lily had knelt down, the old woman saying nothing, reached out to touch Lily's hair and then her face. In a soft voice Hanine said, "When you were born, you had little wisps of blond hair. Your mother brushed it every day so it would grow." Hanine sighed, "You come too late for me to see you. I can only see you as you were back then. So small. No matter what we did you did not gain enough weight." She patted Lily's face and then leaned down. "Come, give me a kiss, Lily. Put your arms around me. It has been a long time since I have felt arms around my poor old body."

Lily kissed Hanine and held her, rocking Hanine as tears ran down both their faces. It was Hanine who pulled away first.

"God is merciful. Now, at the end of my life I may hold you again as I did when you were so very small."

"I promised Frau Walther I would make sure you would eat your lunch," Lily said.

"Yes, we can play the game I used to play to get Emma to eat. 'One for you, one for me, one for Mammi, one for Pappi'." Hanine cocked her head towards Lily. "Your mother, Lily? In my heart I already know the news is sad."

Lily pulled the visitor's chair from the corner of the room next to Hanine's chair and took the old woman's trembling hands into her own. Lily realized her hands were also shaking.

"Yes, Hanine. Theresa died seven years ago."

"Tell me it was a peaceful death. She deserved to die peacefully after such a difficult life, so much grief."

Lily lied because there was nothing to be gained by telling this caring woman her mother had died painfully. "It was a peaceful end."

Hanine nodded, content. "And Emma?" she asked. "She is not with you in Germany?"

"No, Emma could not come with me."

Hanine seemed to think her own thoughts before asking Lily questions about her life, her husband, whether there were children, a profession, how and where she lived. Was she happy?

Lily laughed at the number of questions Hanine asked. As she answered, she played Hanine's remembered food game. For each bite of lunch Hanine took, Lily would answer a question. Lily remembered feeding her mother tiny bits of food as she lay dying and knew how much time to allow Hanine to swallow the tiny bits of food.

When Hanine indicated she had had enough of the very uninteresting, institutional food, Lily wheeled the tray outside the room into the hallway. As Lily re-entered the room she saw that Hanine was taking off a slender filigreed necklace of gold chain and small black opals.

Lily sat down again next to her. Hanine said, touching the necklace, "Your mother gave me this when you were 6 months old and Emma was just two." Lily could tell the necklace had enormous significance for Hanine. "But I must ask something. Why did you make this trip now to Germany?"

Lily thought before she answered, wondering what to include in her answer. "I promised my mother before she died that I would visit her mother's grave in Weissensee Cemetery if I could. I did find the grave. And laid flowers on it."

"Is the inscription still there on the headstone? The one your mother told me she had made?"

Lily smiled in surprise. "You mean `To the sweetest mother of them all'? Yes, it is there still."

Hanine said, "I was there only once - with your mother, to visit the grave. Your mother was heartbroken by the death. She told me often how close they were. She often spoke of how lonely she had been, until your sister Emma, and then you, were born.

She loved you so much. Did she speak to you, Lily, about me? Did she tell you stories of the days when we were all together?"
The old woman broke down. She cleared her throat, shuffling her shoulders from side to side as if physical adjustment would regain her emotional composure. Lily waited with her answer.
"Near the end of her life she told me that…you had helped us leave Germany. But that you could not come with us. Why didn't you?" Lily asked.
The old woman turned her head towards Lily. She patted Lily's hand, clutched in her own, the fingers so thin Lily could feel the bones.
"I am sorry you know so little. Lily, I was not considered a refugee. The U.S. Embassy in Switzerland would not issue me a visa, said they could not do so. I was returned to Germany and sent to what the Nazis called a re-education camp. I was a trained nurse, which is why your mother first hired me, and I spent the years of the war in field hospitals. So long ago…I married a man I met in the hospital. We were caught in the Soviet sector and stayed. I was widowed, grew old …and blind. Now I am here. But at last, so are you, for a while."
"You said that my mother was lonely. Where was my father?" Lily asked.
"Toward the end, he was only permitted to see you and your sister one time a week, and always in the presence of an 'observer'. Much of the time he was away making films."
Lily took a breath before asking, "Did he make Nazi films?"
Hanine seemed to be rustling memories from fields of the mind unvisited for a half-century.
"He had no choice, or thought he had no choice. It is not up to me to judge, Lily. I have known and seen so much sorrow that I leave it up to God to judge."
Hanine furrowed the brow of her aged face.
"I know that without his help you would not have escaped Germany. I took Emma out. He took you out. Did you think, my child, that your father was an evil man? Yes, he made Nazi films, but it could not have been easy for him - a Jewish wife and two children. He too was in danger."
Lily was shaken.

"How could a Nazi film maker be in danger?"

"He was much more than that, Lily." She shook her head impatiently at Lily. "He was a talented man in a dreadful situation. Perhaps not as strong as he might have been."

Hanine paused, as if uncertain that she wanted to tell the story.

"The time came when your mother knew she had to get you out of Germany. It was already very late. You were not to be allowed to leave. That was a direct order from Goebbels. Yet when your mother decided to try to get you and Emma out, your father risked his own life to get you to the Swiss border. For that, if for nothing else, Lily, you must try to see him clearly as more than a man who made a few films for the Nazi cause. Open your heart."

Again, Lily thought: the Swiss border.

"I don't think I understand what you're saying, Hanine. Swiss border?"

"I wish your mother had told you the whole story herself."

"So," said Lily, "do I."


BERLIN, 1940

The areas that surround Greater Berlin and make up its outskirts are filled with lakes. A glance at borough names shows how many bear the suffix "see." But the countryside is lush as well with trees and various other greenery.

In mid-September, 1940, the green was going to red and gold. Leaves had begun to fall. The massive military mobilization had not extended yet out into this Berlin countryside.

Franz Weitrek had stationed himself, waiting for night to fall, in the cover of the trees around their country house. He moved from tree to tree to get as close as he could without being seen from the front door. He kept his attention on one window where a single light darkened, then appeared again.

Franz expected to see what had become a familiar sight in the last months, a uniformed guard at the front door.

Franz stepped sideways, keeping the guard in his view, until he could turn the corner of the house and head to the rear undetected.

A side door opened slightly. Twenty-seven year old Hanine Hoffman held it open just long enough for Franz to get inside, where, once the door was closed again, he looked directly at Hanine.

She whispered, "The housekeeper is asleep. You can go upstairs. The guard just made his rounds and is back outside. But he will return. You must be very quiet."

Franz nodded. He moved quickly to a central staircase and hurried up the stairs. He went immediately into what was obviously an upstairs sitting room. Only a dim light illuminated the space, and the outside was shut out by heavy damask draperies that were tightly drawn across and over the two windows in the room.

Theresa Weitrek had been closing one of two suitcases when Franz came in. She was startled at his entry, her nervousness on the surface of her skin.

"Theresa. It is Franz."

Theresa ran to him. She sought his arms around her. He complied.

"Where are the children?" he asked.

"You look so tired, Franz. They are in the next room. I moved them there. I am worried about Emma."

Franz followed her to the next room where the door was partially open. "Why? What is wrong with Emma?"

No answer was required. Lily was asleep in a crib, but Emma lay on top of two mattresses that were high enough so that she was at the level of the crib. She too was asleep, but her arm was through the bars of the crib and she was holding one of the baby's hands.

"She cries continually, Franz," Theresa said in a whisper. "She continues to say someone will take Lily away."

"But you told her that it would only be for a short while?"

"I do not think she believes that," Theresa said, "and I am not sure that I do completely either. I am frightened. What if your plan does not work? What if they catch us?"

"The plan will work. It has to."

Hanine appeared at the door with an armful of clothing. She waited there.

"Come in, Hanine. Come in. Put all the girls' clothing into the drawers. Nothing of theirs can be taken."

Hanine looked at Franz. "You must leave soon. The guard will be back soon."

Franz took two train tickets out of his inside jacket pocket and handed them to her.

"You are clear about what you must do tomorrow, Hanine?" he asked. "Quickly, rehearse."

"Tomorrow," Hanine recited, "I will tell the housekeeper that I will take Emma to the park so that she does not see her mother leave Germany. But I will go with her instead to the Friedrichstrasse train station and board the 9 a.m. train to Zurich."

"You have her health pass?"

"Yes. If anyone asks, I am to show the temporary visa which allows us to travel to the Swiss health camp for children two to five years old."

"Good," said Franz.

Theresa re-stated what she had already said again and again.

"You must not get off the train for any reason. I will be on the next train to Zurich, one hour behind yours. When I get to the Swiss border and do not see your train, I will then know that you crossed safely and that you and Emma are with our friends in Zurich.

Hanine nodded patiently and added to the much-rehearsed list of instructions.

"If there has been any trouble at any of the train stops within Germany, or we have been taken off, I am to leave Emma's doll on a bench on the platform."

"It is good the Germans are so honest," Theresa said bitterly. "They would never take a child's doll, only the child's life. Or its mother's life."

"Mrs. Weitrek and I," said Franz, "are very much aware of the risk you will take. If you are caught at the border on one train

with a health pass and Mrs. Weitrek is found with a permanent
exit order on another train, it would be very dangerous for you.
We cannot find a way to thank you."

Hanine replied softly, "I love the girls."

Franz continued. "Do not talk to anyone. If there are other
children on the train, try to sit near them. There is nothing more
to say, except 'thank you'"

"God willing," said Hanine, "I will get Emma across the
border safely."

After Hanine left the room to assume her normal duties
downstairs so as to not arouse the guard's suspicion when he next
made his rounds of the house, Theresa threw herself into Franz's
arms. Just then, Emma awoke and sat up.

"Papa, do not leave me. No bye-bye on a train. No
'Friedrichstrasse'."

She could not pronounce the name so it came out
'Fweedsaase', but her intention was clear.

"I never will. I never will leave my girls. Go back to sleep
now," he said, as he placed her back on the makeshift bed, and
drew the blanket over her.

They stepped out of the room into the hall. Franz fixed his
eyes on Theresa's.

"As soon as you have left tomorrow morning, I will be able to
come to get Lily. We will be on our way out of Berlin by the time
your train to Zurich leaves the station. Do not worry. I will get
her across the border."

"How?"

"We will try to cross at Gottsberg. It is possible that you may
have to wait one day or more, but we will get there."

Franz then went quickly down the stairs, and as he turned to
the kitchen, through the door that Hanine had opened for him,
the guard entered the front door and proceeded directly upstairs.

The guard had three responsibilities. The first was to see to it
that the children were not taken from the house.

The second was to ascertain that Theresa Weitrek, expelled
from Germany, was indeed finally going to leave.

The third was to make sure there was no contact except under
his watchful eyes between the Jew and the Aryan. Once the

woman was gone, the famous director could return to live with his two children, and he, the guard, could then go on to other similar duties. He smiled in satisfaction that, one by one, the mixed-race households were being cleansed.

He took particular satisfaction in having discovered the Jewish family hiding in one of the outlying buildings on the estate. He had watched with curiosity as Frau Weitrek made her nightly walks around the grounds, always at the end entering one particular building. He had called the Security Police, the SS, and let them do the dirty work, pulling up the floorboards and dragging the family out. Only a pair of crutches remained in the building now, dropped by the young boy as he was taken away with his mother and father.

His rounds upstairs satisfied him that the woman was packing to leave.

By the time the guard had finished his inspections, Franz Weitrek had wended his way back through the trees away from their house. He stopped at the far property line, about 200 yards from the house itself. He looked back briefly, and then moved on.

At eight o'clock the next morning, the front door of the Weitrek country house opened. Hanine Hoffman, holding two-year old Emma Weitrek by the hand, left. Hanine carried her purse. They both wore warm coats, but they carried nothing else. They were, after all, headed for the park.

Theresa watched their departure from the upstairs window of the room in which she had been packing her last belongings. She was crying openly, the sounds sobbing makes muffled by the closed window.

When Emma and Hanine had disappeared in the direction of the park, Theresa left the room and headed downstairs. The two suitcases were all she could manage without having to get a porter. She dared not attract attention or questions.

A disdainful and even surly housekeeper greeted her at the first floor. Goebbels had assigned this housekeeper as watchdog over Theresa Weitrek. Her real task was not keeping house, but to make certain that Theresa's departure was real, if very uncomfortable.

The housekeeper offered no help, used no words; she only shut the door firmly once she was satisfied that Theresa, shut up in the special car that had been waiting, was on her way out of Germany.

The housekeeper could now report that fact to the authorities.

The Friedrichstrasse train station bustled that morning with the great number of military personnel who were in the process of coming or going.

Theresa had entered the station after the special car dropped her there and had gone up to the platform. Small as she was, she assumed a partially hidden position behind a column from which vantage she could look for Hanine and Emma.

At first, she could not locate them. The platform clock at Trains 3 and 4, at the gate for the 9 a.m. train to Zurich, read 8:50 a.m.

Suddenly, a commotion developed surrounding a group of young children, some only toddlers. Chaperones or governesses accompanied the children. The children had signs around their necks that announced their destinations in handwritten script: "Health Camp - Swiss Alps."

Theresa found Hanine and Emma in the middle of the small crowd. No doubt because these were true German children, aryans, a photographer took pictures of them as they boarded the train, and the uniformed military police digressed from their sterner duties to help the children get aboard, and did so with smiles and jovial banter.

The children and their guardians were finally aboard. The train left, only delayed one minute by the need to accommodate precious cargo. Theresa was drained. She slumped against the column.

One hour later, Theresa boarded, as planned, the next train to Zurich. She rode through the rest of the day and into the next night. Around midnight, a uniformed conductor stationed himself at the end of the car and spoke loudly.

"We will reach the border between Germany and Switzerland in only a few minutes. First German Passport Control will come through this car, and all others. That will be followed by Swiss Passport Control. Your papers must be ready. Heil Hitler!"

The train coasted slowly into the border station and came to a halt. There was another train stopped directly across. Theresa realized that this train must be the 9 a.m. train from Berlin, the one carrying Hanine and Emma, just as the conductor explained it.

"There will be a short delay. There is a group of children on the train across from us. Some of them have become ill. They are being taken off at this time."

Theresa panicked. She watched in fright as children came off the train. Emma was not among them. But, because she was scanning the children, she did not see Hanine one car behind the children who were being taken off. Hanine looked frantically up and down the train that Theresa was on to try to locate her.

They saw each other across the platform. Emma was held up facing Hanine so that Theresa could see her child was safe. Emma held her doll out toward Hanine for her to kiss as the earlier, delayed train began to move again.

Emma suddenly pulled away and turned around in time to see her mother in the stationary train that they were beginning to pass. She began to form the sounds of "Mama." Hanine stifled the sounds with her hand over Emma's mouth.

By the time Passport Control began its way through Theresa's car, Hanine and Emma were through the border and on Swiss soil. Theresa sank back into her seat, her permanent exit orders in her hand.

# SIXTEEN

On an isolated area on the German/Swiss border, a German border official was sitting in a small kiosk that served as his field office. The Nazi swastika flew at the top of a short flagpole above the kiosk. The kiosk was on the northern edge of the "no man's land" between the countries. At the southern edge there was another kiosk flying a Swiss flag.

The German border official saw that a truck and two cars were making their way slowly, sometimes lurching over the rural landscape, toward him and the border. He stepped out of the kiosk and stood erect and at attention, prepared to salute if the occupants of the vehicles were important military officials or to demand papers if they were not.

The spire of a church could be seen in what was apparently a small Swiss village very close to the border kiosk.

The truck pulled up first, the two cars behind, and stopped. The panel sign on the side of the truck read, "Tobis Films: Locations and Properties."

Franz Weitrek sat in the seat beside the driver of the truck. The official approached.

"Papers! Heil Hitler!"

Franz Weitrek, seemingly an actor as well as a director, replied in a hearty, if phony voice.

"Heil Hitler. And good day, good day. We do not plan to cross the border. We wanted to come to inform you that we are here to film some scenes for a movie for the Fatherland. The film is about the heroes in the Hitler Youth."

Franz pointed grandly to a small, wooded area about 100 yards away, in the direction of the border barbed wire, but considerably short of it.

"We will be over there."

"It will be necessary for me to see your papers in any case," the officer said.

The driver handed a leather folder which held his own papers to the officer, and then relayed Franz' papers also. The border officer studied them carefully.

As the officer proceeded with his painstaking review of the documents, Franz Weitrek said to the driver, "We will film first the scene with the baby. There. Do you agree? See, the sunlight is perfect."

The officer, having completed his review of their papers, was now studying Franz.

"I have heard of you."

Franz felt his heart jump.

"You have?"

"Yes. A few years ago... I was here then also... you made a film in this area. Yes. You had just won first prize at the Hitler Film Festival. Am I not correct?"

"I did. I did. Such an honor."

The official afforded his memory a self-rewarding smile.

"Perhaps you will need another man in your film...?"

"Of course. You. What a splendid suggestion."

Franz reached across the driver's seat to extend his hand, and the official reached into the car to join the handshake.

The exchange completed, the driver of the truck turned it somewhat to the right going away from the kiosk, and headed it toward the wooded area. The two cars followed.

Having traveled the 100 yards, the truck and cars stopped and shut off their engines. When the truck and the cars were emptied of their passengers, they constituted only a small crew: Franz, the driver of the truck, two other men, presumably those who drove the cars, and a woman.

She carried a small child, perhaps six months old, sleeping in her arms. She walked a few steps to a more shaded area in the little grove and lowered herself carefully into a sitting position on the ground. Settled, she began to rock the baby slowly.

Franz had set up his camera quickly and now peered through its lens, which was focusing on the woman and child. He spoke, more loudly than needed, loud enough in fact for the officer in the kiosk to hear him.

"That is fine, Gisella. I want you and the child right there. Right by that tree. I want a sound test; say your lines."

249

The officer in the kiosk had responded to the generous volume of Franz' directions, and had become a rapt audience of one.

"That is fine, Gisella. Once again…"

"And when you grow up, little Lily, like your sisters and brothers you will march for the Fuehrer and the Fatherland."

"Excellent," Franz concluded.

Much activity followed from the film crew. While someone with reasonable knowledge would have recognized that the activity was pointless, and had little if anything to do with the normal process of filmmaking, the officer in the kiosk was fascinated. It was as if he had been able to order personally a famous person to come to his lonely border outpost and entertain him.

Thus did the rest of the morning pass, and the film crew stopped somewhat short of noon.

Franz and the others made their way back toward the kiosk. They brought with them the lunches that they had packed.

"Officer," said Franz, "will you join us for lunch, or may we join you? You can do your duty as a border guard even as we dine together."

The officer agreed, and brought out his own food. His kiosk had the only chair available, and he brought it out to offer it to Gisella, still carrying Lily.

Gisella thanked him and sat down.

Franz uncovered a bottle of aquavit. He offered to pour a drink of it for the guard, and for the others, but the guard alone accepted.

"My crew is fearful their work will suffer if they turn to aquavit," said Franz, "but I have no such fear, and, I see, neither do you."

Three glasses of aquavit later, the guard inhabited a somewhat blurred world. He was happy with the company, with the food and drink. But that good cheer was suddenly assailed by an outburst of crying from the baby. Both the volume and the pitch of her staccato cries increased. Gisella tried altering the rocking pattern, but the cries continued.

Suddenly, the baby threw up. Gisella was frightened. The officer came quickly to see what could be done; this incessant shrieking had to stop.

"Look," said Gisella to Franz, "her face is mottled with red welts. She is sick, very sick. We must find help."

"Well," said the guard, "a physician. She must have a physician. Right there, across the border, is a little village. Likely a physician there. On this side. two hours to a town. What is there to be done?"

Franz, Gisella and the others waited, with hope, and patiently.

"I cannot leave my post here," the guard said, "nor can I allow…"

The guard's training had not prepared him to face this kind of need for decision. He was trained to follow orders, and the orders clearly stated that he could not leave his kiosk until relieved by another officer and that he was not allowed to permit anyone to cross the border without the proper visa.

Perhaps the aquavit helped him find a middle ground.

"Are you," he said to Gisella, "the child's mother?"

Without hesitation, Gisella said, "Yes."

"Then this is my decision. I must keep you here with me. You, Herr Weitrek, may take the child across the border to find a physician. You cannot drive a German car onto foreign soil, so you must walk. That is my decision. The child's mother will be under arrest until you return with the child."

Franz nodded acceptance. He showed no signs of satisfaction. He simply moved to join the other two men, who already had taken a kind of carrier, a baby bed but without wheels from the truck.

The guard, apparently anxious to re-establish his military prevalence in this situation, marched Gisella off to the kiosk.

Franz came back to the kiosk. He exchanged a look with Gisella, one that might have been said to combine the apprehensiveness of lovers when they are faced with the prospect of unwanted separation.

The two crewmen followed, bringing Lily lying in the carrier.

Franz moved to take the burden from the two crewmen. It weighed more than he had expected, it was evident, and his knees almost buckled. This unexpected surprise elicited suspicion in the guard. He looked at Franz, at Gisella, at the crewmen, back and forth. Before it was evident what he would decide to do, or perhaps before he could even address that question, Gisella crossed the meter between her and Franz and broke into hysterical sobs.

"My baby. My baby. Please let me go with her."

"No!" the guard shouted.

The baby started to cry again.

"Go," said the guard angrily to Franz, "just go. And return soon. This woman will not be released from arrest until you both return."

The guard raised the control bar. Franz, carrying the baby, crossed the no man's land to the Swiss Border Patrol kiosk.

The Swiss Border guard had been puzzled by what he could see of what was taking place on the other side. He had been able to conclude that a film of some kind was being made, because the camera suggested it. He had also, in fact, however surprised he was about it, been able to hear some of the instructions being shouted, for some reason, by the film's director.

So, the guard reasoned, one extraordinary event is to be followed by another. The director was crossing on foot over to his kiosk. What for?

When it had become clear to him that a medical emergency existed, and that it was the reason for the German guard's permission for this man to walk across to Switzerland, he beckoned to the driver of an official automobile parked near the Swiss kiosk.

Franz and the carrier were loaded into the vehicle, and it quickly covered the short distance to the little village with the church spire and a physician, who the German border guard had correctly assumed would be there.

The physician's office was, as was common, a part of his family's house. The knock on his door by the Swiss official brought him quickly to open it. He studied what was in front of him: the guard, a tired and harassed-looking man, and what appeared to be an outsized, cumbersome baby carrier.

The physician, Dr. Rupert Diehl, beckoned them in. The guard declined, saying that he would wait in the car to take them back to the border and to Germany after the infant had been given medical treatment.

Once the guard had retreated to the outside, Franz put the carrier down where the physician indicated, on an examination table. He straightened his back in relief of the heavy burden.

Theresa emerged from another room and went quickly to the carrier.

Franz opened the carrier's half-top, and lifted a sleeping Lily out of it. He then opened the apparent floor of the carrier and revealed a hidden compartment where another infant lay, blond like Lily and of similar age.

The physician's examination of both children was thorough.

He looked up at Franz and Theresa.

"What did you use, belladonna?"

"Yes. We mixed ipecac with belladonna for Lily," Franz answered. "We had to make her throw up."

"How did you know to do that? That it would work?"

"A close friend of ours is a nurse."

"Which child is the one who will go back to Germany?" Dr. Diehl asked.

Franz pointed to the other child, the one who had traveled with him in the hidden compartment.

"Then keep her very warm. She should be fine. I have a bit of advice to offer you..."

He was suddenly very aware of the intensity with which Theresa was cuddling Lily. "Ah, who knows what any of us would do, will have to do, in these most difficult times. I'll have the driver take you back."

Dr. Diehl bowed, turned and left the examination room.

Theresa, still holding the still sleeping baby close, looked up at Franz.

He stood uncomfortably, restive under her intense stare, and then began to pace the room as he gave her a full report of the day's events, leaving only Gisella 's name out of the narrative. Then he fell silent, and the silence grew between them. Theresa concentrated her gaze on Lily. Franz turned away as Theresa began softly to cry.

"I am begging you, Franz. Please leave with us. I am so afraid. I have already lost so much, my mother dead, Aunt Franziska and Uncle Misha and Ludwig God knows where. Uncle Daniel dead. Now I am to lose everything else — the country I grew up in, the language I speak. Must I lose you too? Please come with me and our children. Aren't we more important than your ambition?" Theresa was sobbing audibly.

Franz, both hands already in his pockets, thrust them deeper, too embarrassed to look at the woman he promised once to love and to protect. He turned towards the door.

"I have to go back, Theresa.

"Is she with you? Gisella. Is she with you?"

He said reluctantly, "Yes."

Theresa kept her eyes on Lily, but addressed him. "The gossip columns say you will marry her. Is that true?'

She looked up defiantly at him then. "Is she more beautiful? More intelligent? Better?" She added angrily, "Or is it that she is easier than I am?"

Almost anyone is easier than you, he thought; but instead he said, "You promised to let me go if I helped you get your children out of Germany."

"'My' children'?" Her voice rose. The baby in her arms began to move restlessly. "Are they not your children also?"

Franz was shamed. "Of course."

The nurse in the physician's office entered the examination room without knocking. She moved efficiently to place the child who would be returned into the top half of the carrier where Lily had lain. She covered the child with a blanket, picked up the carrier, opened the outside door and left.

Theresa and Franz followed and stopped at the vehicle into which the nurse had placed the carrier. By now it was dusk moving on to darkness. They looked at each other, Theresa holding on to Franz one last time across Lily's sleeping shape.

"I must go, Theresa," he said removing Theresa's arm.

"Why could you not have loved me enough, loved your children enough to give up everything for them?" Theresa cried out.

He leaned over to kiss Lily.

"Tell the girls about me. Tell them I did what I could."

Theresa's look changed. Her face moved from the fluid softness of sorrow, deep sorrow, to the rigid permanence of sculpture. She had found the beginnings of the disguise she would wear in the many years to come.

"I will tell them... nothing."

Theresa turned abruptly and moved away from the vehicle to stand just inside the physician's office. She watched as Franz entered the Swiss vehicle.

Theresa could see a series of headlights climbing the mountain towards the German kiosk. Men in black uniforms ran from the cars. Their guns were drawn. She could see Franz getting out of the Swiss vehicle. The Swiss driver quickly put the baby carrier on the ground near the German kiosk. He then drove back to safety as quickly as he could. Franz moved towards the German kiosk. Theresa could hear voices yelling orders. The words were unclear.

Theresa could not watch. Carrying Lily, she opened the door to the physician's house.

She did not look back towards the border as the shot rang out. Theresa closed the door.


1991


"I knew some of this story because I had been part of its planning," Hanine said, "the rest I learned over a decade later. Your mother wrote only one very long letter to me; the rest were more hurried, short. That one long letter... I no longer have it... was one, she said, she needed to write, to tell someone the story

255

which she otherwise would never tell. I was the one she chose, Lily. I do not think there was anyone else she felt she could tell. Now, Lily, you must tell me what happened to Emma. Your mother, when she wrote, referred mostly to you. So I always feared that something about Emma was being hidden. Was I right?"

The old woman was nearing exhaustion. It was unlikely she had taken part in such an extended conversation for many years, and seldom, if ever, one so intense. Her breath was coming in irregular gasps and her hands shook. Lily was afraid for Hanine. And for herself. Theresa, she said silently, where did it go so wrong?

Throughout her life Lily had observed an almost terminal struggle between her mother and her sister. The adult struggled for supremacy in the battle over the small child, Emma's, memories of a man she called "Papa."

As a young child, Emma found a safe place to remember out of range of her mother's fury. It was under her bed. Lily would creep under the bed with her and listen to Emma's childish fantasy that once there had been a father who was always with her until he disappeared in a great train station.

Emma always struggled to remember the name. It was something that sounded like "Freed." She would whisper to Lily that their father was kind and loving.

After a while Emma stopped speaking to her mother, and only spoke to her through Lily, using her younger sister as a shield. It became clear to school officials, social workers and later institutional staff that Emma needed a protected environment.

From what Emma needed the protection was never quite clear to her guardians.

In answer to Hanine's question, Lily finally said, "Emma has good days and bad." Lily stopped. She groped for a ray of hope for her sister's future.

"I think if I tell her much of what you told me it will bring her comfort, help her in a way nothing else could."

Hanine took the necklace that had been in her hand throughout the long meeting and reached it towards Lily. "I want you to give this to Emma. It comes indirectly from your father.

He gave it to your mother and she to me the day I took Emma to Switzerland. Give it to her and tell her that her father loved her very much."

Lily could see that Hanine was too tired to go further. The old woman said, "I hope it will help her, with all my heart." Lily took the necklace.

Hanine then turned her head at an angle, cocked toward Lily. "And what will help you?"

"Time, perhaps," Lily whispered.

Hanine was quiet, as if she were listening to something Lily could not hear.

"Perhaps, Lily, not time, but forgiveness. Forgive both your mother and your father."

# SEVENTEEN

Lily knew as soon as she opened her eyes that this was her last day in Germany. She tried to put the thought of Wolfgang and the almost certain defeat of her claim for property out of her mind and concentrate instead on the last event that would still take place, an event Lily herself had arranged.

She called room service, ordered a coffee, a small defiant act of self-indulgence given its exorbitant cost, and requested that a copy of the Berlin morning newspaper be delivered with the coffee.

While she waited, Lily stood at the window and studied the Friedrichstrasse train station and thought of Hanine. "Bless you, Hanine, for saving our lives. For taking Emma out of Nazi Germany." Lily could hear Emma's young voice years ago hiding under the bed, whispering the name of the train station to Lily. "Freedsomething." So not only had the Berlin air evoked some long buried childhood memory the night Lily arrived in Berlin, but so had the name of the train station when Lily first read it in a spy book. Lily suddenly thought of Wolfgang's laughter in response to her confessing to a love of spy novels on the first day they met. Lily moved away from the window, restless at the wait and unwilling to start the packing process until the newspaper arrived.

Lily surveyed the hotel room which had served as a safe haven during the traumatic discoveries of her family's history and her own. She doubted the walls had ever witnessed so much grief in such a short amount of time. But then to herself she said, "That may not be true. The Hotel Metropol, given its location just inside the Wall and so close to the 'Palace of Tears,' probably played host to countless visitors, bedeviled by hope, guilt, fear and loss."

After the coffee tray arrived Lily pounced on the newspaper, quickly turning the pages until she found what she was looking for.

She flattened the obituary page, folded it back. There, as she had ordered it yesterday, appeared her public notice. It had been expensive, but she had taken the advice she had heard Michael give many times to people who, like her in this case, had only one chance to get the attention they wanted: make the advertisement as large as possible.

The notice was framed in a wide black band, a one-quarter page on the lower right; "recto," Michael had also said, was better than "verso," the left page.

There, among the death notices and the longer notices called obituaries, as well as the commemorative insertions, and in very large type, was Lily Weitrek's choice about the best fashion in which she would leave Germany for America.

In a box it said:

"THE PEOPLE OF BERLIN
ARE INVITED TO A SPECIAL CEREMONY TODAY,
WEDNESDAY, MAY 15, 1991, AT NOON
IN THE JEWISH CEMETERY OF WEISSENSEE

WE WILL REMEMBER"

Because of her blindness Hanine still saw Lily as the child she had been on that flight out of Germany. It was Hanine who prompted Lily to think of other children.

Ludwig Sagal, a child whose life was canceled by Nazi hatred; Mauer, whose child's face was scarred by a competing hatred; and Emma, her own sister who had paid a high price for holding on to memories of a father.

Then Lily had added to the list the young boy who had hidden all during the war in Weissensee Cemetery and was now its aged caretaker. It was the children - and Lily now knew she was one with them - who had grown into adulthood around the world, whose souls were forever shadowed by the ghosts of the past.

The ghosts had always been there, walking side by side with Lily, waiting for recognition. Lily knew that now, knew that throughout all of her mother's re-casting of the truth into fiction, the past had been waiting to catch her, either in restless sleep, in dreams with remnants of forgotten images from long ago, or in awkward moments of childhood when Lily would suddenly say something in a language that Lily's mother said she did not speak, did not know.

"How many are there like me around the world still asking themselves who they are?"

As Lily dressed and packed, her thoughts returned again to the last few minutes with Hanine.

The ordeal of Lily's visit and the need for Hanine to recount the story of escape had worn the old woman out. As is often true in the very old, fatigue punishes coherence. Hanine needed to rest, probably to sleep.

The nurse had helped her into bed. Lily waited at Hanine's request until the old woman who had helped save her life slept. She knew with virtual certainty that she would never see Hanine again. Hanine had said she was ready to meet her God, now that Lily's real history had been told her, a burden of silence lifted from the wonderful brave woman. Lily wept as she leaned over to kiss Hanine's sleeping face. Then Lily left.

Lily was so tired herself that she decided to take a taxi directly back to the Metropol, thereby avoiding the effort of the S-Bahn, especially at a time of day when the system became crowded.

Midway back to Berlin, Lily asked the cab driver if he would take her to Berlin's largest daily newspaper. When they arrived Lily asked if he would wait, to which the driver replied with a one-word response, "Yes."

Placing the ad didn't take long. The ad taker was not only helpful but also intrigued by Lily's short text. "Are you sure you want to do this?" she asked. Lily had been emphatic in her response.

The woman promised that the ad would appear exactly as Lily specified. "Maybe you are right to do this. I'm surprised, now that I think of it, why no one else has ever held such a ceremony." She looked up at Lily, who thought the woman appeared to struggle with herself. She finally said, "I have an hour for lunch. I will be there. And try to bring others with me."

Lily had dined that night in the restaurant off the lobby, not noticing the curiosity with which the maitre d' studied her or the special emphasis he added to the word 'alone'. His question had been, "Are you dining `alone,' Madame?" The waiter, remembering her generous tip from before, served her efficiently, if not with great charm. But he was content with the speed with which Lily ordered, ate and left.

Before going to her room Lily requested that a bellhop pick up her suitcase at 11 a.m. promptly the next morning and that a cab be ordered for the same time.

Between sips of coffee Lily looked ruefully at the mess she had created by jamming rather than folding her clothes neatly in the large suitcase that had caused such grief at so many train stations.

The knock on the door surprised her. She looked anxiously at the clothes still scattered on the bed and wondered why the bellhop would be a half-hour too early. The knock repeated. Lily called out, "I'm not ready. Please come back in half an hour."

A louder knock followed. "Damn it," she muttered aloud, tripping over her shoulder bag on the floor as she headed toward the door. Lily planned to be very firm in dealing with the bellhop.

She threw open the door and stopped just short of delivering her speech.

Wolfgang stood in the doorway. Instinctively Lily turned back into the room. "May I come in?" he asked.

Reluctantly Lily said, "I suppose so," and went back to her packing, ignoring him.

Her quick impression of Wolfgang was that he looked tired, not at all like the fastidious attorney she had first met.

Wolfgang watched the haphazard manner in which Lily tossed her clothes into the suitcase. "Your clothes are going to be very wrinkled."

"I really don't care." Furious at him, Lily snapped, "Is that what you came for? To discuss wrinkled clothes?"

"No, not at all," he replied.

"Why don't you just spit it out and then leave." Lily had to move around Wolfgang to get a blouse off the chair. As she passed him Wolfgang took her arm and forced Lily to face him.

Hesitantly, as if afraid Lily might laugh at him, or worse, start to yell, he said, "What I came to say is, I want to apologize for what I did. For what I said to you. I let you down when you needed me." Wolfgang dropped her arm and turned away as if to leave. He turned back to Lily from the door and said, "I also let myself down, became again the frightened boy who needed stability and order."

"Please, don't go," Lily said, surprising herself.

"Can you forgive me?" Wolfgang asked, standing awkwardly at the door.

"Whatever I learned here about my family was because of you. When I got discouraged, you were there. When I got depressed or sad, you gave me the energy to go on. So there is nothing to forgive, Wolfgang." Lily reached out her hands to Wolfgang, who took them into his own. Lily whispered, "There is only a need for me to thank you."

A hesitant smile broke Wolfgang's tired face and he asked, "So you will let me stay as your German attorney?"

Lily backed away to study him from a greater distance. "What are you talking about?"

"I am a poor, lonely lawyer looking for a client. Will you be my client, Lily?" A sheepish grin spread across his face as he saw Lily's eyes widen in amazement.

"Wolfgang, did you quit that big, glitzy firm?"

"Yes, Ms. Weitrek, I did."

"But what about your career, Wolfgang?"

He grabbed Lily's hands and pulled her to him. Into her hair he said, "I knew because of you, Franziska, given a choice between honor and dishonor, I had to choose honor. So I can look my sons in their eyes and say I did what was right to make up for the horrible things done in the past. Thank you, Lily, for showing me - letting me see who I can be. Without you I would have always wondered if I could have been different than my father and his father. I know now, I am different. I'm not afraid anymore."

Lily was so taken aback by Wolfgang's speech she sank into one of the two chairs and stared at him. "What happened?" she asked.

"Mr. Gast called me into his office yesterday and told me, ordered me, to turn over your file to him. The firm is going to represent the Von Jaegerlieds against you if your claim goes to court. And believe me, I intend to take it to court so you get something. I have copies of some of the documents you and I found. I refused to turn them over. I always suspected Gast represented Nazi clients, got them off with light fines back when the firm started in 1947. Until your case came up I had not given much thought to how many people these `industrial criminals' had harmed, caused some of them - like Daniel Brodsky - to take their own lives. But the people who took the firms just moved on with their stolen companies, particularly after the West German amnesty of Nazis in 1951, and grew larger and more powerful as Germany's `economic miracle' took place in the 1950s and 1960s."

Lily blanched. Wolfgang was speaking contradictions of what she had expected.

He continued.

"Today their children or grandchildren run these companies and never look back. They do not remember that the companies were stolen from innocent people. I realized, Lily, I do not want to represent these people. Those rich in money and poor in memory. I know now and I will remember." He smiled again, "And I will make sure others remember also. I will start to look at those products we market so proudly and ask about the origin of the companies that make the shoes, the plastics, the gas, the steel, the guns, the tanks, the chemicals."

Lily looked worried as she said, "You're sounding more like an anarchist than a lawyer."

"For us, Lily, looking back and finding the truth and recognizing it may be the only road to our long term survival as a 'democratic country'."

Wolfgang looked around the messy room and said, "Can I help you finish packing? We will be late if we do not hurry."

Lily jumped up saying, "You're right, I will be late." She stopped and turned to Wolfgang. "How did you know it was me?"

"No one else I know would place a large ad in a newspaper inviting the entire city of Berlin to come for a memorial service at Weissensee Cemetery at noon today. Only you, Lily, would dare to ask us to go to a Jewish cemetery to show respect for the dead."

Wolfgang watched as Lily crammed the last of her clothes in the suitcase and jammed it shut.

"Was it the wrong thing to do?"

"No, Lily. It is about fifty years overdue."

Finished packing, Lily quickly opened each drawer to make sure it was empty when the bellhop knocked at the door. "Do you think people will actually come, Wolfgang?"

"Some. It is pretty short notice, but if only a few come today, it will cause a lot more people to question why there is no national day of remembrance and mourning. You will have made your point." He stopped, "You will let me go with you?"

Lily replied, "Yes, Wolfgang. I would like to have you with me - as I say goodbye to my family, one last time."

Lily checked out at the lobby cashier, smiled in response to the professional smiles bestowed on her by those behind the desk, and left the Hotel Metropol for the last time.

Lily knew that she would always remember that the Metropol's main door was a revolving one, and that on each side of the revolving door were two conventional glass doors. For some reason she could not articulate - and she had thought about it a number of times - those doors had assumed a mystical quality the very night she passed through them ten days ago.

And she wanted to remember them. So after the luggage had been put into the trunk of the waiting taxi, she stopped and turned to face the hotel one last time, photographing, so to speak, its entrance purposively within that random album of images of her visit to Germany that she knew time would assemble.

Lily stood, grateful that Wolfgang seemed to understand that she needed to do this. What Lily was doing as she stared at the Metropol Hotel was to capture in one non-verbal moment the image of what had been her 'home' during most of her journey into the past.

Wolfgang, after a moment of indecision, climbed into the cab. He would have preferred to take his own car but Lily had been adamant. She wanted to retrace her first ride to Weissensee Cemetery by taxi. And to leave from the cemetery alone. "I will say goodbye to you there, not at the airport with hundreds of people around." How he was going to handle Lily's leaving was unclear to Wolfgang.

As the cab drove past the Friedrichstrasse train station Lily turned to look at it for as long as it was in view. They rode, each lost in their own thoughts. If either had spoken they would have discovered their thoughts were identical.

Of a morning nine days earlier, both of them had made their way to Weissensee Cemetery independent of each other, to meet each other for the first time. Now they went together to that cemetery for a second and probably last time. And quite possibly, they would not see each other again.

Their conversation, when they happened to speak, centered on the events of the last two days. Wolfgang had been thoroughly briefed about what Lily had been told at the Treuhand, although Wolfgang was quite surprised, he said, that the Deputy Director had been assigned to tell it. It foreshadowed a major battle between the Von Jaegerlieds and Lily if she persisted in her claim. Wolfgang promised himself again that Lily would win, if not the property, some compensation.

He also had heard about Kroner, he told her, and he had found that aggressive act on Kroner's part, and on the part of the Von Jaegerlieds, so offensive that it heated his terminal discussion with Heinrich Gast even more.

When he asked Lily about Hanine, she told him that Hanine was old and blind.

Wolfgang asked whether Hanine had been able to furnish any more information about her father.

Lily would only say, enigmatically, that Wolfgang's information about Franz Weitrek disappearing on the Swiss border was close to the story Hanine told. The cab driver listened as best he could to the conversation of his two passengers. They seemed quite unaware of his presence.

When they fell silent, the driver, whose name was Rudi Winkler, thought back to the strange events of the morning. The taxi yard had been thrown into chaos. Call after call, about 60 according to the dispatcher, had already come in by 9:00 a.m., all ordering a cab with the same destination: Jewish Weissensee Cemetery. And all callers were very clear in their instructions. They had to be picked up so they would arrive at the cemetery at precisely 11:55 a.m.

Max Hein, the dispatcher, usually a calm sort, lost his temper. "Do these fools think I am a magician?" Hein wondered aloud as to what would be going on at, of all places, the deserted Jewish cemetery. He barked orders at his secretary to start calling all drivers in, even those on the afternoon shift.

But it was that dumb 'Ossie' driver Schultz who really blew the lid off the situation. Schultz, hearing the name of the destination, refused to come to work early, point blank refused! Rudi Winkler almost laughed out loud as Hein, having grabbed the phone from his secretary, cajoled, screamed, threatened, cursed and finally hung up on Schultz.

What could have gotten into Schultz, who was usually so eager to work overtime, Winkler wondered? One of the first cab drivers called in early was able to answer Max Hein's question as to why so many people had the same destination. He placed the ad on Hein's desk. "Well, I will be damned," said the dispatcher, reading Lily's announcement.

Hein addressed the two dozen men standing around the room and asked if anyone knew how to get to the Jewish cemetery. There was a general shaking of heads indicating, "No."

The dispatcher took a pointer to the large wall map of Berlin and after a few false starts found the streets leading to Weissensee Cemetery. "Does anyone object to going out there?" he finally curtly asked. Two men stood up. One left the room without a word. The other said, "Take Jews to their cemetery? No." He stalked out.

Of the remaining group one said, "I did not think any Jews were left in Berlin."

"A couple of hundred here in the East Zone, I read somewhere," someone said.

"I have never even seen a Jew. Is it true they have long noses?" said another.

"No longer than yours," said Winkler. Everybody laughed except the driver with the long nose. "I for one would like to go to this forgotten place," said Winkler.

Max Hein felt relieved. The tension in the room dissipated. "That is good, Winkler, because you get the pick-up at the Hotel Metropol on Friedrichstrasse. That call came in last night."

It had been one hell of a morning, Winkler thought as he studied his passengers through his rear view mirror.

The woman had a short, straight nose, so she was not Jewish, not that he believed such rubbish. He found her attractive. Not beautiful, but definitely attractive. Her face was serene. The man was definitely a German. He looked, thought Winkler, who was in his late 20s, like a stuffy old German, smug, content with himself and his orderly world. Why would these two people be going to Weissensee Cemetery, particularly since the woman had told him she would be going on to the airport?

Wolfgang looked with curiosity at the number of cars entering the streets towards the cemetery.

Is it possible that many people read Lily's notice and are going to Weissensee Cemetery? Wolfgang wondered.

Wolfgang looked at his watch. They would arrive about twenty minutes before noon, he decided.

He was right. It was 11:40 a.m. when the cab entered the small parking lot. It was full.

Wolfgang was surprised by two things; Lily seeming surprised at neither.

First, the old caretaker, the one who had found them wrestling with grave markers on their first visit to Weissensee Cemetery, was in the parking lot to greet them.

Second, there were about 150 people already waiting outside the gates.

The old caretaker unlocked the gate so Lily could enter the cemetery, Wolfgang behind her. Inside the gate Wolfgang saw a large box filled with yarmulkes, quite old, he thought, as if they had been stored away for years waiting to be worn again, which was of course the case.

"Frau Weitrek. As you requested the gates will open exactly at noon. A friend will do that for me so I can show you the spot I chose." He threw a glance at the crowd gathered and said, "It is very nice. Some I see have brought flowers." He turned to Lily and said, "It is possible you have given people a chance to do something they wanted to do but were afraid - to visit all these here." He waved his arm wide to cover the cemetery's huge expanse. "And remember those missing."

He reached into the box and gave a yarmulke to Wolfgang, who without hesitation put it on. Wolfgang put a five Deutschemark piece on the tray next to the box. The caretaker hurried down the central path, "Come, come with me. I did just as you asked on the phone."

The caretaker led them through the central wagon wheel from which all the cemetery's paths spread out and they quickly found themselves under the umbrella of trees, amidst the untended vines creeping over the fallen headstones that stretched to the outer edge of the large cemetery.

As much as Lily felt she had changed or been changed in ten days, Weissensee Cemetery was exactly as it had been on the first day she and Wolfgang had met. Deserted, and except for the sound of the birds and the rustling leaves of the tree branches, a silent world.

Because of Lily that silence was finally going to be broken. Those of other faiths would mourn for those of one faith who had few of their own left to mourn in this troubled country. The caretaker stopped and pointed them to a small, secluded spot.

The outer perimeter they saw was planted with new flowers. Lily flashed the old man a smile. She knew he must have worked very hard to prepare the ground and find the flowers. A large single tree with branches like feathery arms covered the space.

Wolfgang saw that some object, covered with a small cloth leaned against the tree trunk. Next to it was a mound of palm-sized rocks.

"Is it as you wished, Frau Weitrek?"

"Yes, Mr. Stein. Thank you. We will wait now for the others."

Jakob Stein fussed at the flowers as they waited. Wolfgang looked at Lily with unasked questions in his eyes. She seemed unnaturally calm, he thought, almost regal. Content with whatever it was she had created.

What Lily had created was a reminder for the years to come that those who were buried in Weissensee Cemetery were not forgotten, and that those whose burial grounds were unknown, often in the ash-pits of Nazi camps, would be especially remembered.

And the children. Those who had died, those who had suffered and those who still carried scars on their bodies or in their souls.

They did not have to wait long. Wolfgang looked down the path. He could hear the silent procession of people come towards the secluded spot. The sound of many pairs of feet announced their progress as they struggled over the ill kept paths.

But no one spoke.

Lily stood erect as the uneasy congregation of several hundred fanned out around the small area the caretaker had created for the occasion.

"The first observance by Germans for Hitler's victims in a Jewish cemetery," thought Wolfgang, amazed at Lily's audacity. "Only Lily - an American - would dare fly in the face of all our guilt, our fear, our shame at what our parents and grandparents did and create a moment of remembrance."

Looking at the faces around him, Wolfgang saw young and old people, students, a Catholic priest, workers, suited men and elegantly dressed women. Wolfgang realized all the men wore yarmulkes. He was amazed at what he saw. He felt his spirit soar. At long last he saw in others a longing to publicly address their doubts about who they might be as descendants of murderers, and their hopes that what had happened in Germany in the past could never happen again. These people would not let it happen again. Wolfgang felt a kind of peace he had never felt before in his life.

The group, the congregation, it might be called, crowded closer and cleared their throats as the caretaker moved to the tree, lifted the sheeted object and placed it in the center of the clearing.

Tania Wisbar and John Mahoney

Jakob Stein, keeper of the history of Weissensee Cemetery, assumed the speaker's role. After all these years of exclusion, of unimportance, and of sorrow, Jakob Stein was proud. He was proud of this woman who knew nothing of her family, who came to Germany to claim property and money, who did not know how to say Kaddish. He did not know how her quest had turned out, but he knew that she had found family, and a legacy.

"I, Jakob Stein, caretaker and stone craftsman, a trade taught me by my father, have created this memorial at the request of Frau Lily Weitrek, some of whose family members are buried here in Weissensee Cemetery, and some who are forever missing."

He gestured to Lily to move to him and remove the covering of the memorial. As she lifted it to reveal the memorial a murmur, then a gasp ran through the crowd.

The memorial read

TO THE CHILDREN OF BERLIN
1933-1945
MAY YAHWEH WATCH OVER THEM

Wolfgang felt tears spring to his eyes. In her memorial Lily had included even him. It was an act of kindness and healing he never expected. Neither did the others standing near him. He could hear the sound of weeping.

The caretaker led Lily to the mound of rocks and, placing one in her hand, said, "It is our way to place a rock. It is for remembrance. To show that we will not forget."

Lily knelt and placed the first rock in front of the memorial tablet. She stayed that way and said loudly enough to be heard, "For Ludwig Sagal and my sister Emma." She went back to the remembrance rocks, picked one up and crossed to give it to Wolfgang.

Wolfgang lay it next to Lily's rock and said softly so he could not be heard, "For the child, Lily."

Helmut Holder had also read the ad in the newspaper. When it was his turn he said, "For Bernie Feldstein. I have never forgotten."

270

Before Lily turned to leave she sought out Jakob Stein who was authoritatively keeping the procession orderly. "Please accept my thanks, Mr. Stein."

Instead of shaking Lily's hand he took her in his arms and kissed her on both cheeks. "It is for me to thank you. I will not forget you."

"Nor I you," she replied. "Or all these here."

It was time to go. Lily and Wolfgang made their way through the line of people still coming. Wolfgang followed Lily as she left the path they were on. He knew where she was going. Lily stopped first at her grandmother's grave and left a stone of remembrance for Emma Auerbach Brodsky. Then they walked, as they had that first day, to the Auerbach mausoleum, to leave another palm-sized rock.

Lily and Wolfgang studied the names familiar only to them from the caretaker's recounting of that service so long ago in 1932. There they were: "Arthur", "Marie," "Isador." Wolfgang knew them best and knew them only as the family that had celebrated Misha and Franziska's engagement at the Berlin Foundation.

"We'll never really know anything about them, will we, Wolfgang?"

"Probably not."

Hand in hand they slowly made their way towards the entrance.

Rudi Winkler, curious at what was taking place to attract such a large crowd, had been among the first in line as the gates were opened at noon. Winkler started to follow the path everyone was taking and then stopped. He wanted to get a sense of this strange place by himself. Privately. He left the path he was on and walked deeper into the cemetery.

Awe formed slowly over and around his body. "For many, many years," he thought to himself, "the leaves and branches of these trees must have fallen, unheard by the living, to cover these graves. The vines have grown around and up the headstones, obliterating the names of the dead and causing the headstones to

271

fall." Winkler looked around at the grave markers that lay askew, on top of each other, one row indistinguishable from the other.

Winkler moved further, walking until he found himself standing in front of a mausoleum still largely intact. Winkler studied its rich marble facade. The mausoleum, he realized, had a central large tablet with the name "Aaronsohn" at the top. Underneath was a marker with the name "Otto Aaronsohn, born 1858, died 1930. Beloved husband, father and grandfather."

It was the blank tablets like wings on each side of the mausoleum that troubled Winkler. The name `Aaronsohn' was at the top of each but there were no names of Aaronsohn's children or their children. The tablets were blank eyes looking out at a silent world.

Winkler knew in his heart where the missing children had died. He did not turn away from the knowledge. He was a deeply religious man who celebrated his love of God every day. He knelt down and prayed. When he was finished, he took off the cross he wore around his neck. Uncertain as to whether anyone might take offense at the presence of a Christian cross in a Jewish cemetery, Winkler dug a small hole at the foot of one of the blank tablets, brought the cross to his lips and then buried it.

"Rest with God, Mr. Aaronsohn." After fifty years someone had come to mourn the Aaronsohn family.

Winkler looked at his watch and walked rapidly towards the entrance. The woman had been very precise. She had to leave the cemetery at exactly 1 p.m. to catch her plane to Frankfurt and make the Lufthansa connection to Los Angeles/San Diego. Winkler had promised he would be at the entrance at exactly 1 p.m. As he passed through the gate he took off the yarmulke. He waved away the five Deutschemark the gatekeeper offered him.

The man and woman were already standing by his cab when Winkler arrived in the parking lot. Cars and cabs spilled out in the street. Winkler quickly got into his cab realizing the couple needed the few remaining minutes to say goodbye privately.

Lily said, "It's time."

Wolfgang took Lily into his arms and whispered into her hair, his voice breaking, "Franziska, remember me. I would have done anything to keep you from harm. Remember I loved you."

"I will, Misha. Remember I loved you."

"Goodbye, Lily."

"Goodbye, Wolfgang."

Lily moved out of his arms. They stood looking at each other for another minute.

Winkler knew it was time to leave. He opened the back door and helped the woman, whose name he now knew was `Lily,' into the back seat.

He turned the cab into the street. Winkler's last view of Weissensee Cemetery included the gates, the umbrella of trees overhanging the cemetery, and the man standing alone in the parking lot.

Wolfgang said, "Goodbye, Lily," to himself as the cab disappeared from view. He was at a total loss as to what to do next. His glance fell on his shoes. The expensive Italian shoes had dried. Without thought, Wolfgang had put them on that morning, not expecting they would carry him back to Weissensee Cemetery.

Wolfgang walked over to the telephone booth on the street outside the cemetery's parking lot. He knew what he had to do.

Greta answered as he had anticipated she would. It was her day off. Wolfgang was direct in his instructions to her. Wolfgang told his wife that he wanted Peter and Klaus to be put in a cab and driven to Weissensee Cemetery. He hung up before giving Greta an opportunity to argue. Wolfgang's voice left little doubt in Greta's mind that her husband expected her to obey his order.

Waiting the hour Wolfgang knew it would take for his sons to arrive, he re-entered the cemetery, sat on a bench by the caretaker's hut and watched the people leave. Some looked stunned, some disturbed, some smiled at him as they walked by his bench.

By 2 p.m. Weissensee Cemetery was quiet again.

Wolfgang, anticipating his sons' arrival, waited at the entrance gate. To his surprise it was not a cab but Greta's car that pulled into the parking lot. The boys ran to greet Wolfgang. Greta followed more slowly, barely nodding to her husband. Wolfgang saw that Peter, who loved flowers, had a white rose in

273

his hand. Wolfgang had to conclude that Greta had told the boys they were going to a cemetery. Peter associated cemeteries with flowers. He always took a white rose to his grandmother's grave when he went there.

Entering the cemetery, Wolfgang picked two small yarmulkes out of the box, dropped a ten Deutschemark note in the tray and carefully placed one on each of his sons' heads. Whatever questions they had died on their lips as they saw the expression on their father's face.

Wolfgang led them through Weissensee Cemetery to the children's memorial, Greta following slightly behind her family.

The caretaker was still there. After all the people had left Jakob Stein had studied the plaque he had worked on yesterday and through the night. Stein was satisfied with the result. But he had begun to worry about the rabbi of the tiny East German congregation. Fortunately the rabbi was out of the country. But that might not make much difference to the elders of the congregation whom Stein had failed to notify about Lily's impromptu ceremony.

Stein sighed, "Was it better to have people come on such short notice? Or should he have waited until such an event had been given approval? But by then Frau Lily Weitrek would have been gone." Stein sighed again. He was old, tired and it had been a long night and tumultuous day.

Stein looked up at the sound of people approaching. It was Mr. Schmidt coming back. "Now why would he come back? And who was the woman? Who were the two young boys?" A smile broke on his face as he got up to greet them. "This must be Mr. Schmidt's family," Stein said to himself.

"We have come, Mr. Stein, to ask you to say Kaddish," said Wolfgang.

The two boys were drawn to the plaque. Peter read it aloud. He was having trouble in school with reading, but by taking his time, he accurately read, "To the Children of Berlin 1933-1945. May Yahweh watch over them." He turned to his father and asked, "What does it mean, Pappi? Who is `Yahweh'?"

His older brother Klaus provided the answer. "This is a Jewish cemetery. 'Yahweh' is probably another name for `God'. Is that right?" He looked at Stein for confirmation.

"Yes, Yahweh is our name for God," Stein replied.

"Doesn't God love all children the same?" Peter asked.

"Yes," said Wolfgang.

"What happened to the children? The children on the tablet?" Peter looked very unhappy at the thought someone would hurt a child.

A silence fell. To Wolfgang's astonishment it was Greta who finally answered her young son's question. "Many years ago we allowed things to happen we are all ashamed of. Tonight your father and I will talk with you about the past. It is important you know about it."

Wolfgang looked at his wife in amazement. He felt enormous gratitude that she would be part of what was going to be a very painful discussion, which would include revealing something about the man the two boys fondly called 'Opa Gast', 'Grandfather Gast'.

"We will start then," said Stein.

"Wait," Peter said. "Before you start I want to put the rose by the children." They waited until Peter had placed his white rose on the top of the rocks of remembrance.

The Schmidt family stood, heads bowed, as Jakob Stein's voice rang out, saying Kaddish in Hebrew. The sound of the ancient language echoed in the otherwise silent cemetery, filling the paths, rolling over both fallen and upright headstones. Wolfgang closed his eyes and said to himself,

"Franziska."

*Tania Wisbar and John Mahoney*

# EPILOGUE

## IMPERIAL BEACH, CALIFORNIA
## 2002

"Whoever has never eaten bread in sorrow, /Or has never spent his nightly hours/ Weeping, waiting for tomorrow,/ Has yet to know you, Heavenly Power." (Goethe, *Benjamin Meisters Lehrjahre*)

The story is now complete. If there is more to this story, I will never know it. Nor will you.

Except for a small footnote.

It fell to me in 1991 in one of life's ironies not only to meet Lily at the airport when the flight arrived from Berlin but also to tell her that the factory had been closed down by the German government even as her plane took off from Berlin. The phone had rung as I was leaving for the newspaper office. Through the static of another bad connection the voice of the factory director, Otto Gesset, reported that the Treuhandandstalt had sent a representative to Fehleen that day to notify him and the workers that the famed old shoe factory would be closed by week's end. Gesset sobbed as he reported the loss of his job as well as the lost jobs of hundreds of workers. He asked me to tell Lily that the Treuhand representative explained the abrupt closure by saying the American heiress had decided not to pursue her claim.

And so Lily and I had made a full circle of phone calls from Otto Gesset. The first of his calls started Lily on her journey, and his second and last call ended her journey.

The claim was lost.

Lily's attorney, Wolfgang Schmidt, wrote occasionally for a time, but not now for several years, reporting on his attempts to take Lily's claim through the drawn-out German court hearing process – a strange unfamiliar process because no witness is ever called.

Tania Wisbar and John Mahoney

Lily thought that she would like Schmidt to take her case to a higher court. Would I agree?

How could I not agree? It was a matter of justice.

For a while we discussed the role of justice when a government in the name of the greater good tramples on individual rights.

Those in charge of reparation for the thefts and brutalities perpetrated by the Nazis dealt daily with this valley of the unclear, this limbo. They rendered the present whole by making the least of both the claims and of the deeds in the past that created the claims.

In the case of Lily and her family, the decision over the factory and the other properties that these had been "bought fairly" in 1933 was self-serving. It benefited the state, and excluded the claimants from the right, or need, to come home.

No amount of substantiation could be put forward to persuade those in charge of reparation to move old indictments into the present. And therefore there was not, could never have been enough substantiation, and therefore the claim was finally void.

This analysis was of short comfort to Lily. Justice will not be explained away; nor will injustice.

What we were looking for, what Lily was looking for, was some shadow of justice.

I realized this slowly, and it took me some while to propose the idea to Lily.

Justice is quite different from being dealt with justly.

When justice abides within a culture, its signs can be found. Perhaps not everywhere, and perhaps sometimes can even be denied. But the signs will still be there.

Lily was looking for signs of justice not only for herself, but for others.

Any hope for Lily's claim for the factory, the properties, or the hope of some compensation all now rest in the cemetery of justice.

Much has changed over the years since Lily's trip and her lost causes of property and justice became part of the fabric of our lives.

Germany exists today in a new world order as a member of a community of other, mutually resolute European nations. These nations have no past, nor any need to acknowledge one. Just the future. They are the shining new forces in the world.

There are press accounts every day of attacks on foreigners and vandalism of Jewish gravesites in Germany, also in France and Austria, maybe Romania, but none are organized by governments or supported by public opinion.

Lily goes to see Emma, her sister, several times a month. On the first visit Lily gave Emma the necklace from the old woman, the one who died shortly after Lily arrived home. Evidently the necklace and learning about her father brought Emma confort. She is doing quite well in a less restrictive residential program.

Lily asks me from time to time whether I believe people live parallel lives in different dimensions of time. As I have said, before I became a small-town newspaper publisher I taught philosophy. I tell her that current research, widely accepted, if not by all, suggests that time exists at many levels — most of which we barely understand. It is called "Superstring Theory." I answer that I think such parallel existences are possible. She seems content with the answer. And so am I.

It is my choice finally to join her as she travels these other dimensions. It surprises me that I can feel her arms reach out to me across all forms of separation in another existence as I whisper into her hair, "Franziska, remember me. I would do anything to keep you from harm, keep you safe, my love."

It is important to me that you remember my name.

Printed in the United States
909000004B